Hors d'Oeuvres

THE ICE BOWL

(FOR SHRIMP, RAW VEGETABLES, ETC.)

*"You've always wanted to know how to make
one and didn't know whom to ask!"*

Use two mixing bowls, one 2 or 3 inches smaller in diameter than
the other. The metal bowls are good. Tape the two bowls together,
so that the tops of both bowls are level with each other.

Fill the space between them partly with water. Place in freezer
overnight. The next day, add more cold water, almost to the top of
the bowls. Again, place in freezer for a day.

When completely frozen, remove from freezer. Take the tape off,
and fill the smaller bowl with hot water.* Then remove the smaller
bowl. Dip the outer bowl in hot water for a few minutes until it
slips off, and you will be left holding a bowl of ice.

Quickly wrap the ice bowl in foil, and return to the freezer
until ready to use. At serving time, remove foil and place it on a
serving platter that has a rim to catch the drippings. Surround it
with lots of greenery, parsley for example, and fill it with shrimp
or vegetables. It will keep for several hours without melting away.

*If desired, you may insert garnishes, such as parsley, lemon slices,
etc., before the first or second layers are added.

Editors' Note:
   The following two recipes can be made quickly and the supplies
are easy to keep on hand for unexpected guests.

CHOPPED EGG AND ANCHOVY DIP

3 eggs, hard-boiled
1 tbsp. chopped onion
5 or 6 anchovies
1 tbsp. mayonnaise

Mash eggs and mix all ingredients together. Serve as a dip
with crackers.

HOT CREAM CHEESE HORS D'OEUVRE

1 package (3 oz.) cream cheese
2 tbsp. mayonnaise
sprinkle of garlic powder or
   any other seasoning

Mash cheese and blend all ingredients together. Now spread
on crackers and broil about 1
minute. Serve immediately.

Anchovy Dip

"Serve with crackers."

1 package (8 oz.) cream
   cheese, room temperature
¼ lb. sweet butter, room
   temperature
1 tin (2 oz.) boneless
   filet anchovies
1 small onion

Blend first two ingredients until soft. Drain and mash anchovies. Add to above. Grate onion and blend with all other ingredients.

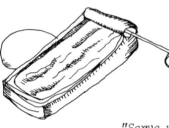

Daffodil Dip

Serves: 8
Cooking Time: 20 minutes

*"Serve with celery, cucumbers, radishes
cherry tomatoes, etc."*

½ cup mayonnaise
1 package (8 oz.) cream cheese
½ cup parsley, chopped
1 egg, hard-boiled
2 tbsp. onion, chopped
1 clove garlic, minced
1 tbsp. anchovy paste
dash pepper

Gradually add mayonnaise to soften cream cheese, blending well. Add parsley, chopped egg white, onion, and other seasonings. Mix well. Sprinkle with sieved yolks.

Fresh Raw Vegetable Dip

Serves: 8 - 10
Chill: 2 hours or more

"Very versatile."

1 cup mayonnaise
1 cup sour cream
1 grated onion
4 tbsp. mustard
¼ cup chopped parsley

Mix all ingredients together and blend. Can be used with all assorted fresh raw vegetables. Chill for minimum of 2 hours before using.

Curry Dip with Fresh Raw Vegetables

Serves: 8
Chill: Overnight

1 pt. mayonnaise
1½ tsp. mild curry powder
3 tbsp. ketchup
3 tbsp. honey
3 tbsp. grated onion
1¼ tsp. lemon juice
7-9 drops Tabasco

Mix all ingredients together and refrigerate overnight. Serve with broccoli, cauliflower, celery, carrots, cherry tomatoes, cucumbers.

Herbed Cream Cheese Dip

Yield: Approximately 1 cup

"Good with raw vegetables or seafood."

1 clove garlic, minced
1-2 tsp. minced onion
¼ tsp. salt
pinch dry mustard
1 package (3 oz.) cream cheese
¼ cup mayonnaise
1 tbsp. lemon juice
2 tbsp. chopped olive
¼ tsp. thyme
dash Tabasco
chopped parsley or chives

Blend together garlic, onion, salt, and mustard. Add cream cheese; cream until smooth. Add rest of ingredients and sprinkle with parsley or chives. Serve with seafood or raw vegetables, such as celery, cauliflower, or radishes.

Clam Dip

Serves: 8
Chill: 1 hour

"Dipper's delight."

1 cup minced Doxee clams
1 package (8 oz.) cream cheese
½ tbsp. chopped onions
½ tsp. Worcestershire sauce
dash garlic powder
dash pepper

Drain clams, reserve 2 tablespoons clam juice. Soften cream cheese with clam juice. Add remaining ingredients and beat into cheese mixture. Mix in clams. Chill and serve on crackers or with vegetable dippers.

SHRIMP DIP

Serves: 6
Chill: Ahead

paprika
1 small can (4 oz.) petite
   shrimp, drained and mashed
1 cup Hellman's mayonnaise
few sprinkles onion flakes
few sprinkles garlic powder
salt
pepper
lettuce leaves

Mix ingredients together. Put on lettuce leaf with paprika. Chill.

SPICY BEEF DIP

Yield: Approximately 2 quarts
Cooking Time: 30 minutes

1 lb. ground beef
½ cup chopped onion
1 clove garlic, minced
1 cup tomato sauce
¼ cup ketchup
1 tsp. sugar
¾ tsp. dried oregano leaves,
   crushed
1 package (8 oz.) cream cheese,
   softened
⅓ cup grated Parmesan cheese

Cook ground beef, onion, and garlic in skillet until meat is lightly browned and onion is tender. Stir in tomato sauce, ketchup, sugar, and oregano. Cover; simmer gently 10 minutes. Spoon off excess fat. Remove from heat. Add cream cheese and Parmesan cheese. Heat and stir until cheeses melt and mixture is well blended. Keep warm in chafing dish and serve with crackers.

CHEESE BALL

Preparation Time: 10 minutes

2 packages (8 oz.) cream cheese,
   room temperature
½ cup chopped chutney
2 tsp. curry powder
½ cup chopped pecans
½ tsp. dry mustard

Mix all ingredients together. Roll into three balls. Wrap in aluminum foil. Can be frozen.

OLIVE CHEESE "PORCUPINE" HORS D'OEUVRES

Chill: 2 hours

4 oz. blue cheese
1 package (8 oz.) cream cheese
1 lb. Cheddar cheese
1 tbsp minced onion
1 tsp. Worcestershire sauce
½ cup walnuts, finely chopped
Spanish green olives

Allow cheeses to soften at room temperature. Mix well, with parsley, onion, Worcestershire sauce, nuts. On wax paper form mixture into oval shape. Refrigerate 2 hours. Roll "porcupine" in paprika. Let stand at room temperature one-half hour before serving. Serve with crisp crackers. Garnish with Spanish olives on wooden picks for quills.

PINEAPPLE-CHEESE BALL

Yield: 40

2 packages (8 oz.) cream cheese, softened
1 can (8½ oz.) crushed pineapple, drained
2 cups chopped walnuts
¼ cup green pepper, finely chopped
2 tbsp. onion, finely chopped
1 tbsp. seasoned salt
canned pineapple rings
maraschino cherries
parsley sprig

In bowl, mash cheese with fork till smooth. Stir in crushed pineapple, one cup nuts, pepper, onion, and salt. Shape into ball. Roll in remaining one cup nuts. Wrap in Saran Wrap and refrigerate overnight.
To Serve: Place on board. Decorate with pineapple slices, cherries, and parsley. Surround with crackers. Leftovers may be reshaped and used another day. Keeps well.

PARMESAN CANAPÉS

Yield: 24
Cooking Time: 5 - 10 minutes

4 slices white bread, crusts removed
½ cup mayonnaise
¼ cup grated Parmesan cheese, freshly grated, if possible
2 tbsp. packaged minced onion

Cut each slice of bread into 6 pieces. Combine remaining ingredients. Drop three-quarters teaspoon on bread squares. Place under broiler until lightly browned. Toaster oven may be used. Set control on "Top Brown Only." Serve hot.

Bacon/Cheese Puff Hors d'Oeuvres

Yield: 24 pieces
Cooking Time: 20 minutes

6 slices thin white bread
12 slices bacon
2 packages (3 oz.) cream cheese
   with chives

Trim crusts off bread. Flatten bread. Spread one side of bread with cream cheese and chives. Cut each slice bread into four pieces, diagonally. Do other sides of bread with chive cheese. Cut each slice bacon in half. Roll bacon around bread slices and secure with wooden toothpicks. May be frozen at this point. Heat in oven at 400° for 20 minutes or until bacon is done.

Cheese Puffs

Yield: 30 - 40
Cooking Time: 15 minutes

2 cups sharp, grated Cheddar
   cheese (8 oz.)
½ cup butter
1 cup flour
½ tsp. salt
1 tsp. paprika
pineapple chunks or olives

Mix all ingredients, except pineapple or olives, together with fork or fingers. Cut pineapple chunks in half or use olives, and roll in cheese mixture into balls; or make plain cheese balls. Freeze on an ungreased cookie sheet until hard. Can be put into containers and kept frozen. Bake frozen on ungreased pan in preheated 400° oven for 15 minutes.

Tuna and Cheese Canapés

Yield: 16 canapés
Cooking Time: 5 minutes

1 cup grated Cheddar cheese
½ cup canned tuna
2 tbsp. dry vermouth
black pepper (freshly ground)
toast squares

Combine first 4 ingredients and blend well. Spread on squares of lightly browned toast and bake in preheated oven (350°) for 5 minutes.

Gruyère and Anchovy Canapés

Yield: 24
Cooking Time: 5 minutes

4 slices white bread
sweet butter
4 oz. Gruyère cheese, shredded
8 flat anchovy fillets, finely
   minced
½ cup mayonnaise
4 tbsp. grated Parmesan cheese

Preheat oven to 450°. Toast bread under broiler on one side only. Spread untoasted side with butter. Mix remaining ingredients together. Spread mixture evenly on untoasted sides of bread. Place bread, cheese side up on baking sheet. Bake 5 minutes. Cut each slice into six pieces. Serve hot.

Spanakopita

(SPINACH-CHEESE CANAPÉ)

Yield: 40 - 50 pieces
Cooking Time: 20 minutes

"More difficult to prepare, but a marvelous taste treat."

1 package (10 oz.) frozen
   chopped spinach
2 medium onions
½ lb. feta cheese
½ lb. pot cheese
3 eggs
¼ cup bread crumbs
salt to taste
¼ lb. butter
½ package filo pastry

Cook frozen spinach 3 minutes and drain. Sauté onions and add to spinach. Add cheeses, eggs, bread crumbs, and salt to above mixture. Melt butter. Unroll filo pastry on tea towel. Brush with melted butter. Spread 1-inch strip of filling. Roll up on 2 layers of pastry. Place on cookie sheet. Bake at 400° about 20 minutes, turning once.

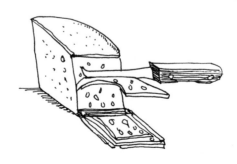

PICKLED MUSHROOMS

Cooking Time: 5 minutes
Chill: Overnight

⅔ cup vinegar
¼ cup water
3 cloves garlic, minced
dash of Tabasco
2 cans (4 oz.) whole mushroom
    crowns

Simmer first four ingredients in saucepan 5 minutes. Drain the mushrooms; pour hot liquid over them. Refrigerate overnight. To serve, drain and spear with toothpicks.

STUFFED MUSHROOMS

Yield: 15
Cooking Time: 15 - 20 minutes

"One extra for the cook!"

16 large mushrooms
¼ lb. butter
½ cup Italian flavored bread
    crumbs
2 eggs, lightly beaten
1 tsp. chopped parsley
2 tbsp. minced onion
salt
pepper
Parmesan cheese
broth

Wash mushrooms (wipe with damp cloth). Remove stems and chop fairly fine. Heat 2 or 3 table-spoons butter in skillet and sauté chopped stems slightly. Mix these with bread crumbs, eggs, parsley, onions, one-half teaspoon salt, and fresh black pepper. Brush caps with butter and arrange on buttered baking dish. Stuff, sprinkle with cheese. Dot with butter and add a little broth to pan. Bake at 375° 15-20 minutes or till tender. Baste during cooking with butter or white wine.

Variations

Seafood: substitute shrimp, crab meat, or lobster for mushroom stems.

Meat: substitute chopped meat for mushroom stems.

CRAB MEAT STUFFED MUSHROOMS

Yield: 12 - 16
Cooking Time: 15 minutes

"Can be prepared early in the day and baked at serving time."

12 - 16 large mushrooms
¼ lb. butter, melted
1½ cups crab meat
2 eggs
3 tbsp. mayonnaise
¼ cup minced scallions
2 tsp. lemon juice
½ tsp. Worcestershire sauce
½ cup bread crumbs

Preheat oven to 375°. Wash mushrooms and remove stems. Dip mushrooms in melted butter and place upside-down in buttered baking dish. Combine crab meat, eggs, mayonnaise, scallions, lemon juice, Worcestershire sauce, and half the bread crumbs. Fill mushrooms with mixture. Note: Favorite meat loaf mixture can be substituted for crab meat filling.
Sprinkle remaining crumbs and butter over mushrooms. Bake 15 minutes.

MUSHROOM-ONION TART

Serves: 4 for lunch; 6 for appetizers
Cooking Time: 30 minutes

pastry for 1-crust pie
7 large mushrooms, sliced
3 tbsp. shortening
3 eggs, slightly beaten
3 tbsp. dry onion soup mix
dash pepper
2 tbsp. fresh parsley, chopped
1 cup sour cream

Bake pie crust for 10 minutes at 400°. Cook mushrooms in shortening and put in bottom of baked crust. Save shortening. Mix remaining ingredients and add saved shortening. Pour over mushrooms in pie shell. Bake at 350° for 20 minutes or until golden brown.

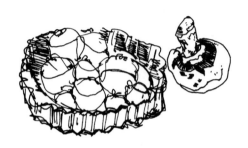

Mushroom Turnovers

Yield: 50
Cooking Time: 15 minutes (refrigerate 30 minutes to 1 hour)

3 packages (3 oz.) cream cheese
½ cup butter, softened
1½ cups flour
1 minced onion
2 tsp. butter
1 cup chopped mushrooms
salt
pepper
thyme
¼ cup sour cream
2 tsp. flour

With hands, mix cream cheese and butter together. Add flour and work into a dough. Refrigerate 30 minutes to one hour. Sauté onion in butter and add chopped mushrooms. Sprinkle with salt, pepper, thyme, and sour cream. Stir together. Set aside. Roll out dough, very thin, on floured surface. Cut into 3-inch circles with glass. Fill each circle with one-half teaspoon filling. Fold and seal edges like a turnover. Prick each one. Bake at 450° for 15 minutes or until brown.

Vegetarian Derma

Serves: 8 - 10
Cooking Time: 1 hour

12-oz. box Ritz crackers
2 large pieces celery
2 large carrots
1 medium onion
1 stick margarine, melted
1 envelope MBT bouillon

Put through meat grinder crackers, celery, carrots, onion. Add melted margarine and MBT powder. Mix thoroughly and shape into 3 loaves, 2 x 6 inches. Wrap each loaf in aluminum foil. Bake on cookie sheet for one hour at 350°. Cool before slicing. Reheats well. Freezes well. Very good as an hors d'oeuvre. For dinner, use instead of potatoes.

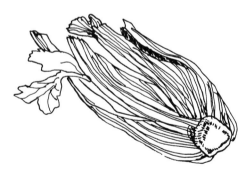

Asparagus Rolls

Serves: 8 - 12
Cooking Time: 5 minutes

4 oz. sharp Cheddar cheese,
   grated
1 loaf white bread, sliced
1 can (8 oz.) medium-sized
   white asparagus
butter

Remove crusts from bread and flatten each slice. Butter bottom edge of bread, especially corners. Sprinkle on grated cheese up to butter. Place one asparagus on each slice of bread. Roll bread toward self, holding with thumbs. Refrigerate. Cut each slice in half and brush with melted butter. Broil.

Tempura Batter and Dip

Cooking Time: 30 minutes

Batter:

2 eggs, beaten
1½ cups flour
½ cup cornstarch
2 cups cold water

Blend all ingredients and mix until smooth (use mixer or whisk). Set aside.

Dip Sauce:

2 cups water
1 bouillon cube
½ cup sugar
2 tbsp. MSG
¼ cup soy sauce
¼ cup saké
lemon juice to taste
crushed peppers, to taste
dash salt
1 sauce dish of Japanese
   horseradish (if available)

Prepare dip sauce, set aside. Use all or as many of the following ingredients as you desire: sliced carrots; sliced sweet potatoes (or white potatoes); sliced green peppers (about 1-inch square); large, dry Japanese mushrooms soaked 30 minutes and sliced in half or quarters; raw shrimp; Japanese seaweed; green onions; cooked sliced pork.

Dip each vegetable or fish in batter and deep fry in hot vegetable oil until golden. Drain well, then set on paper toweling. Heat a few minutes on cookie sheet in 350° oven before serving. Dip cluster of carrots and hold together until set.

SHRIMP RÉMOULADE

Serves: 6 - 8
Marinate: 24 hours

"Without the shrimp this makes a good dip for vegetables."

1 lb. shrimp, cooked and
   deveined
½ cup sour cream
4 tbsp. mayonnaise
juice of 1 lemon
1 bottle (12 oz.) Heinz chili
   sauce
garlic
salt
onion powder
fresh scallions
parsley

Combine all ingredients and marinate for 24 hours before serving.

CHINESE FRIED SHRIMP BALLS

Serves: 5 or 6
Cooking Time: 15 minutes

1 lb. raw shrimp cleaned,
   grind or chop fine
1 tsp. salt
2 tbsp. cornstarch
dash of pepper
1 egg
oil for deep frying

Mix ground shrimp, salt, cornstarch, and dash of pepper. Beat egg separately and slowly add to shrimp mixture (you may not need all the egg as mixture should not be too soft).

When making shrimp balls, put a little cornstarch on your hands to prevent sticking and roll balls between the palms of your hands. Make balls walnut size and deep fry about 2 or 3 minutes until golden brown. Put only 5 or 6 shrimp balls into hot oil at a time.

Serve with sweet and sour sauce or soy sauce with mustard.

SHRIMP TOAST

Yield: 24 pieces
Cooking Time: 30 minutes

"You're never caught short with this in your freezer."

½ lb. raw shrimp, minced,
  not too finely
4 water chestnuts, chopped
1 tsp. salt
½ tsp. sugar
1 tbsp. cornstarch
1 egg, lightly beaten
2 tbsp. chopped scallion,
  white only
6 slices white bread, stale
2 cups vegetable oil

Mix shrimp with chestnuts, salt, sugar, cornstarch, egg and scallions. Trim crusts off bread. Spread each slice with one-sixth of above mixture. Heat oil (to 375°) in pan. Gently lower bread into oil, shrimp side down. After one minute, turn and fry a few seconds till golden. Fry only a few at a time. Drain very well. Chill, slice into triangles. Can be frozen at this time. Heat in oven quickly. Serve with duck sauce.

SHRIMP PUFFS

Yield: 20, approximately
Cooking Time: 15 - 20 minutes

white bread
½ lb. raw shrimp
½ lb. grated American
  cheese
1½ cups mayonnaise

Trim crusts from white bread and cut into quarters. Place on cookie sheet and top with shrimp. Top shrimp with mixture of grated cheese and mayonnaise. Bake at 350° for 15-20 minutes.

CRAB MEAT SPREAD

Serves: 6
Cooking Time: 10 minutes

"Horseradish is an added tang."

1 can (7½ oz.) crab meat
1 package (8 oz.) cream cheese
2 tbsp. grated onion
½ tsp. white horseradish
dash salt
1 tbsp. milk

Soften cream cheese with milk. Separate crab meat and mix together with rest of ingredients; add to cream cheese mixture. Heat in oven-proof dish for 10 minutes and serve hot on crackers.

HOT CRAB COCKTAIL SPREAD

Serves: 6
Cooking Time: 15 minutes

"A new combo — almonds and clams."

1 package (8 oz.) cream cheese
1 tbsp. milk
2 tsp. Worcestershire sauce
1 can crab meat (7½ oz.)
2 tbsp. onion
2 tbsp. toasted slivered
   almonds

Thoroughly combine cream cheese with milk and Worcestershire sauce. Drain and flake crab meat. Add to cream cheese mixture along with onion. Turn into greased 8-inch pie plate or small, shallow baking dish. Top with almonds. Bake at 350° for 15 minutes or until heated through. Keep spread warm over candle or on hot tray. Serve with crackers.

CRAB CANAPÉS

Yield: 16 - 20
Cooking Time: 10 - 15 minutes

1 package refrigerator rolls,
   flaky type
1 package (3 oz.) cream cheese
1 tbsp. mayonnaise
¼ tsp. Worcestershire sauce
⅛ cup finely chopped onion
6 oz. frozen crab meat
paprika

Separate rolls in half and place on ungreased cookie sheet. Bake one-half the recommended time. Mix together remaining ingredients and spread on rolls. Sprinkle with paprika. Broil until hot and bubbly.

CRAB MEAT TOASTIES

Serves: 8 - 12
Cooking Time: 8 - 10 minutes

"Easy — can use on regular slice of bread for a nice open sandwich for lunch."

1 can (7 oz.) king crab meat
2 packages (4 oz.) shredded
   Cheddar cheese
2 tbsp. mayonnaise
1 package cocktail rye bread

Drain liquid from crab meat and flake it. Mix with Cheddar cheese and mayonnaise and spread (not too thickly) on rye bread. Broil until bubbly and light golden brown.

IMPERIAL CRAB APPETIZERS

Yield: 3 dozen

"Can also be used as a luncheon dish using larger tomatoes or green pepper shells. Lots of eye appeal."

1 package (6 oz.) frozen snow crab
1 package (3 oz.) cream cheese
1 tsp. mayonnaise
¼ tsp. dry mustard
8 capers, minced
½ tsp. onion salt
2 drops Tabasco
1 tbsp. minced pimento
18 cherry tomatoes
parsley sprigs
18 ¼-inch thick slices cucumber
sliced stuffed olives

Thaw snow crab; thoroughly drain and chop coarsely. Blend cream cheese, mayonnaise, and mustard together in small bowl until smooth. Stir in next three ingredients, crab, and pimento; chill. Cut thin slices from tops of cherry tomatoes; scoop out some seeds and pulp. Fill each with about one teaspoon of crab mixture. Top each with small sprig of parsley. Top each cucumber slice with about one teaspoon of crab mixture, garnish with olive slice.

HOT CRAB AND CHEESE CRESCENTS

Yield: 16
Cooking Time: 15 - 18 minutes

1 package (6 oz.) frozen snow crab or 1 can (7 oz.) king crab
½ cup mayonnaise
½ cup shredded sharp Cheddar cheese
1 tbsp. minced green onion
1 package (12 oz.) refrigerated crescent dinner rolls
1 tbsp. capers (optional)

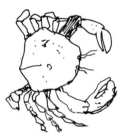

Canned king crab can be used in place of snow crab. Thaw snow crab, drain thoroughly and chop coarsely. Combine with mayonnaise, cheese, and onion; mix well. Separate roll dough at perforations; shape into triangles. Then cut lengthwise down middle of each to make a total of 16 triangles; press into shape. Spread with equal portions of crab mixture; sprinkle each with 4 to 5 capers. Roll up loosely; place on lightly greased cookie sheet. Bake at 375° 15 to 18 minutes until golden brown.

CRAB MEAT AND DILL — THE FILLED BREAD ROLL

Yield: 20 - 30
Cooking Time: ½ hour (must be made ahead and frozen.)

"You are never caught short with these in the freezer."

1 loaf thin-sliced white bread*
¾ cup sweet butter
1 package (6-7 oz.) frozen crab
  meat, thawed
salt to taste
pepper to taste
handful of chopped fresh dill
  (feathers only)
little sherry or curry powder,
  if desired

*For these rolls, you must use square-cut white bread, thin-sliced, of the Tip-Top or Wonder Bread variety. It will not work if you use Arnold or Pepperidge Farm brands.

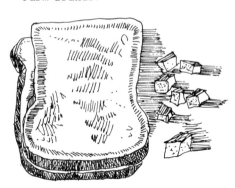

Cut off the crusts of bread (save them for bread crumbs), and roll out each slice with a rolling pin so it will be thin and flat. Melt the butter. Add the crab meat, salt, pepper, dill, and seasonings to taste. Spoon the filling along one end, roll up the bread very tightly, using lots of butter to seal them. Place the rolls very close together, seam side down, in a pan you can place in the freezer. Freeze.

Bake on buttered baking sheet at 350° for about 30 minutes, turning once. Remove when golden brown. Can be cut in half if desired.

Note: When solidly frozen you can separate the rolls and store them in a plastic bag in the freezer. You MUST bake them when they are frozen. This enables you to use them as last-minute hors d'oeuvres, since you can remove them from freezer to oven when drop-in guests arrive.

LOBSTER (OR CRAB) AND CHEESE ROLLS

Yield: Approximately 60
Cooking Time: 15 minutes

"Make ahead and freeze."

1 small Velveeta cheese
¼ lb. butter
1 lb. lobster or crab meat
1 loaf white bread, sliced

Melt cheese and butter in double boiler. Add lobster or crab meat and mix together. Remove crusts from bread and roll each slice flat with a rolling pin. Spread mixture on bread and roll up. Freeze. When removed from freezer, cut into thirds and put on cookie sheet; drizzle with butter. Bake for 15 minutes in a preheated 350-400° oven. Serve.

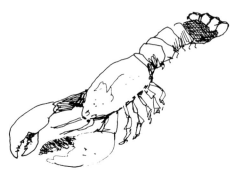

CLAM PIE

Serves: 6 - 8
Cooking Time: 15 minutes, unfrozen; 30 minutes, frozen

"Can be frozen."

2 cans (10 oz.) minced clams
  (Doxee), use juice from clams
1 tsp. lemon
1 onion
1 small green pepper
¼ cup parsley flakes
3 cloves garlic (add lots more
  to taste)
1 tsp. oregano
¼ lb. butter, melted
¾ cup unflavored bread crumbs
Parmesan cheese

Simmer clams and juice and lemon for 10 minutes. In blender, add onion, pepper, parsley, garlic, oregano to mash; add mixture to melted butter and sauté. Add clams and juice to bread crumbs, then to butter pan and stir to right consistency. FREEZE NOW.

Sprinkle Parmesan cheese on top and bake at 350° for 15 minutes, if not frozen, and 30 minutes, if frozen (brown on top). Serve with Ritz crackers.

BAKED CLAMS OREGANATO

Yield: 24
Cooking Time: 30 minutes

"Topping can be made in advance and frozen for up to a month."

2 tbsp. olive oil
2 tbsp. light vegetable oil
2 cloves garlic, minced
1 medium onion, finely minced
1½ cups fine, fresh bread
   crumbs
¼ cup fresh parsley, finely
   chopped
¼ tsp. ground black pepper
1 tsp. salt
2 tbsp. grated Parmesan cheese
1 tsp. oregano
24 littleneck clams on half
   shell

Heat oils, add garlic, and sauté until just turning golden. Scoop out garlic and discard. Add onion and sauté until soft. Place onion and oil it was cooked in into a mixing bowl, together with the bread crumbs, parsley, pepper, salt, cheese, and oregano, stirring well to mix. The mixture may seem dry. Clam juice or water may be added to moisten. Place one teaspoon of mixture on top of each clam, place under broiler about 5 inches from heat and broil 5 minutes at 375° or until topping is brown. Serve hot.

Note: This topping or stuffing (for artichokes without clam juice) may be made in advance and frozen for up to one month, then placed on top of fresh clams for heating and serving.

BAKED CLAMS

Yield: 12
Cooking Time: 20 minutes

"Quick and easy."

3 cans (8 oz.) Doxee minced
   clams
liquid from one can
½ cup of bread crumbs
3 cloves crushed garlic or
   garlic powder (to taste)
4 tbsp. olive oil
4 tbsp. Parmesan cheese
2 tsp. oregano
2 tsp. chopped parsley
12 shells

Combine all ingredients and place in shells. Bake at 350° in oven for 15 to 20 minutes.

BAKED CLAMS

Serves: 15
Cooking Time: 30 minutes

"A generous sprinkling of Tabasco and green peppers adds a punch to the clams."

3 cans (10½ oz.) clams and
   juice or 4 (8 oz.) cans
4 tsp. lemon juice
½ lb. margarine or butter
1½ large onions, diced
1 large green pepper, diced
3 cloves garlic
4 tsp. parsley
4 tbsp. oregano
¾ to 1 tsp. Tabasco
1½ cups bread crumbs
paprika
½ cup Parmesan cheese

Simmer clams and lemon juice for 10 minutes. Melt butter or margarine. Blend diced onion, pepper, garlic, and parsley in blender. Combine margarine and blended vegetables in large bowl, mix well. Add oregano, Tabasco sauce, mix well. Add simmered clams, mix well. Add bread crumbs, mix well. Spoon into large clam shell. Sprinkle paprika and grated Parmesan cheese onto filled shell. Bake at 350° for 20 minutes.

BAKED CLAMS ITALIAN HORS D'OEUVRES

Yield: 2 dozen
Cooking Time: 15 minutes

"May be frozen for future use."

2 dozen cherry stone clams,
   scrubbed
½ inch water
¾ cup melted butter
1 cup bread crumbs
2 cloves garlic, crushed
2 tbsp. chopped parsley
2 tbsp. Parmesan cheese
4 tsp. lemon juice
1 tsp oregano
dash of Tabasco

Put water in pot and bring to boil. Add clams and simmer 7 to 8 minutes until they pop. In bowl combine remaining ingredients. Remove clams from shells. Chop them coarsely and add to mixture. Spoon mixture into shells. Broil clams for 5 minutes at bottom of oven. May be frozen and reheated at 350° for 10-15 minutes. Serve with lemon and fresh parsley.

BAKED STUFFED CLAMS

Serves: 8
Cooking Time: 35 minutes

"White wine is something new."

2 tsp. garlic powder
2 tbsp. minced onion
2 tsp. parsley
oregano, to taste
½ cup bread crumbs
olive oil
2 cans (8 oz.) minced clams
1 clam can of dry white wine
¼ tsp. salt
Parmesan cheese

Sauté garlic, onion, parsley, oregano and bread crumbs in olive oil for about 2 minutes. Remove mixture from pan and mix one can clams with juice and one can clams with juice removed and replaced with white wine and salt. Spoon onto shells. Sprinkle lightly with Parmesan cheese. Bake at 375° for 25-30 minutes.

"LINDY'S" PICKLED HERRING

Serves: 2
Chill: 24 hours

"Serve as an appetizer and enjoy!"

1 jar Vita Bismark Herring,
   cut in pieces
1 pt. heavy cream
2 onions, sliced

Drain herring, cut in pieces, discard juice. Make layers of herring, sweet cream, onions. Let stand in refrigerator 24 hours in a covered jar.

HORS D'OEUVRE EGG AND CAVIAR MOLD

Serves: 12
Preparation Time: 15 minutes (refrigerate overnight)

1 package (8 oz.) cream cheese
2 packages (3 oz. each) chive
   cheese
9 hard-boiled eggs
1 small jar red or black caviar
½ pt. sour cream

Chop hard-boiled eggs very finely; add cream cheese and chive cheese and blend thoroughly. Pack into a lightly oiled 2-cup ring mold and refrigerate overnight. To Serve: Unmold on serving plate and frost with sour cream. Make an indentation around top of mold and fill with caviar. Serve with crackers or party rye bread.

Coconut Chicken Puffs

Yield: 24
Cooking Time: 30 minutes

1½ cups flour
2 tsp. baking powder
¾ tsp. salt
1 egg, beaten
1 cup milk or water
1 package Lipton onion soup mix
6 chicken cutlets
oil
1 package shredded coconut

Mix flour, baking powder, salt, egg, and milk in a bowl. Add soup mix dry. Skin and bone chicken cutlets. Boil until tender. Cut chicken into chunks. Dip into batter, then coconut, and deep fry. Drain and serve.

Chicken Yak-Tori

Yield: 12 pieces
Cooking Time: 5 minutes
Marinate: 15 minutes

1 chicken breast, boneless
1 can pineapple chunks
½ cup soy sauce
⅓ cup sugar
1 clove garlic, minced

Cut chicken breast into 1-inch pieces. Drain pineapple, reserving one-third cup syrup. Combine this syrup, soy sauce, sugar, and garlic, bring to a boil and cool. Place chicken and pineapple on skewers. Marinate in sauce 15 minutes. Broil 6 inches from heat. Turn once.

Chinese Chicken Wings

Yield: 24
Cooking Time: 45 - 60 minutes
Marinate: Overnight

2 dozen chicken wings
3 tbsp. hoisin sauce*
3 tbsp. sherry
3 tbsp. soy sauce
1 tbsp. dry mustard
1 tsp. Accent
3 tbs. grated fresh ginger root*

*These items may be purchased at the Oriental Gift and Gourmet, 74 N. Franklin, Hempstead, N.Y.

Marinate chicken in above mixture overnight. Roast on foil lined cookie sheets, do not crowd pieces. Bake at 350° for 45-60 minutes. Serve hot! Spareribs, pork butt strips, chicken pieces may be substituted for the wings. Increase marinade and adjust cooking times accordingly.

Rumaki

3 tsp. soy sauce
¼ tsp. garlic powder
1 tsp. sherry
1 tsp. horseradish
20 mushroom caps or water
   chestnuts, cut into slices
½ lb. chicken livers, cut in
   half
½ lb. bacon, cut in half

Mix soy sauce, garlic powder, sherry, and horseradish. Marinate chicken livers in this mixture overnight. Roll mushroom caps and liver in one-half bacon slice. Secure with toothpick and broil until done, turning once, approximately 12-15 minutes.

Chopped Liver

Serves: 4
Cooking Time: 20 minutes

"Serve with crackers or on a bed of lettuce for an appetizer."

2 medium-size onions, cut up
1 tsp. margarine
1 lb. chicken livers
1 hard-boiled egg

Cut onions into small pieces. Place in fry pan with margarine. Sauté, covered, over low flame until onions are brown and soft. Add a drop of hot water if onions are dry. Add chicken livers and continue cooking with cover on until liver looks done (about 10 minutes). Drain juice into a bowl and reserve. Chop the liver, onions, and egg together. If consistency looks too dry, add some juice. Season with salt to taste.

CHOPPED LIVER PUFFS

Yield: Approximately 80
Cooking Time: 10 minutes

"Monte Cristo style."

1 loaf egg or white bread, sliced
1 lb. chopped liver (more if desired)
4 - 6 eggs, beaten

Cut crusts off bread. Spread liver between bread slices like sandwiches. Cut diagonally twice to make four triangles. Dip each triangle into beaten eggs and fry in hot oil on both sides until brown. They can be frozen at this point. If too large, cut into smaller pieces for easier handling.

BARBECUED CHICKEN LIVERS

Serves: 8 - 10
Cooking Time: 25 minutes

1 lb. chicken livers
2 tbsp. honey
2 tbsp. soy sauce
¼ cup corn oil
1 tbsp. white wine
1 clove garlic, crushed
1 hard-boiled egg, more may be added if desired

Rinse chicken livers. Drain on absorbent paper towels. Let stand 30 minutes in combination with remaining ingredients. Spoon livers with sauce into greased, shallow baking pan. Bake at 375° about 25 minutes, turning once.

SWEET AND SOUR MEATBALLS

Serves: 15 - 20
Cooking Time: 30 - 40 minutes

"This is an easy one."

2 lb. chopped meat
2 eggs, beaten
2 slices wet bread
salt to taste
pepper to taste
1 can whole cranberries
1 can Arturo spaghetti sauce (found in most Hills and A & P supermarkets)

Combine meat, eggs, bread, and seasonings. Form into small balls. Fry until lightly brown. In a saucepan, combine cranberries and spaghetti sauce. Add meatballs when sauce is blended and cook over low flame for 30 minutes.

24

SWEET AND SOUR MEATBALLS

Serves: 8 - 10
Cooking Time: 1 hour

"Quick, easy, and good."

1 lb. ground beef
1 egg
¼ cup bread crumbs
salt
pepper
garlic powder
¼ cup water
1 bottle (12 oz.) Heinz chili
   sauce
6 oz. grape jelly

Mix beef, egg, bread crumbs, salt, pepper, garlic powder, water, and shape into small balls about three-quarter inch in diameter. Heat chili sauce and grape jelly until they blend. Drop raw meatballs into sauce and simmer, covered, approximately 45 minutes.

COCKTAIL MEATBALLS

(MINIATURE)

Yield: 60
Cooking Time: 35 minutes

*"I have made this recipe for about 15 years and found
it in the Daily News Magazine!"*

1 lb. finely ground lean beef
½ cup soft bread crumbs
¼ cup milk
1 tbsp. finely minced onion
salt
2 tbsp. butter or margarine
½ cup sherry wine
½ cup ketchup
¼ tsp. oregano

Combine beef, bread crumbs, milk, onions, and one teaspoon salt. Mix well. Shape lightly but firmly into small balls. Allow about one teaspoon mixture per meat ball. Melt butter in heavy skillet. Brown meat balls nicely on all sides. Pour off most of the fat. Blend wine, ketchup, and oregano. Add salt to taste. Pour over meatballs in skillet. Cover, simmer gently, shaking pan now and then to assure even cooking, about twenty minutes. Transfer meatballs and sauce to attractive chafing dish or pottery casserole, set over candle warmer. Provide a supply of cocktail toothpicks. Also, accompany the meatballs with a basket of French rolls, sliced crosswise and buttered, for those who like bread with their meat.

MINIATURE MEAT TURNOVERS

Yield: 32
Cooking Time: 15 minutes

1 envelope Lipton beef flavor
  mushroom mix
½ lb. ground beef
1 cup drained bean sprouts
½ cup sliced water chestnuts
2 tbsp. chopped onions
2 packages refrigerator
  crescent rolls

Preheat oven to 375°. In medium skillet combine first five ingredients. Brown well. Separate roll dough as package directs. Cut in half. Place spoonful of mixture in center of each triangle. Fold and seal. Place on ungreased cookie sheet and bake 15 minutes, until golden brown.

BACON ROLLS WITH COTTAGE CREAM

Serves: 10
Cooking Time: 1 hour

24 prunes
12 slices back bacon
1 package (8 oz.) cottage
  cheese with chives
salt
pepper
paprika
butter
wooden cocktail sticks
¼ pt. sour cream

Cook prunes in water over low heat for about 15 minutes. Drain and remove pits. Lay the bacon on a board and spread each slice with cottage cheese, salt, pepper, and paprika lightly. Put two prunes on one end of each bacon slice, roll up, securing the roll with a wooden cocktail stick. Put into a covered dish and bake in a low 350° oven for 30 minutes. Remove dish from oven, add the sour cream and cook for another 15 minutes at 325°. Serve hot.

Blini

(HOT PANCAKE HORS D'OEUVRE)

Yield: 25
Preparation Time: 45 minutes

2 egg yolks
2 eggs
1 cup milk
1 cup buckwheat flour
1 tbsp. melted butter
melted butter
black or red caviar
sour cream

Beat together egg yolks, eggs, and milk with whisk. Add buckwheat flour. Add one tablespoon melted butter and whisk until smooth. Heat pan, butter lightly (only once). Cover blini pan lightly with batter. Turn as soon as edges are slightly brown. Stack pancakes and keep them warm in covered casserole. To serve, cover with melted butter and accompany with dish of black or red caviar and dish of sour cream. Pancakes have a better texture if batter sets in refrigerator from one-half to two hours.

Plum-Glazed Franks

Yield: 24
Cooking Time: 20 minutes

"Great for chafing dishes."

¼ cup plum jelly
¼ cup finely chopped chutney
1 tsp. vinegar
dash garlic salt
1 package cocktail franks or
   Viennese sausages

Mix jelly, chutney, vinegar, and garlic salt in small chafing dish. Add franks, heat through, stirring constantly. Serve hot with wooden picks for serving and eating.

Nut Candy

Cooking Time: 35 minutes

"To be served with drinks. Easy."

1 lb. unsalted nuts, mixed or
   of your choice (no peanuts)
¼ lb. unsalted butter
2 egg whites
1 cup sugar

Preheat oven to 400°. Brown nuts for 10 minutes. On a cookie sheet with sides, melt butter in oven. Beat egg whites stiff. Add sugar and nuts. Pour over butter in cookie sheet. Bake 25 minutes. Turn the mixture with spatula every 10 minutes. Watch last five minutes so as not to scorch.

Sangria

(PUNCH)

Serves: 12

"Double, triple, and enjoy, enjoy, and enjoy!"

3 peaches, peeled and sliced
3 oz. peach brandy
1 lemon
2 oranges
½ large apple (optional)
1 qt. sangria (more if desired)
chilled club soda (up to 24 oz.)

Let peaches stand in brandy for one hour. Cut lemon and oranges into ¼-inch slices. Cut apple into wedges. Combine fruit, brandy, and sangria in pitcher. Stir with long wooden spoon. Refrigerate at least one hour. Add chilled club soda just before serving. Stir again and serve in chilled wine glasses.

Soups

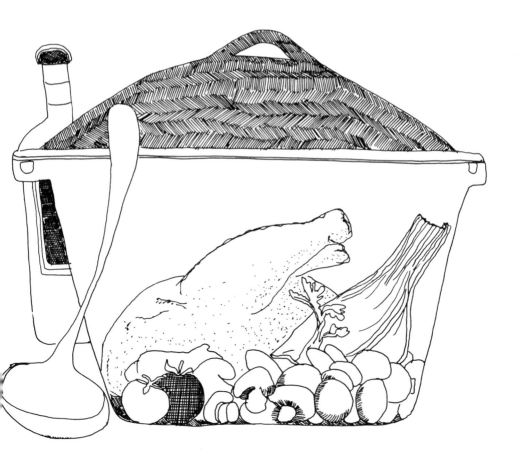

CHILLED ASPARAGUS SOUP

Serves: 8
Cooking Time: 15 minutes
Chill: 4 hours

"Refreshing summer soup."

2 large leeks, chopped (1 cup)
¼ cup butter or margarine
3 envelopes or tsps. instant
    chicken broth
3 cups water
2 packages (10 oz. each)
    frozen asparagus pieces
¼ cup flour
1 tsp. salt
⅛ tsp. pepper
2 cups light cream

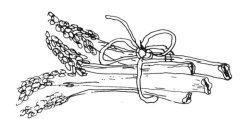

Sauté leeks in butter or margarine (in a large skillet) until soft. Combine chicken broth and water in a large saucepan; bring to boil; add asparagus and cook 5 minutes. Remove with a slotted spoon and add to leeks. Stir flour into the asparagus and leeks until absorbed; add chicken broth, salt and pepper. Simmer 3 minutes. Pour part of the soup at a time into container of electric blender, cover, blend until smooth. Pour into large bowl. Stir in light cream; cover, chill at least 4 hours. Pour into chilled serving bowl. Garnish with lightly salted whipped cream and parsley, if you wish. Serve icy cold.

JELLIED MADRILENE

Serves: 6
Cooking Time: 15 minutes
Chill: 4 hours

"Great in summer; low in calories."

2 envelopes unflavored gelatin
1 can (18 oz.) tomato juice
3 packages onion-flavored MBT
    broth
2 cups boiling water
⅛ tsp. salt
dash of pepper
lemon wedges
caviar
6 tsp. sour cream

Sprinkle gelatin on tomato juice to soften. Dissolve broth in boiling water. Add to gelatin, stirring until dissolved. Add seasonings. Cool. Chill in individual serving cups or bowls until set. Garnish with lemon wedges or caviar and teaspoon sour cream.

QUICK GAZPACHO

Serves: 4 - 6
Cooking Time: 1 minute
Chill: 2 hours

"Blender recipe."

1 clove garlic, sliced
1 small onion, sliced
½ green pepper, sliced
1½ cups chilled tomato juice
½ medium cucumber, peeled
    and sliced
2 medium tomatoes, peeled,
    seeded, and quartered
1 tsp. salt
¼ tsp. pepper
½ cup chilled chicken
    bouillon or 1 bouillon cube
    dissolved in ½ cup hot
    water and chilled
2 tbsp. olive oil
3 tbsp. wine vinegar

Blend first three ingredients and one-half cup tomato juice 30 seconds or until very finely chopped. Add cucumber, tomatoes, salt and pepper.

Blend 20 seconds or until ingredients are finely chopped, but not smooth. Pour into bowl. Stir in remaining one cup tomato juice, bouillon, oil, and vinegar. Cover. Chill well.

Serve in small soup bowls in crushed ice. Garnish with watercress and cucumber slices or serve with an assortment of buttered croutons, diced cucumber, green pepper, onion and tomato, as desired. Yield: about four cups.

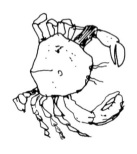

CRAB MEAT BISQUE

Serves: 8 - 10
Cooking Time: 15 minutes

"Elegant but easy."

1 can tomato soup
1 can green pea soup
1 can beef bouillon
½ cup heavy cream
½ cup sherry
½ lb. crab meat
¼ tsp. salt

Mix undiluted soups. Bring to a Boil. Add cream, sherry, crab meat, and salt. Make early in the day and let stand. Reheat before serving. Add extra sherry if desired.

ALASKA CRAB CHOWDER

Serves: 4
Cooking Time: 15 minutes

"Hot and hearty."

¼ cup minced onion
2 tbsp. chopped green pepper
¼ cup butter or margarine
1 can cream of celery soup
1½ cups milk
1 package (10 oz.) frozen whole kernel corn, thawed
½ tsp. seasoning salt
1 package (6 oz.) frozen king or snow crab, partially thawed
1 tbsp. minced pimento

In 1½ quart saucepan, sauté onion and green pepper in butter until tender. Stir in remaining ingredients except crab and pimento. Simmer, stirring occasionally, about 5 minutes. Stir in crab and pimento; heat a few minutes longer.

MANHATTAN CLAM CHOWDER

Serves: 12 - 16
Cooking Time: 1 hour, 15 minutes

"Wonderful on a cold night."

8 oz. lean salt pork, diced
2 large onions, diced
3 stalks celery, sliced chunks
2 green peppers, diced
2 carrots, sliced in rounds
4 medium potatoes, cubed
4 tsp. salt
¾ tsp. pepper
1½ tsp. thyme
2 large cans Redpack tomatoes (6 cups)
5 cups water
3 dozen large chowder clams, chopped
1 qt. clam liquid

Cook pork until brown. Brown onions, then celery and peppers. Add remaining ingredients and simmer one hour.

Shrimp and Corn Chowder

Serves: 4
Cooking Time: 8 minutes

"This is a quickie and very nice."

1 lb. can cream-style corn
2 cups chicken consommé
salt
pepper
1 can shrimp (4 oz.)
1 tsp. snipped fresh dill
1 tsp. parsley, chopped

Combine corn and chicken consommé in saucepan and simmer for five minutes. Taste for seasoning and add salt and pepper, if needed. (This depends on the amount of seasoning in the chicken consommé.) Add deveined shrimp, dill, and parsley and simmer, but do not boil, for three minutes longer. Serve hot.

Spiced Lobster Bisque

Serves: 6 - 8
Cooking Time: 30 minutes

6 tbsp. butter
6 tbsp. flour
1 tsp. salt
¼ tsp. ground black pepper
½ tsp. celery salt
4½ cups milk
1½ cups chicken stock
3 tbsp. instant minced onion
3 cups diced cooked lobster
1 tbsp. paprika
½ cup light cream

Melt butter. Stir in flour, salt, pepper, and celery salt. When smoothly blended, add milk and chicken stock slowly. Cook over low heat, stirring constantly, until mixture begins to thicken. Add onion, lobster, and paprika. Heat 10 minutes. Add cream. Reheat to serving temperature.

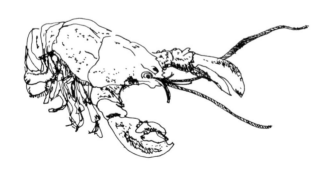

Beef 'n' Barley Vegetable Soup

Serves: 12
Cooking Time: 3 hours, 10 minutes

"Hearty enough for a wintertime meal, served with salad."

3 lb. soup meat (short rib or flanken)
2 tbsp. fat
2 qt. water
1½ tbsp. salt
¼ tsp. pepper
2 tbsp. minced parsley
½ cup barley*
1 cup cubed carrots
¼ cup chopped onion
½ cup chopped celery
2 cups canned tomatoes, drained
1 cup fresh or frozen peas

*Add more barley for thicker soup; less barley for thinner soup. If leftover soup becomes too thick, dilute with beef broth. Can be doubled or tripled and freezes well.

Brown meat with bones in hot fat. Place meat, soup bone, water, seasonings, and parsley in soup kettle. Cover tightly and cook slowly one hour. Add barley and cook one hour longer. Cool and skim off excess fat. Remove soup bone. Add carrots, onion, celery, and tomatoes; cook 45 minutes. Add fresh peas and continue cooking 15 minutes.

Beef-Barley Soup

Serves: 8 - 10
Cooking Time: 2½ hours

2 lb. beef short ribs
1 can (16 oz.) cut green beans
1 can (16 oz.) lima beans
4 cups water
1 cup carrots, chopped
¾ cup onion, chopped
⅓ cup barley
1 tbsp. salt
1 tbsp. sugar
1 bay leaf
½ tsp. basil leaf
1 lb. peeled tomatoes in purée

In soup pot, place short ribs, liquid from both cans of beans (not beans), water, carrot, onion, barley, seasonings, and tomatoes. Bring to boil then let simmer two hours partially covered. Cut meat from bones and discard bones. Put meat back in pot, add beans and heat and serve. If possible, place soup in refrigerator overnight and skim off fat.

Lentil Soup

Serves: 10
Cooking Time: 1 hour, 30 minutes

½ lb lentils
2 carrots, cut into small
  pieces
2 stalks celery, cut into
  small pieces
2 medium onions, finely
  chopped
2-3 sprigs parsley, finely
  chopped
olive oil
salt
½ lb. elbow macaroni, cooked
Parmesan cheese
ham bone (optional)*

*If ham bone is used, put it in
with onions, carrots, etc.

Rinse lentils in cold water. Put lentils in four-quart pot, add cold water to fill pot a little more than half (lentils will swell). Add carrots, celery, onions, and parsley. Bring to a boil, then simmer for one and one-half hours. Add water if needed (warm or hot water only). About five minutes before soup is ready, add salt to taste and one tablespoon olive oil. (Salt added while soup is cooking in early stages will toughen lentils.)

I put in a (small) serving of elbows in a soup dish, add soup, sprinkle with cheese, and serve.

Green Split Pea Soup

Serves: 4
Cooking Time: 2 hours

1 cup green split peas
leg of lamb bone
6 cups water
salt to taste
pepper to taste
whole onion
2 carrots, sliced in rounds
3 stalks celery, diced
1 tomato, cut up

Wash peas and put in pot with lamb bone and water. Season to taste. Boil ½ hour. Add onion, carrots, celery, and tomato. Boil 1 to 1½ hours. Stir occasionally. Should be thick. (Package of soup greens may be used.)

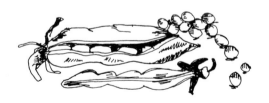

Mock Split Pea Soup

Serves: 4
Cooking Time: 15 minutes

"This is a great tasting soup and has very few calories."

1 can (1 lb.) asparagus
1 can (1 lb.) French-style
  string beans
1 envelope or cube chicken
  or beef bouillon
½ envelope onion broth
dash salt
dash pepper
dash garlic
1 tsp. dried soup greens
  without potato
1 tsp. dried mushrooms

Blend asparagus and string beans in blender. Pour into 1¾ quart pot. Add all other ingredients. Add water to fill pot. Cook for about 15 minutes or until it boils, and carrots and soup greens get soft.

Mushroom Soup

Serves: 4
Cooking Time: 45 minutes

"This is a real mushroom lovers treat!"

½ oz. dried mushrooms
3½ cups water or stock
½ cup minced onions
½ cup carrots, diced
½ cup minced celery
½ tsp. dill
½ tsp. parsley
2 tbsp. butter
2 tbsp. flour

Cook mushrooms and onion for 20 minutes in water at a slow simmer. Add carrots and celery and cook 20 minutes more. Add herbs. Make a roux of flour and butter and add to soup. Stir for 5 minutes and serve hot.

Onion Soup

Serves: 10
Cooking Time: 3½ hours

"You don't have to be French to make this well."

2 lb. onions, sliced
2 tbsp. oil
8 cups water
3 envelopes G. Washington
   broth
soup bones
¼ tsp. salt
½ cup white wine
Italian or French bread,
   sliced thin
grated Parmesan cheese
Swiss Gruyère cheese

Slice onions. Sauté with oil until cooked and light brown. Add water, broth powder, and soup bones. After cooking a while, add salt to suit your taste. Add white wine. Simmer very slowly 2 - 3 hours. Butter slices of bread and sprinkle with Parmesan cheese. Place slices on cookie sheet and bake to delicate brown. Put slice of bread in each bowl and pour soup over. Top with grated Swiss Gruyère cheese.

Scallion Soup

Serves: 6
Cooking Time: 30 minutes

¼ lb. sweet butter
5 bunches of scallions, finely
   chopped
1 tsp. salt
½ tsp. pepper
2 tbs. flour
5 cups chicken stock
¾ lb. fresh mushrooms,
   sliced
1¼ cups cream

Place the stick of butter in a large pot. Add scallions, salt, and pepper. Mix thoroughly and cook slowly without browning for about ten minutes, stirring all the while. Remove from heat and stir in the flour. Smooth. Add the stock and stir over flame until the mixture boils. Simmer for ten minutes uncovered. Remove from heat and add one-half pound of the mushrooms. Place all in electric blender and blend. (For easier handling, cool first.)

    To reheat, add one and one-quarter cups of cream without boiling. Serve garnished with raw, sliced mushroom if desired.

Seafood

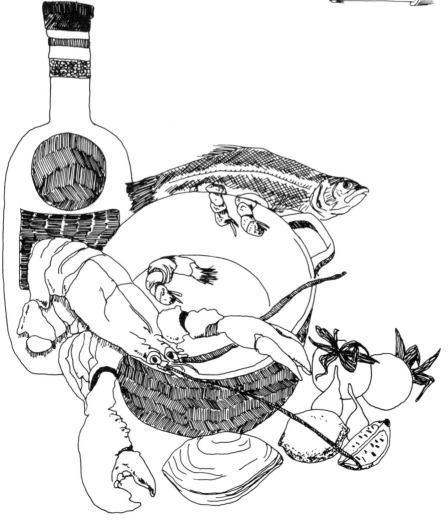

STUFFED FILET OF FLOUNDER

Serves: 4
Cooking Time: 15 - 20 minutes

"Easy as can be and delicious too."

8 slices filet of flounder
salt
pepper
oregano
parsley flakes
¼ lb. butter, lightly salted
1 can (6½ oz.) crab meat
oil

Preheat oven to 350°. Oil bottom of pan. Take four pieces filet of flounder and place in baking dish. Add a pinch of salt, pepper, oregano, and parsley to each filet. Slice two pats of butter per filet and put on top. Divide crab meat into quarters and place on top of each filet. Top each filet with one of the remaining filets. Add a little oil to top of filets. Baste frequently while baking. Bake at 350° for 15 - 20 minutes.

FISH BAKED IN HERB SAUCE

Serves: 5
Cooking Time: 25 - 30 minutes

2 lb. cod filets
3 tbsp. minced onion
3 tbsp. minced celery
4 tbsp. butter or margarine
2 tbsp. flour
2½ cups canned tomatoes
1 tsp. salt
⅛ tsp. pepper
1 tbsp. sugar
½ tsp. thyme
1 tbsp. minced parsley
buttered crumbs

Cut fish into one-inch pieces. Sauté onion and celery in butter or margarine until tender. Stir in flour until smooth. Add tomatoes, salt, pepper, sugar, thyme, and minced parsley and bring to a boil. Add sauce to fish and mix thoroughly. Pour into greased casserole. Top with buttered crumbs. Bake at 400° for 25 - 30 minutes, until fish flakes easily.

Filet Sole Marguery

Serves: 6 - 8
Cooking Time: 30 minutes

"Fish going fancy."

6 filets of sole or flounder
1 medium onion, peeled
4 or 5 parsley sprigs
1 carrot, peeled
2 packages (10 oz.) frozen
  spinach
½ lb. sliced mushrooms, fresh
  or canned
½ lb. shrimp
pepper to taste
salt to taste
2 cans shrimp soup, undiluted
¼ lb. grated Swiss cheese
bread crumbs
tufts of butter or margarine

Cut filets in half lengthwise to make 12 filets. Boil in salted water to cover with onion, parsley, and carrot. Cook 10 to 15 minutes. Throw off water. Let fish cool so that they can be handled without breaking. Cook spinach as per package directions. Spread spinach to cover bottom of baking dish. (Use dish that is brought to table and served from.) Lay filets on top of spinach. Cut shrimp and spread over filets with small amount of salt and freshly ground pepper to taste. Pour over all the cans of soup (if too thick add two tablespoons milk). Spread grated cheese, a little bread crumbs, and small tufts of butter here and there. Bake in 350° oven until top is lightly browned. Serve with tossed salad.

Fish Steaks à la Grecque

Serves: 4
Cooking Time: 30 - 40 minutes

1½ lb. halibut steak
salt
pepper
1 tbsp. lemon juice
2 tbsp. olive oil
1½ cups sliced onions
1½ cups diced celery
3 medium carrots, diced
¼ cup finely chopped parsley
1 clove garlic, peeled, finely
  chopped
1 can (8 oz.) tomato sauce
1 cup dry white wine

Sprinkle fish with salt and pepper and lemon juice. In large heavy skillet, heat the oil and sauté the onion, celery, carrots, parsley, and garlic gently, stirring often, until onion is soft, about 7 minutes. Add tomato sauce, wine, one teaspoon salt, and one-quarter teaspoon pepper. Cover and simmer about 20 minutes. Place half the sauce in a shallow baking dish, arrange the halibut over the sauce, then spoon on remaining sauce. Bake uncovered, in preheated 350° oven for 20-30 minutes or until fish flakes with a fork.

Sweet and Sour Fish

Serves: 6
Cooking Time: 2 hours, 5 minutes
Marinate: Overnight

"Best when served cold."

1 cleaned carp (about 4 lb.)
cider vinegar
2 large onions, thinly sliced
pepper
2 lemons, thinly sliced
⅓ cup raisins
6 gingersnaps, crumbled
brown sugar

Place fish in bowl. Cover with cider vinegar and let stand overnight, covered. (This considerably firms the fish preventing its falling apart while cooking.) Drain the fish the next day. Place in cooking pot. Add enough water just to cover fish. Remove fish, draining it on paper towels. Add the onions to the water and bring just to a boil. Replace the fish in the pot, reduce heat, and simmer gently for 1¾ hours. After one hour add pepper, lemon slices, and raisins. When fish is done, remove to platter. Add crumbled gingersnaps to sauce as a thickening agent. Add more for a thicker sauce. Correct the sweet and sour flavoring by adding brown sugar or, for tartness, some cider vinegar.

Seafood Crêpe

Serves: 8 as appetizer; 4 as main dish
Cooking Time: 15 minutes

"Good as an appetizer also."

8 crêpes made from Basic
  Crêpe Batter (see page 139).
5 tbsp. butter
1 shallot diced fine or 2 tbsp.
  minced onion
4 mushrooms, diced fine
6 tbsp. flour
1 cup milk
½ cup chicken broth or clam
  juice
½ cup heavy cream
¼ tsp. dry mustard
1 tsp. salt
½ tsp. white pepper
1 tbsp. cognac
2 cups seafood or poached fish
2 egg yolks
½ cup whipped cream
2 tbsp. sherry
2 tbsp. Parmesan cheese

Prepare Cream Sauce: Melt two tablespoons butter in a sauce pan. Sauté shallot and mushrooms for two minutes. Add remainder of butter. Blend in flour and stir well. Remove from flame and add milk, broth, and cream a little at a time. Season with mustard, salt, pepper, and cognac. Return to flame and allow to thicken. Cook for two or three minutes. Remove from flame and cool slightly.

Blend seafood or fish with 1½ cups sauce. Set aside remaining one-half cup of sauce. Taste and adjust seasonings. Divide mixture between eight crêpes by placing two or three tablespoons of it along center of each crêpe and roll up. Place on buttered oven-proof dish and bake for ten minutes at 400°. Stir egg yolks well and slowly add one-half cup cream sauce to yolks. Fold in whipped cream, sherry, and cheese. Pour this over crêpes. Place under broiler until sauce bubbles and browns, about one minute.

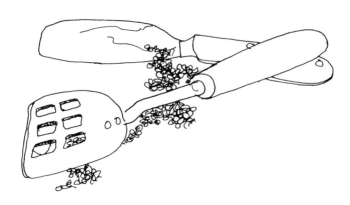

CLAM DIGGERS SCALLOP

Serves: 4
Cooking Time: 1 hour

1 can (10½ oz.) minced clams
  (Doxsee)
1 can (10¼ oz.) baby clams
  (Progresso), save juice
1 cup milk
2 eggs, beaten
½ cup melted margarine
30 crushed unsalted saltines

Add clam juice to milk to make 1½ cups. Mix clams and blend ingredients well. Bake at 350° for one hour. If using fresh clams, match proportions given.

HOT CRAB PASTRIES

Serves: 6
Cooking Time: 20 minutes

"Lovely ladies' luncheon."

1 tbsp. butter
1 can cream of mushroom soup
¼ cup white wine
6 oz. frozen crab
½ cup shredded American cheese
parsley
pimento
¼ cup peas
4 oz. mushrooms
6 pastry shells, baked (I use
  Pepperidge Farm)

Melt butter in sauce pan. Add soup and wine. Cook over medium heat, stirring constantly until creamy. Add crab and stir. Stir in cheese and, if desired, any of the remaining ingredients. Reduce heat and cook until cheese has blended in. Serve in pastry shells.

MARYLAND CRAB CAKES

Serves: 2
Cooking Time: 10 minutes
Chill: 2 hours

1 can (7 oz.) fresh white
  crab meat
2 slices cubed soft white bread
2 eggs
1 level tsp. mustard
⅓ cup mayonnaise
chopped parsley
cracker meal
oil

Mix crab meat, cubed bread, one egg, mustard, mayonnaise, and parsley. Form mixture into four or five cakes. Dip into one beaten egg then cracker meal. Refrigerate at least two hours. Fry in deep oil until golden brown. Serve on hamburger buns, with tartar sauce or relish.

44

CRAB CAKE ON BUNS

Yield: 6 sandwiches
Cooking Time: 10 minutes

*"Good luncheon dish or fun for an evening snack.
Simple and super!"*

2 (6 oz.) or 1 (12 oz.) package
  snow crab
½ cup soft bread crumbs
½ cup finely minced celery
2 tbsp. finely minced onion
½ cup mayonnaise
1 tbsp. chili sauce
1 tbsp. prepared mustard
1 tbsp. lemon juice
½ tsp. salt
⅛ tsp. pepper
fine dry bread crumbs
6 sesame seed buns, split,
  toasted, and buttered
lettuce
tomato
sweet pickle relish

Thaw snow crab; drain thoroughly and chop coarsely. Toss with soft bread crumbs, celery, and onion. Stir in mayonnaise, chili sauce, mustard, lemon juice, salt, and pepper; chill. Shape into six patties; coat with fine dry bread crumbs. Brown in lightly oiled skillet over medium heat about five minutes; turn once. Serve open face on bottom halves of buns. Arrange lettuce leaf, slice of tomato, and dab of pickle relish on top halves of buns.

SPINACH CRAB MEAT CASSEROLE

Serves: 4
Cooking Time: 30 minutes

"Different buffet or luncheon dish."

2 packages (10 oz.) frozen
  spinach
butter
¼ cup sour cream
1 lb. frozen (canned) Dungeness
  crab meat
toasted croutons
¼ lb. butter, softened
1 cup sour cream
2 tbsp. minced scallions and
  tops
2 tsp. minced parsley
salt
pepper
cayenne

Cook and drain spinach. Place in bottom of buttered casserole. Spread on a layer of sour cream and crab meat and then a layer of rough, crisp toasted croutons. Make a paste of butter, sour cream, scallions, parsley, salt, pepper, and cayenne; use this to top casserole. Bake about thirty minutes in a 350° oven.

Avocado and Crab en Casserole

Serves: 6
Cooking Time: 35 minutes

"Elegant and easy. Can be prepared in advance and cooked 20 minutes prior to serving."

¼ cup diced green pepper
2 tbsp. minced onion
2 tbsp. minced celery
2 tbsp. butter or margarine
2 tbsp. flour
1 cup milk
¼ cup dairy sour cream
1 cup shredded sharp Cheddar
  cheese
½ tsp. seasoning salt
½ tsp. Worcestershire sauce
2 (6 oz.) or 1 (12 oz.) package
  frozen king crab, thawed
1 ripe avocado, cut in crescents
1 tbsp. lemon juice
½ cup soft bread crumbs or
  ⅓ cup sliced almonds

Sauté green pepper, onion, and celery in butter in sauce pan. Blend in flour; add milk, then sour cream, stirring constantly. Cook over medium heat, stirring until thick and smooth. Add next three ingredients; stir until cheese is melted. Fold in king crab. Pour into one-quart baking dish. Can be prepared ahead up to this point. Sprinkle avocado crescents with lemon juice; arrange over top of crab mixture. Sprinkle with bread crumbs or almonds. Bake at 375° twenty minutes until mixture is bubbly and crumbs or almonds browned lightly.

Crab Casserole

Serves: 5 - 6
Cooking Time: 15 - 25 minutes

"Great with salmon or tuna."

1½ cups soft bread crumbs
1½ cups milk
2 cups crab meat (13 oz. can)
5 hard-cooked eggs
⅓ tsp. dry mustard
1½ tsp. salt
dash of pepper
½ cup melted butter or
  margarine

Moisten bread crumbs with milk. Remove fibers and bones from crab meat. Mix with bread crumbs and milk. Also add finely chopped eggs, mustard, salt, pepper, and butter. Pour into buttered baking dish (not too deep). Sprinkle with dry bread crumbs. Dot with butter. Bake for 15 - 25 minutes at 375 - 400°.

CRAB MEAT CRÊPES

Yield: 15
Preparation Time: 2 hours (30 minutes to heat before serving)

*"Not easy, but certainly worth the extra effort.
Must be made ahead."*

Crêpes:

½ onion
½ cup water
½ cup milk
2 eggs
2 egg yolks
1¼ cups flour
salt
1 tbsp. melted butter

Blend onion, water, milk, eggs, and egg yolks together. Add flour and salt to moist mixture. Add melted butter and beat until smooth. Refrigerate at least thirty minutes. Make individual crêpes and fill with crab meat, chicken, or mushroom filling.

Crab Meat Filling:

1 lb. (or 2 cans) crab meat*
2 eggs
⅓ cup minced parsley
½ tsp. dry mustard
½ tsp. salt
2 tbsp. dry sherry
1 tbsp. instant flour
enough Bechamel Sauce to hold mixture together

Combine all ingredients.

*Shredded cooked chicken or sautéed mushrooms chopped coarse can be substituted.

Bechamel Sauce:

2 tbsp. butter
2 tbsp. flour
1 cup milk
1 small onion, studded with
   cloves
½ small bay leaf
½ cup grated Parmesan cheese
1 cup broth
salt

Melt butter. Add and blend flour over low heat. Slowly stir in milk. Add remaining ingredients and cook, stirring with wooden spoon until thickened and smooth. Strain sauce and correct seasonings. To thicken add a little more cheese.

Spread layer of sauce at bottom of casserole. Fill crêpes with filling and arrange in casserole. Cover with sauce and heat through in a 350° preheated over for approximately thirty minutes.

Stuffed Lobster Tails

Serves: 12
Cooking Time: 25 minutes

"For those special parties. Can be prepared ahead."

12 lobster tails
3 cans frozen cream of shrimp
  soup
⅓ cup sherry
2 cans (4 oz. each) sliced
  mushrooms, drained
dry bread crumbs, buttered
paprika

Boil lobster tails. Cool; cut shells and remove meat. Cut meat into chunks. Reserve shells. Heat soup; add sherry and mushrooms. Mix with lobster meat. Stuff into shells; sprinkle with crumbs and paprika. Bake at 350° for 25 minutes or until browned lightly.

Baked Stuffed Lobster

Serves: 1
Cooking Time: 45 - 50 minutes

"For those extra special times."

1 lobster (1½ to 2 lb.)
juice from ½ lemon)
1 tbsp. butter
paprika

Stuffing:

roe from lobster
½ cup seasoned bread crumbs
1 tbsp. melted butter
1 tbsp. white wine

Ask fish store to split and clean live lobster for broiling and baking and use same day. Place stuffed lobster in large baking pan. Sprinkle with lemon juice and paprika. Dot with butter and place open and uncovered into 375° oven for 45 - 50 minutes to bake. Melt butter and lemon to use as a sauce dip and enjoy.

Sweet and Sour Shrimp and Vegetables

Serves: 6
Cooking Time: 30 minutes

"Quick and easy. Stir, fry — should be crisp."

2 lb. cleaned, shelled shrimp
cornstarch for rolling shrimp
oil for deep frying
1 cup water, warm
3 tbsp. sugar
3 tbsp. soy sauce
½ tsp. salt
¾ tsp. garlic powder
3 tbsp. wine vinegar
3 shakes Eno Itchi Ban, rice
   seasoning, or MSG
¼ cup sake or dry vermouth
3 tbsp. cornstarch
3 tsp. oil
6 shakes cayenne pepper
1 carrot, cleaned and sliced
   into thin strips
1 can (15 oz.) bamboo shoots,
   drained
5 dry black mushroom tops
1 large onion, sliced
   lengthwise in chunks
1 box (10 oz.) frozen
   Chinese pea pods

Dredge shrimp in cornstarch and deep fry until golden. Make sauce: Combine warm water, sugar, soy sauce, salt, garlic powder, vinegar, Eno Itchi Ban, wine, cornstarch, and cayenne. Mix well.

In large frying pan, sauté carrot slices in three tablespoons oil. Stir well. Add bamboo shoots, sauté. Soak mushrooms in hot water thirty minutes then cut in about six parts. Add cut up mushrooms, discard stems (reserve water to use in soup or stock). Add onion, fry fast, do not wilt. Blend sauce into pan and stir well until thickened. Add green pea pods. Stir well. Add shrimp and just barely heat. Check seasonings. Serve with rice.

French Fried Shrimp

Serves: 6
Cooking Time: 2 - 3 minutes

"Can also be used as an hors d'oeuvre."

1 cup flour
1 tsp. baking powder
½ tsp. salt
1 egg
⅔ cup milk
1 tbsp. oil
1½ lb. shrimp, shelled
   and deveined
1 pt. Mazola oil for frying

Combine flour, baking powder, and salt. Mix egg, milk, and one tablespoon oil and add to first mixture. Stir until smooth. Dip shrimp into batter, drain well. Pour one pint Mazola oil into heavy pan and heat. Carefully add shrimp, a few at a time and fry 2 - 3 minutes until golden brown. Decorate with parsley and lemons.

CURLED SHRIMP

Serves: 3
Cooking Time: 10 minutes

1 lb. raw shrimp, peeled and
  cleaned
1/2 tsp. salt
1/2 tsp. pepper
2 tbsp. oil
2 tbsp. ketchup
2 tbsp. soy sauce
2 tbsp. vinegar
2 tsp. sugar
1 tsp. minced ginger root*
6 scallions, sliced
1 clove garlic, minced
1 tsp. cornstarch
1 tbsp. water

*Minced ginger root is available
in Oriental food stores.

Wash and drain shrimp; sprinkle with salt and pepper. Heat oil, sauté shrimp one minute. Add a mixture of the ketchup, soy sauce, vinegar, sugar, ginger, scallions, garlic. Cook over low heat three minutes, stirring frequently. Mix together the cornstarch and water. Add to the shrimp and cook an additional two minutes.

SHRIMP CREOLE

Serves: 3 - 4
Cooking Time: 50 minutes

"Good for buffets and supper parties. Can be done ahead."

1 or 2 large green peppers,
  cut in chunks
1/2 cup diced onion
1/2 cup celery cut in 1/2-inch
  slices
1 clove garlic
2 tbsp. oil
1 can (7 oz.) imported tomato
  paste
1 1/2 cups water
1/8 tsp. pepper
1/4 tsp. thyme
2 bay leaves
1 tsp. salt
2 cups cooked and cleaned
  shrimp

Sauté peppers, onions, celery, and garlic in oil until tender. Stir in remaining ingredients except shrimp. Simmer fifteen minutes, stirring occasionally.* Add shrimp to sauce and simmer ten minutes. Serve with rice.

*Sauce can be prepared in advance and refrigerated for two days or frozen.

SHRIMP MARINARA

Serves: 4
Cooking Time: 15 minutes

"Quick and easy."

⅓ cup olive oil
¼ cup butter (2 oz.)
⅓ cup parsley flakes
1 tbsp. sweet basil leaves
1 tbsp. Parmesan cheese
1 tsp. oregano
3 cloves garlic, crushed
1 can (8 oz.) drained, minced clams
1 jar (16 oz.) Buitoni Marinara sauce
1 lb. cooked shrimp

Put oil and butter in pan. Combine parsley, basil, cheese, oregano, and garlic. Add to oil mixture and simmer for a minute. Add clams and marinara sauce. Simmer for about ten minutes. Add shrimp to sauce and heat about five minutes longer.

SHRIMP IN WINE SAUCE

Serves: 3
Cooking Time: 30 minutes

"Simple preparation."

1½ lb. small shrimp
½ cup flour
½ cup oil
½ cup dry white wine
2 tsp. tomato paste
4 tbsp. water
1 tsp. salt
½ tsp. pepper
½ tsp. garlic
1 tbsp. parsley
2 tsp. lemon juice

Peel and devein shrimp. Roll shrimp in flour. Heat oil in skillet, add shrimp and brown on both sides. Drain oil and reserve. Add wine, cook over low heat until absorbed. Combine oil, tomato paste, water, salt, pepper, and garlic. Cook over low heat five minutes. Pour over shrimp. Cook five minutes. Add parsley and lemon juice.

SHRIMP MILANESE

Serves: 4
Cooking Time: 30 minutes

"This also makes a delicious appetizer if kept in a chafing dish."

¼ lb. butter
1 clove garlic
2 lb. shelled, raw shrimp
1 tbsp. parsley flakes
½ tsp. Tabasco
½ tsp. paprika
salt to taste
pepper to taste

In iron skillet, melt one-third of the butter. Add garlic and shrimp. Sauté slowly. As shrimp simmers, pour off juice into a bowl. When shrimp are simmering dry, add remaining butter. Scrape pan with spatula and keep turning shrimp as brown crust forms. Add remaining ingredients, pour back shrimp juice, stir and serve.

SHRIMP SCORPIO

Serves: 4
Cooking Time: 1 hour

"Can be prepared ahead of time."

3 tbsp. olive oil
2 cups onion, finely chopped
1 clove crushed garlic
¼ cup finely chopped
   parsley, fresh
1 tbsp. dill, finely chopped
⅛ tsp. dry mustard
¼ tsp. sugar
2 cups canned peeled tomatoes,
   chopped
½ cup canned tomato sauce
1½ lb. raw shrimp, cleaned,
   deveined, and peeled
1 cup feta or mozzarella
   cheese, crumbled*

*If feta cheese is not used, season tomato sauce with salt and fresh pepper to taste.

Preheat oven to 425°. Heat oil in sauce pan and add onions, stirring until onions start to brown. Add garlic, parsley, and dill. Stir in mustard and sugar. Add tomatoes and tomato sauce; simmer 30 minutes. Add shrimp to sauce and cook until shrimp are almost done (approximately 5 - 8 minutes). Don't overcook! Pour mixture into a casserole and sprinkle with crumbled cheese. Bake 10 - 15 minutes or until cheese is melted. Serve on bed of white rice or on pasta. Note: Allow casserole to come to room temperature before heating if it is prepared earlier and refrigerated.

Shrimp in Lobster Sauce

Serves: 4 to 6
Cooking Time: 30 minutes

"Go Chinese."

½ lb. ground fresh pork
1 tbsp. chopped green onion
1 tbsp. chopped carrot
1 tbsp. chopped celery
salt
pepper
2 tbsp. salad oil
2 lb. raw shrimp
1 cup chicken stock
1 beaten egg
2 tbsp. cornstarch
2 tbsp. cold water
1 tbsp. soy sauce

Combine pork, vegetables, and seasonings in pan with hot oil and cook about five minutes. Add cleaned, washed, and deveined shrimp and sauté until they turn pink (about five minutes). Add chicken stock and cook covered for ten minutes. Add egg and stir rapidly for two minutes. Blend cornstarch, water, and soy sauce to mixture, stirring until thickened. Serve with boiled rice.

Shrimp and Rice Casserole

Serves: 3
Cooking Time: 30 minutes

1 lb fresh shrimp*
⅔ cup uncooked rice
½ cup chopped onion
¼ cup chopped green pepper
3 tsp. margarine
1 envelope Lipton tomato-
    vegetable soup mix
1½ cups boiling water

*If shrimp are purchased already cooked and cleaned, use approximately one-half pound.

Boil and clean shrimp and set aside. Cook rice without salt. Sauté onion and pepper in margarine until tender, about five minutes. Add shrimp and cook for five minutes more. Next add rice. Prepare soup separately with water and then add to mixture. Cover and cook for ten additional minutes.

CIOPPINO

(SEAFOOD STEW)

Serves: 4 - 6
Cooking Time: 1 hour, 45 minutes

"Great for informal supper."

3 tbsp. olive oil
2 onions, chopped
2 stalks celery, chopped
2 tbsp. parsley, chopped
¼ tsp. thyme
1 bay leaf, crumbled
2 cloves garlic, minced
¼ tsp. pepper
1 tsp. salt
1 lb. can tomatoes
1 cup dry white wine
4 lobster tails
16 - 20 clams
16 - 20 shrimp*
16 - 20 scallops*

*Other seafood may be substituted for shrimp and scallops. Crab and oyster are good.

Heat oil in skillet (large and heavy). Cook onions, pepper, and celery in oil until soft but not brown. Add seasonings and tomatoes. Simmer one hour covered. Add wine and simmer five minutes longer.

Scrub and rinse shellfish (do not remove shells) and place in large pot. Pour sauce over, cover, and simmer 20-25 minutes. Note: Sauce can be prepared in the morning. Then reheat sauce in large pot before adding shellfish to simmer.

SEAFOOD AU GRATIN

Serves: 6
Cooking Time: 30 minutes

"Delicious dish for those special evenings."

½ lb. cooked shrimp
½ lb. crab meat
½ lb. lobster
½ lb. sole
2 tbsp. butter
2 tbsp. flour
¾ cup milk
¾ cup grated cheese, sharp
   Cheddar
½ cup white wine
1 tbsp. sherry
bread crumbs*

*I use Pepperidge Farm stuffing to make my bread crumbs.

Cut seafood into bite-size pieces and arrange them in baking dish. Mix butter and flour over low heat and stir in milk and grated cheese. When slightly thickened, add wine. Pour sauce over seafood and top with buttered bread crumbs. Bake at 325° for 20-25 minutes until browned. Serve over plain white rice.

SEAFOOD POTPOURRI

Serves: 6
Cooking Time: 10 - 20 minutes

7 tbsp. butter
1 large (7 oz.) can crab meat*
1 large (7 oz.) can lobster*
½ lb. cooked shrimp*
1 tbsp. chopped onion
2 tsp. sherry
½ tsp. pepper
3 tbsp. flour
1 cup milk
½ cup bread crumbs
½ cup Parmesan cheese, grated

*Or any combination of your choice.

In large frying pan, melt four tablespoons butter. Add seafood and tablespoon chopped onion. Cook four minutes, stirring occasionally. Sprinkle with sherry and pepper. Melt three tablespoons butter and stir in flour until smooth, then add milk. Stir until thick and smooth, over low heat. Combine with seafood. Sprinkle with bread crumbs and Parmesan cheese. Bake 10 - 20 minutes in individuals shells or large casserole. If not brown, put under broiler.

CREOLE JAMBALAYA

Serves: 8 - 10

2 tbsp. butter
1 tbsp. oil
3 cloves garlic, minced
2 onions, chopped
1 slice ham, cubed (approximately ½ cup)
3 tomatoes, chopped
½ cup tomato juice or 1 can (8 oz.) tomato sauce
1 bay leaf
salt
pepper
pinch of thyme
dash of chili pepper
4 cups chicken broth
1 cup rice
2 Italian sausages, cut in slices and fried until well done (optional, but gives a nice flavor)
1 cup raw shrimp, cleaned
1 cup frozen or cooked lobster tails, cut in bite-size pieces
1⅓ cups cooked chicken, diced
1 cup crab meat (optional)
4 oz. sherry

In a large pot, sauté garlic and onions in butter and oil. Add ham. When onions are brown and ham is slightly browned, add tomatoes and tomato juice or tomato sauce. Add bay leaf and season generously with salt, pepper, thyme, and chili pepper. Simmer for ten minutes. Then add chicken broth. When mixture starts boiling, add rice. After the rice has cooked for about fifteen minutes, add sausages and whatever shellfish is available, such as uncooked, shelled, deveined shrimp, and chunks of frozen lobster tail. Add chicken and then add crab meat at the last minute. Stir frequently until rice is tender. Add a wine glass of sherry. Cook five minutes longer and serve with crusty, warmed French sourdough bread, Brie cheese and a light, lovely salad.

SALMON CROQUETTES

Serves: 3
Cooking Time: 20 minutes

1 large can (1 lb.) salmon
2 eggs
½ cup bread crumbs
3 medium, cooked potatoes,
  mashed
½ cup grated carrots
½ cup minced onions
cooking oil or butter

Drain salmon and place with all other ingredients (except oil) in bowl. Mix together and form into patties. With extra bread crumbs, coat patties. Fry in oil or butter for ten minutes on each side.

SALMON MOUSSE

Serves: 10 - 20
Chill: Overnight

"Good luncheon dish or hors d'oeuvre spread."

1 envelope Knox unflavored
  gelatin
2 tbsp. lemon juice
1 small onion, sliced in
  quarters
½ cup boiling water
½ cup mayonnaise
¼ tsp. paprika
1 tsp. dried dill
1 can (1 lb.) salmon, drained
1 cup heavy cream

Empty gelatin into blender, add lemon juice, onion, and boiling water. Blend well at high speed. Add mayonnaise, paprika, dill, and drained salmon. Blend briefly at high speed. Add heavy cream, one-third at a time, blending after each addition. Blend all ingredients 30 seconds. Run a mold under cold water and then coat with oil. Pour mixture into prepared one-quart mold. Chill overnight. (Should be covered with Saran wrap while chilling.) To Unmold: Fill sink to immerse bottom of mold just a few seconds. Unmold. Return to refrigerator for a few minutes after unmolding to resolidify

SWEET AND SOUR SALMON WITH LEMON SAUCE

Serves: 6
Cooking Time: 25 minutes

1 cup vinegar
⅛ cup sugar
2 cups water
½ tsp. salt
3 lb. salmon, cut 1-inch thick
3 eggs
juice of 1 lemon

Combine and boil vinegar, sugar, water, and salt. Cook fish in this mixture 20 minutes. Whip eggs, add lemon juice. Stir in juice of fish in bowl of eggs very slowly (so as not to curdle). Pour back over fish and simmer five minutes. Serve cold.

RIVIERA CASSEROLE

Serves: 6
Cooking Time: 20 - 30 minutes

"Quickie, economical. Make it early. Bake it later."

2 cups cooked rice
2 cups tuna, salmon, crab meat, or chicken
2 cups frozen peas
2 cups condensed cream of mushroom soup
¾ cup milk
⅔ cup herb seasoned bread crumbs, buttered

Preheat oven to 350°. Grease casserole. Combine rice, tuna, and peas. Combine soup and milk; add to tuna mixture. Pour into casserole. Top with buttered crumbs. Bake 20-30 minutes until bubbly and crumbs are browned.

TUNA CASSEROLE

Serves: 3 - 4
Cooking Time: 25 minutes

"Marvelous for meetings! Very easy!"

1 can (7 oz.) tuna fish (white chunk style)
1 can cream of mushroom soup
¼ cup water
1 cup diced (not too small) celery
¼ cup diced onions
3 oz. Chinese noodles
cashews (optional)

Mix together tuna fish, soup, water, celery, diced onions, 1½ ounces Chinese noodles, and nuts. Pour into baking dish. Sprinkle reamining noodles on top. Bake at 350° for 25 minutes.

Tuna Sandwich Puffs

Serves: 4
Cooking Time: 30 - 40 minutes
Refrigerate: 40 minutes

"Good luncheon dish!"

8 thin slices white bread (crusts removed)
1 can (7 oz.) tuna
1 tsp. minced parsley
1 tsp. finely chopped onion
1 tsp. lemon juice
1 tbsp. mayonnaise
4 slices American cheese
2 eggs
½ tsp. dry mustard
½ tsp. salt
1 cup milk

Place 4 slices bread in greased Pyrex pan. Mash tuna and blend in parsley, onion, lemon juice, salt, mayonnaise, and dry mustard. Spread over bread. Top with slice of cheese, top with bread slice. Beat eggs and milk. Pour over all. Let stand or refrigerate 40 minutes. Bake at 350° for 30-40 minutes until all is puffed and golden brown. Serve at once.

Confirmation Tuna

Serves: 4 - 6
Cooking Time: 35 - 45 minutes

"Quick supper or luncheon."

2 cans (7 oz. each) tuna, well drained and flaked
1 can cream of mushroom soup
1 cup milk
sherry (optional)
salt to taste
pepper to taste
½ can (8 oz.) water chestnuts
¼ package green peas
½ cup cashews
1 can Chinese noodles

Mix tuna, mushroom soup, milk, sherry, salt, and pepper. Add water chestnuts, peas, and cashews. Pour over a layer of Chinese noodles in a casserole dish. Sprinkle noodles over top. Bake at 325-350° for thirty to forty-five minutes.

Poultry

BAKED CHICKEN

Serves: 4
Cooking Time: 1 hour

*"Delicious and easy. You can also add one
jar of apricot jam to mixture. Good leftover cold."*

1 bottle Milani 1890 dressing
1 broiler-fryer, cut up
1 package Lipton onion soup mix
garlic powder
salt
pepper

Coat bottom of pan with dressing. Lay chicken in pieces into pan. Mix dressing, soup mix, and seasonings and paint on chicken. Bake in a 350° oven for one hour.

CHICKEN LICKIN'

Serves: 4 - 6
Cooking Time: 1 - 1½ hours

2 packages Lipton onion soup mix
1 chicken cut into pieces
¼ lb. butter or margarine
aluminum foil

Line roasting pan with aluminum foil. Spread the soup mix into pan and place chicken parts over it. Dot chicken with butter or margarine. Spread another package of onion soup on top. Cover completely with foil and place in a 350° oven for 1 to 1½ hours, depending on size of chicken.

BAKED CHICKEN

Serves: 4
Cooking Time: 1 hour

"Easy chicken with a crust."

¼ lb. margarine, salted
cornflake crumbs
1 broiler cut into 8 pieces

Melt the margarine and dip the chicken into the melted margarine. Then cover the chicken with cornflake crumbs and bake at 350° for one hour. (The salted margarine should be sufficient seasoning, but extra salt may be used in the cornflakes.)

Baked Parmesan Chicken

Serves: 6
Cooking Time: 50 minutes

"Very easy to prepare."

2 eggs
1½ cups milk
2 cups bread crumbs
2 cups grated Parmesan cheese
½ cup chopped parsley
1 clove garlic, minced
2 tsp. salt
¼ tsp. pepper
4 lb. chicken, fryer, cut up
¼ cup melted butter

Beat eggs and milk together. In a separate bowl combine bread crumbs, Parmesan cheese, parsley, garlic, salt, and pepper. Dip chicken pieces in egg-milk mixture, then in the bread crumb mixture. Arrange coated chicken in a shallow baking pan. Pour the melted butter over it. Bake at 400° for 50 minutes or until chicken is tender. Use more butter if desired.

Parmesan Chicken

Serves: 4
Cooking Time: 1 hour

"Cheese lovers delight."

½ cup flour
1 tsp. salt
¼ tsp. pepper
2 tsp. paprika
1 chicken, cut up
2 eggs
3 tsp. milk
⅓ cup fine bread crumbs
⅔ cup Parmesan cheese
¼ cup butter
¼ cup margarine

Mix flour, salt, pepper, and paprika in paper bag and shake two pieces of chicken at a time. Dip chicken in mixture of eggs and milk, then roll chicken in bread crumbs and cheese. Melt butter and margarine in pan, add chicken and bake at 400° for one hour, turning once.

Tangy Chicken

Serves: 4
Cooking Time: 1 hour

"Sharp and tangy flavor."

2 tsp. salt
¼ cup melted margarine
¼ cup lemon juice
¼ cup vinegar
1 tsp. garlic salt
1 tsp. onion salt
¼ tsp. black pepper
¼ tsp. thyme
1 fryer, cut up

Mix all ingredients except chicken. Dip pieces of chicken in sauce and place in shallow baking dish or pan, skin side up. Bake one hour at 350°.

Chicken with Italian Dressing

Serves: 4
Cooking Time: 1 hour, 15 minutes
Marinate: Overnight

1 chicken, cut into 8 pieces
1 bottle Italian dressing
  (Wishbone)
1 cup oil
½ cup Kellogg cornflake
  crumbs
½ cup flavored bread crumbs
¼ cup almonds, slivered

Marinate chicken in Italian dressing overnight. Next day, heat up oil, remove from stove, and dip chicken parts into oil. Combine dry ingredients, covering chicken well. Bake in 325° oven for 1 hour, 15 minutes.

Moist BBQ Chicken

Serves: 2 - 4
Cooking Time: 45 minutes to 1 hour

"Bake and BBQ."

1 chicken, cut up
1 brown-in-bag
barbecue sauce (see page 95)

Place chicken in bag. Pour ¾ to one cup sauce over chicken. Tie and punch holes in bag. Make sure chicken isn't touching top of bag. Bake at 350° for 45 minutes or at 350° for 30 minutes, then place on hot coals for 15 minutes, basting with remaining sauce.

BARBECUED CHICKEN

Serves: 4
Cooking Time: 1¼ hours

"BBQ flavor indoors."

3-lb. broiler-fryer, cut up
seasoned flour*
¼ cup margarine
1 cup ketchup
½ cup sherry
⅓ cup water
2 tbsp. lemon juice
1 onion, minced
1 tbsp. Worcestershire sauce
2 tbsp. melted margarine
1 tbsp. brown sugar

*For 3-lb. Chicken:
    ¼ cup flour
    1 tsp. paprika
    ¾ tsp. salt
    ⅛ tsp. pepper

Coat chicken with seasoned flour. In hot, melted margarine, cook chicken till evenly browned. Remove to 2-quart casserole. Heat oven to 325°. In sauce-pan, combine ketchup and all other ingredients; bring to boil. Pour over chicken. Bake, covered, 1¼ hours.

BAR-B-Q CHICKEN OR RIBS

Serves: 4 - 6
Cooking Time: 1 hour
Marinate: Overnight

"Sauce sufficient for two chickens."

1 cup ketchup
½ cup Worcestershire sauce
1 tsp. chili powder
1 tsp. salt
2 dashes Tabasco
2 cups water
4 tbsp. brown sugar
juice of 1 lemon
2 tsp. garlic powder
1 cup Saucy Susan sauce
chicken or ribs

Combine all ingredients except meat. Heat slightly. Pour over chicken or ribs. Marinate overnight. Meat may be baked or barbecued. Before cooking remove meat from sauce; retain sauce. Use extra sauce for basting.

RBECUED TERIYAKI CHICKEN WITH ONIONS AND POTATOES

Serves: 4 or 6
Cooking Time: 1 hour
Marinate: Overnight

"Marinade can be used for beef teriyaki also."

⅔ cup soy sauce
⅓ cup honey
2 tsp. grated fresh ginger or
   ¾ tsp. ground ginger
3 tbsp. dry sherry
½ cup salad oil
1 clove garlic, minced
½ cup green onions, thinly
   sliced
1 large chicken or 6 legs and
   thighs (3 - 3½ lb.)
6 large dry mushrooms (optional)
½ cup butter
4 large onions, thinly sliced
4 large boiled potatoes, thinly
   sliced

First seven ingredients are the marinade. Combine and marinate the chicken overnight (refrigerated) or at least four hours. If you use the mushrooms, soak them in water (warm) 30 minutes, then discard stems. Slice very thinly. When coals are gray, barbecue chicken on grill. Set large frypan on grill. Add butter and sauté onions, potatoes, and mushrooms. Cook covered, stirring occasionally, until onions are soft, about 45 minutes. Turn chicken frequently to avoid burning. Baste after 30 minutes until done. Before serving, add two to four tablespoons of marinade to potato mixture to taste. Chicken serves four and potatoes serve six.

CHICKEN AND HONEY

Serves: 8 - 10
Cooking Time: 1 hour
Marinate: Overnight

"Make extra. Good cold, great for picnics."

¼ cup Golden Blossom honey
¼ cup LaChoy soy sauce
¼ cup ketchup
¼ cup cooking wine (white),
   sauterne
1 can chicken consommé,
   undiluted
¼ cup water
dash ginger
dash pepper
¼ tsp. garlic powder
3 chickens, broilers or fryers,
   cut into pieces

Combine all ingredients except chicken. Place chicken in pan and pour marinade mixture over. Marinate overnight, turning once. Bake, skin side up, at 425° for 30 minutes, then at 375° for an additional 30 minutes.

64

Cinnamon Chicken

Serves: 8
Cooking Time: 1 hour
Marinate: Several hours

"Nice and different flavor."

½ cup sherry
2 tsp. cinnamon
⅓ cup honey
2 tbsp. lemon juice
½ tsp. curry powder
1 tsp. garlic salt
2 frying or broiling chickens, cut up

Blend all ingredients thoroughly. Pour over chicken pieces, mixing so they are well coated. Let stand in refrigerator several hours or overnight. Bake about one hour at 375°. Baste occasionally.

Chicken with Lemon Sauce

Serves: 4
Cooking Time: 1 hour

1½ lb. boneless chicken breast
½ tsp. salt
1 tbsp. dry sherry
1 tbsp. light soy sauce
2 eggs
¼ cup cornstarch
½ tsp. baking powder
2 cups oil

Preheat oven to 350°. In large bowl toss chicken, salt, sherry, and soy sauce. Let stand 15 minutes. In medium bowl, beat eggs, then beat in cornstarch and baking powder. Beat to form a smooth, thin batter. In large skillet heat oil to 350°. Coat chicken breasts well with batter. Deep fry each piece until browned. Drain on paper towels and keep warm in oven.

Sauce:

1 tsp. salt
3 tbsp. sugar
1 tbsp. cornstarch
1 cup chicken broth (from bouillon cube)
1 to 2 tbsp. lemon juice
1 scallion

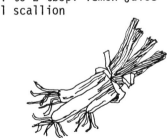

In small bowl, combine salt, sugar, and cornstarch. Mix well. Gradually add chicken broth and lemon juice to taste, stirring to dissolve cornstarch. In large skillet, heat two tablespoons salad oil, add scallion, cut into two-inch pieces. Stir and fry 30 seconds. Slowly add cornstarch mixture to oil mixture. Stir constantly until it becomes a clear thin sauce. Keep hot. To Serve: Cut chicken into small pieces. Mound on heated platter. Pour sauce over chicken.

CHICKEN WITH LEMON JUICE

Serves: 4 - 6
Cooking Time: 1½ hours

4 medium onions, finely chopped
1 tsp. parsley
2 leaves sweet basil or 1 tsp.
1 tsp. garlic salt
1 tsp. salt
½ tsp. pepper
½ tsp. oregano
6 lemons
½ cup olive oil
6-7 pieces of chicken, breasts
    and legs
salted water

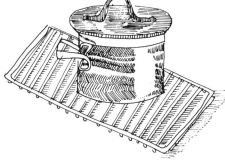

Mix finely chopped onions, parsley, and sweet basil together. Add garlic salt, salt, pepper, and oregano. Add the juice of six lemons and oil. Soak the chicken pieces in cold salted water for 15 minutes. Rinse with cold water and towel dry. Dip chicken in juice mixture. Roast in a 375° oven till brown on both sides.

Then steam as follows: Put some of remaining juice in a pot (large enough to hold all of the chicken). As pieces are browned, place them in the pot in layers, alternating each layer with juice. Cook over low heat for 45 minutes. From time to time cold water may added as needed.

PEACHY GLAZE CHICKEN

Serves: 4 - 6
Cooking Time: 1½ hours

"Peaches, grapes, cherries, make this chicken different."

3 lb. frying chicken pieces
½ tsp. salt
2 tbsp. melted margarine
1 can (16 oz.) peach halves,
    drain and reserve 1 cup of
    juice
1 cup Open Pit barbecue sauce
1 tbsp. lemon juice
1 can (8 oz.) small onions,
    drained
grapes or cherries, canned or
    fresh

Rub chicken with salt, then brush with margarine. Place in shallow pan and bake at 375° for thirty minutes. Combine peach syrup, barbecue sauce, and lemon juice. Pour over chicken and bake thirty minutes longer. Arrange onions and peaches around chicken. Baste with sauce. Bake for another thirty minutes. Add grapes or cherries and serve with rice.

CHICKEN WITH ORANGE JUICE

Serves: 4
Cooking Time: 1 hour, 15 minutes

1 chicken, divided into 8 pieces
1 small can frozen orange juice
¼ cup oil
1 tsp. salt
1 tsp. mustard
1 tsp. paprika

Combine ingredients. Pour over chicken that is skin side down. Bake in 350° oven, and baste with sauce. After 45 minutes turn chicken over and bake remaining time.

POTTED CHICKEN WITH MEATBALLS

Serves: 6
Cooking Time: 1 hour

*"Trick here is to brown chicken well.
Tastes even better next day."*

1 broiler or fryer, cut up
salt
pepper
paprika
garlic powder
butter or margarine
2 or 3 medium onions, diced
1 can cream of mushroom soup
    or cream of chicken soup

Sprinkle chicken with salt, pepper, paprika, and garlic powder. Using a large pot or electric frying pan, brown chicken in butter. Remove from pan. Sauté onions in butter until golden brown. Remove onions from pan. Put chicken legs and thighs in pan, add some onions and ½ can soup. Add remainder of chicken, repeat the onion and soup layers. (Use one can of soup per chicken.) Cover and simmer one hour.

Meatballs

1 lb. chopped meat
1 egg
1 slice bread
bread crumbs
salt
pepper
garlic powder
MSG

Mix together ingredients. Shape into tiny meat balls. After chicken has cooked about 45 minutes uncover and put top pieces of chicken on bottom. Drop meat balls into sauce. Finish cooking 15 to 20 minutes longer. Serve over rice or noodles.

BAKED SESAME CHICKEN BREASTS

Serves: 4
Cooking Time: 45 minutes

"Good company dish."

½ cup flour
1 tsp. garlic powder
2 tsp. salt
½ tsp. pepper
2 chicken breasts, split
1 egg, beaten
1 package (3½ oz.) potato
   chips, crushed
⅓ package (1 lb.) sesame seeds
⅓ cup butter, melted
mushrooms, fresh, sautéed

Mix flour, garlic powder, salt, and pepper in large bowl. Roll chicken in mixture. Place on wire rack. Let stand 30 minutes. Dip chicken in egg. Roll in combined potato chips and sesame seeds. In shallow baking pan, arrange chicken in single layer. Spoon butter over chicken. Bake at 350°, basting frequently with pan liquid, until tender. Sprinkle with lemon juice. Garnish with whole sautéed mushrooms.

CHICKEN KIEV

Serves: 8
Cooking Time: 30 minutes
Refrigerate: 1 hour

*"Chicken can be prepared earlier in the day
and refrigerated until frying time."*

4 whole chicken breasts, boned
   and halved
½ cup chilled butter
2 tsp. salt
1 tsp. black pepper
2 tbsp. chives
2 cloves garlic, crushed
juice of 1 lemon
flour
3 eggs, lightly beaten
unseasoned bread crumbs
oil for deep drying

Pound chicken between sheets of wax paper to flatten slightly. Combine butter, salt, pepper, chives, garlic, and divide into eight pieces. Place a piece of seasoned butter on center of each piece of chicken and roll up, tucking in sides. Dredge each roll in flour, dip in egg, and roll in bread crumbs. Refrigerate for at least one hour. Then fry in hot oil (350-375°). Oil should be about one-inch deep when rolls are frying. Brown all over and drain on paper towels. Serve immediately.

Chicken à la Stacy

Serves: 6
Cooking Time: 45 minutes

"Garlic lovers treat."

1 or 2 chickens, quartered
1 large onion, cut up
garlic (7 cloves if you love
   garlic)
paprika
1 tbsp. oil
salt to taste
½ cup water

Boil chicken 20 to 30 minutes (have soup besides). Cool. In blender, place onion, garlic, enough paprika for rich brown color, one tablespoon oil, salt, and water. Blend. Rub mixture on chicken and marinate if possible. Place in broiler to brown, turning after first side is browned.

Chicken en Cocette

Serves: 6
Cooking Time: 2 hours

"Chicken stew."

4-5 lb. roasting chicken
1 tsp. paprika
1 can cream of chicken soup
12 small potatoes, halved
6 medium carrots, cut in pieces
1 lb. small white onions
1½ tsp. salt
2 tbsp. parsley

Preheat oven to 375°. Sprinkle rinsed chicken with paprika. Fold wings back and tie legs and tail. Place chicken in dutch oven with undiluted soup. Cover and bake 45 minutes. Add vegetables, cover and bake one hour longer or until tender, basting occasionally. Remove cover, cut string, and bake until golden, about 15 minutes more, basting. To serve, sprinkle with parsley.

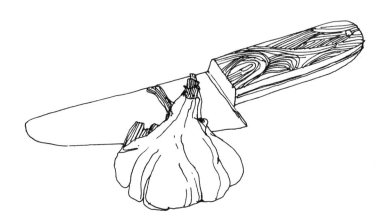

Easy Chicken 'n' Rice

Serves: 4 - 5
Cooking Time: 1½ hours

"Easy meal and delicious!"

3-1b. chicken, cut up
2 cups reconstituted rice
1 (4 oz.) can small mushrooms
2 bouillon cubes
3 cups water
1 tsp. salt
½ tsp. pepper
2 tsp. soy sauce
fresh parsley to taste
2 scallions, cut up, if
   available

Use large baking pan. Add all ingredients. Cover with aluminum foil. Bake at 350° for one hour. Remove aluminum foil and bake for another one-half hour.

Chicken with a Sauce

Serves: 4 - 6
Cooking Time: 1 hour

"Interesting and different."

2 broilers, cut into quarters
1 tsp. salt
½ tsp. pepper
3 tbsp. butter or oil

Sauce

1 cup oil
1½ cups wine vinegar
2 cloves garlic
1 tbsp. dry mustard
1 cup ketchup

Place chicken in a shallow baking pan, season with salt and pepper, dot with butter or margarine. In a sauce pan mix oil, wine vinegar, garlic, mustard, and ketchup, stirring until well blended. Pour the sauce over chicken. Roast in moderate oven, basting often until done (350°).

CHICKEN AND RICE

Serves: 8
Cooking Time: 2 hours

"Easy! Five minutes to prepare. Good for company and children love it too!"

2 chickens, cleaned or parts
2½ cups raw Uncle Ben's rice
2 packages Lipton onion soup mix
2 cans cream of mushroom soup
5 cups water
butter or oil

Chicken can be seasoned according to taste after washing. Sprinkle rice in pan, add dry onion soup over rice. Place chicken parts on rice and onion mix. Spoon or spread mushroom soup over chicken. Pour 2½ cups water around edges of pan. Bake at 350° for one hour. After one hour, pour remaining 2½ cups of water around edge of pan. Bake one hour more.

CHICKEN SHISH-KABOB

Serves: 3 without livers, 6 with
Cooking Time: 20 - 25 minutes
Marinate: 1 hour

"Good indoors or out. A change for barbecue time."

3 chicken breasts
¼ lb. chicken livers
2 green peppers
1 tomato, cut in wedges
6 mushroom caps

Marinade

½ cup soy sauce
⅔ cup Wishbone salad dressing
¼ cup sugar
2 tbsp. lemon juice
½ tsp. Accent
1 small clove garlic

Remove skin and bone chicken breasts. Cut in quarters. Combine all ingredients of marinade. Marinate chicken and chicken livers for one hour. Place chicken, livers, peppers, tomatoes, and mushroom caps on skewers and broil for 20-25 minutes.

71

CHICKEN BREASTS IN SKILLET

Serves: 4
Cooking Time: 1 hour

*"Mushrooms, onions, and peas.
Looks pretty, tastes good."*

1½ lb. chicken breasts
2 tbsp. margarine
2 onions
2 cans (4 oz. each) mushrooms
 (reserve liquid) or 1 lb.
 fresh mushrooms
paprika
garlic powder (optional)
soy sauce to taste
Worcestershire sauce to taste
fresh parsley
1 package powdered chicken gravy
1 package (10 oz.) frozen peas

In large skillet, cut chicken in two-inch pieces and sauté in margarine until white (15 minutes). Remove from pot and set aside. Add onions to pan, cook until soft. Add mushrooms, cook about five minutes. Add all seasonings and parsley and cook few minutes more. Return chicken to this mixture. Mix powdered gravy as directed on package. Add to above and cook, covered, about 25-30 minutes. Add peas just before serving. (If frozen, allow cooking time.) Serve over plain, boiled rice. Salt and pepper to taste.

CHICKEN CHABLIS

Serves: 6
Cooking Time: 1 hour

"Wine and mushrooms, good company fare."

1 egg
½ cup water
6 chicken breasts, boned
unflavored bread crumbs
oil
1 can cream of mushroom soup,
 undiluted
Chablis wine
salt
pepper
garlic powder
1 large can (6 oz.) B & B sliced
 mushrooms

Beat egg with water. Dip the seasoned chicken into this mixture and then dip chicken into unflavored bread crumbs. Fry chicken in oil until brown. Heat soup in small pot until smooth. Add ½ can of Chablis (using cream of mushroom soup can), salt, pepper, and garlic. Cook until smooth. Pour over chicken that has been arranged on a baking dish and garnish with mushrooms. Bake in a 350° oven for ½ hour.

Chicken Breasts in Wine

Serves: 8 - 10
Cooking Time: 1½ hours
Refrigerate: 3 hours

"Very tasty. Can be made ahead of time and reheated. Perfect for company."

4 to 5 whole boned chicken breasts (about 4 lb.)
3 tbsp. lemon juice
salt
freshly ground pepper
thyme
3 tbsp. olive oil
3 tbsp. butter
½ lb. mushrooms, sliced
4 tbsp. flour
2 cups chicken stock or 3 chicken bouillon cubes dissolved in 2 cups boiling water
½ cup dry white wine
1 bay leaf

In the morning wash chicken breasts; dry them well and sprinkle with lemon juice, salt, pepper, and thyme. Don't hesitate to go generously with the thyme. Cover. Store in the refrigerator about three hours. Heat the oil in large deep skillet. Pat chicken dry and sauté breasts, single layer at a time, in the hot oil, until they turn deep golden on all sides. As they brown, remove them to a deep casserole or baking dish that has a cover or use foil. Add butter to the skillet, melt it, and sauté the mushrooms. Blend in flour and add chicken stock and wine, a little at a time. Cook, stirring constantly, until mixture thickens. Add bay leaf and pour over chicken in casserole, making certain first to have blended all the pan glaze from the skillet with the sauce. Sauce seems thick and scarce at this point but will increase in volume. Cover and bake at 325° for about one hour or until tender.

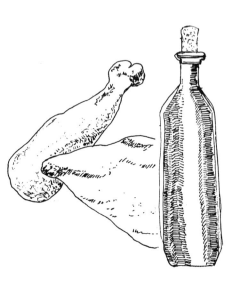

Chicken and Mushrooms

Serves: 4
Cooking Time: 1 hour

*"Can be prepared early in day and partially baked.
A favorite company dish; easy yet impressive when served!"*

¼ cup butter
1 chicken, cut up
½ cup onions, diced
½ lb. mushrooms, sliced
1 can cream of mushroom soup
¾ cup dry sherry
1 tbsp. parsley
1 tsp. salt
1 tsp. paprika
2 lemons, sliced
dash black pepper

Melt butter and brown chicken. Put chicken in a 11 x 7-inch baking pan in one layer. Sauté, but don't brown, onions and mushrooms. Add mushroom soup, seasonings, and lemon. Stir until smooth. Pour over chicken. Bake, uncovered, at 350° for one hour. Don't taste before cooking! Flavor changes after baking.

Chicken in Wine Sauce

Serves: 4
Cooking Time: 1 hour

"Thick sauce and great flavor."

1 chicken, fryer, cut up
salt
pepper
garlic powder
paprika
¼ lb. butter
1 can cream of mushroom soup
½ cup cooking sherry
dash of lemon juice

Season chicken lightly and cover with paprika. Fry in butter until brown. Combine soup and wine. Lower flame under fry pan, add mixture and lemon juice. Cover, simmer until tender.

Coq au Vin

Serves: 6
Cooking Time: 2½ hours

"France's gift to chicken."

5 lb. chicken cut up into
   serving pieces
flour, for dredging
⅓ cup butter or margarine
1 slice raw ham chopped
   (optional)
10 small white onions, whole
1 clove garlic
¼ tsp. thyme
1 sprig parsley
1 bay leaf
8 whole mushrooms
salt to taste
fresh black pepper to taste
2 oz. warmed cognac
1 cup dry red wine

Preheat oven to 300°. Dredge chicken with flour. In a skillet heat the butter and add the chicken. Brown on all sides. Transfer the chicken to a casserole and add the ham, onions, garlic, thyme, parsley, bay leaf, mushrooms, salt, and pepper. Pour the cognac over chicken and ignite. When the flame dies, add the wine. Cover and bake until chicken is tender, about 2 hours.

Chicken Divan

Serves: 5
Cooking Time: 1½ hours

"Can be prepared ahead of time."

2 packages (10 oz.) frozen
   broccoli spears, thawed
5 large chicken cutlets
1 can cream of chicken soup
½ cup mayonnaise
½ tsp. curry powder
½ tsp. lemon juice
cornflake crumbs
1 stick Cracker Barrel sharp
   Cheddar cheese

Place broccoli spears across bottom of 18½ x 13½ x 1½-inch pan. Cut chicken cutlets in half and place them flat on top of broccoli. Mix soup, mayonnaise, curry powder, and lemon juice together and pour over chicken and broccoli. Top with cornflakes. Grate Cheddar cheese over casserole. Bake at 350° approximately 1½ hours. Serve over curried rice.

CHICKEN À LA LILLIAN

Serves: 4
Cooking Time: 45 minutes

"A good company dish, nice and easy."

1 package (10 oz.) frozen
   broccoli
4 boned chicken breasts
4 slices Swiss cheese
1 can Campbell's cream of
   mushroom soup or golden
   mushroom soup
½ soup can of wine for cooking,
   sherry or white wine
   (optional)
sliced mushrooms (optional)

Place broccoli in pan. Insert cheese in chicken breast (roll). Place over broccoli. Combine soup and wine or sherry and pour over chicken. Bake at 350° for 45 minutes.

CHICKEN CASSEROLE WITH ASPARAGUS TIPS

Serves: 6
Cooking Time: 30 minutes

3 cans mushroom soup
1 jar (4 oz.) pimento, cut
¾ cup slivered almonds
3 cans (8 oz. each) cut
   asparagus tips
6 chicken breasts or equivalent amount of cooked,
   leftover chicken
2 cans (3 oz. each) french
   fried onions

Combine mushroom soup, cut pimento, almonds, and asparagus. Pour ½ of mixture in greased casserole. Arrange chicken on mixture, then cover with remaining mixture. Top with onions. Bake at 350° for 30 minutes. Serve over rice or green noodles.

CHICKEN SUPREME

Serves: 6
Cooking Time: 40 minutes

"Easy and good."

6 chicken cutlets
2 eggs
bread crumbs
1 package (10 oz.) frozen
   Japanese vegetables,
   defrosted
1 package (10 oz.) frozen
   broccoli spears, defrosted
½ lb. medium noodles cooked
1 can cream of mushroom soup
½ cup Chablis

Bread chicken in beaten eggs and unseasoned bread crumbs. Fry in margarine until lightly browned. Drain liquid out of defrosted vegetables and place on bottom of casserole. Add noodles and top with chicken. Blend and warm soup and wine together. Pour over chicken. Bake in preheated 350° oven for 30 minutes.

CHICKEN WITH ARTICHOKE

Serves: 4
Cooking Time: 50 minutes

"Artichokes really add the right touch to this."

1 broiling chicken, cut up
½ tsp. salt
¼ tsp. pepper
½ tsp. paprika
6 tbsp. butter
¼ lb. mushrooms, sliced
2 tbsp. flour
1 cup chicken consommé
3 tbsp. sherry
garlic
onion powder
12-15 oz. canned artichoke
   hearts

Salt, pepper, and paprika chicken pieces. Brown chicken in four tablespoons butter and put in a big casserole. Add two tablespoons butter to frying pan and sauté mushrooms for five minutes. Sprinkle on flour and stir in consommé, sherry, garlic, and onion powder. Cook five minutes. Arrange artichoke hearts between pieces of chicken. Pour mushroom-sherry sauce over casserole. Bake at 375° for 40 minutes.

CHICKEN BOMBAY

Serves: 4
Cooking Time: 50 minutes

"Spicy chicken. Nice with rice."

3-lb. frying chicken, cut up
1 tsp. salt
¼ tsp. ginger
¼ tsp. cardamon
¼ tsp. chili powder
½ tsp. turmeric
3 tbsp. butter
1 large clove garlic, minced
2 small onions, sliced thin
  and separated into rings

Wash and dry chicken. On a sheet of wax paper mix spices, spread out, roll chicken in spices. In a 10-inch skillet, melt butter, add chicken, and brown over moderate heat. Sprinkle with garlic and onion. Cover tightly and simmer until tender (about 30 minutes). Turn chicken once or twice to mix with onions and spices.

SZECHUAN CHICKEN

Serves: 4
Cooking Time: ½ hour

"Cut everything small so it cooks fast and is still crisp and fresh when served."

2 whole chicken breasts
2 tbsp. soy sauce
1 tbsp. sherry
1 tbsp. cornstarch
2 tbsp. hoisin sauce
1 tsp. sugar
1 cup oil
¼ cup peanuts or cashews,
  blanched
hot pepper leaves
1 medium bamboo shoot, diced

Remove bone and skin from chicken. Cut into peanut-size pieces. Coat with one tablespoon soy sauce, sherry, and cornstarch. Mix remaining soy sauce, hoisin sauce, and sugar. Heat oil and fry nuts until they are yellow. Remove nuts and oil from wok and pour in more oil and heat. Add three dashes of hot pepper leaves. Add chicken and stir gently so pieces separate. Stir and fry until it turns pink; add bamboo shoot and nuts. Heat and mix thoroughly. Drain off excess oil. Add hoisin mixture and stir until bubbly hot. Serve.

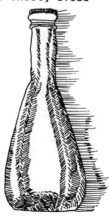

CHICKEN AND WALNUTS

Serves: 3 - 4
Cooking Time: 30 minutes
Marinate: 15 minutes

1 tsp. sugar
1 tsp. salt
1 tbsp. soy sauce
3 tbsp. sherry
2½-3 lb. broiler, skinned and boned (chicken cutlets can be substituted)
cornstarch
1 egg, beaten
¼ cup salad oil
1 cup walnuts, halved
½ tsp. ginger
2 cloves garlic, minced
¾ cup water
Accent
1 can (15 oz.) sliced bamboo shoots, drained

In a bowl combine sugar, salt, soy sauce, and sherry. Cut chicken into bite-size pieces and marinate for 15 minutes. Drain chicken and reserve marinade. Sprinkle lightly with cornstarch and toss with beaten egg. In skillet, lightly toss walnuts in remaining oil. Add ginger, garlic, and chicken and brown. Add ¾ cup water, a little Accent, and remainder of marinade. Cover and simmer 10 minutes. Stir in bamboo shoots. Simmer five minutes.

POLYNESIAN CHICKEN

Serves: 8
Cooking Time: 1 hour
Marinate: Overnight
Reheating: 1 hour

16 chicken breasts with bone, split (8 whole)
3 (1 lb., 1 oz.) cans of fruit for salad
1 bottle (6 oz.) soy sauce
1 clove garlic, crushed
3 jars (8 oz.) sweet and sour sauce

Preheat oven to 350°. Wash and dry chicken. Arrange breasts, skin side up, in pan. Drain fruit (save syrup). Pour syrup, soy sauce, and garlic over chicken. Bake uncovered, baste and brown (approximately one hour). Remove from oven and pour liquid from chicken into large sauce pan. Add sweet and sour sauce. Boil until sauce thickens, about four minutes. Pour over chicken. Refrigerate overnight.

Prior to serving, preheat oven to 350°. Bake chicken 30 minutes. Add fruit and bake 30 minutes longer, basting.

INDIAN CURRY

Serves: 6
Cooking Time: 1 hour, 45 minutes

"For chicken, meat, shrimp, or crab."

1 chicken, cut in quarters
  (meat, shrimp, or crab can
  be used)
1 tbsp. salt
1 onion
3 fair-sized onions
3 heaping tbsp. fat
2 tbsp. curry powder
1 cup chicken broth (use
  chicken. to make broth)
1 tbsp. chutney
1 tbsp. apricot or peach jam
2 tbsp. vinegar
2 tbsp. milk
sugar

Use one chicken or equivalent chicken parts of your choice. Place chicken in pot and add 5 cups water, one tablespoon salt, one peeled whole onion, bring to boil. Cover and simmer 45 minutes to one hour until chicken is tender. Remove chicken, remove bones, and cut meat into bite-size pieces. Reserve broth. (Meat, shrimp, or crab should be cooked or fried until half done). Cut onions finely, brown in hot fat, then add curry powder, stirring constantly to prevent burning, for ten minutes. Add chicken broth; cook five minutes; then add chutney, jam, vinegar, and a little sugar to taste. Add one tablespoon milk and cook ten minutes; then add chicken (meat, crab, or shrimp) cut into small pieces and allow curry to simmer, the longer the better. Just before serving, add 1 tablespoon milk. (Coconut milk is better. This is made by covering grated coconut with boiling water. Let stand for about ten minutes and strain.) Serve with side dishes of tomatoes, bananas, coconut, pineapple, nuts, cucumber, onions. Hard boiled eggs are often served, too. Of course side dishes have contents cut into pieces. Serve with plain white rice.

CHICKEN RICE MARENGO

Serves: 4
Cooking Time: 1 hour

"Dinner in a pot."

2½ to 3 lb. chicken, cut in
   serving pieces
2 tbsp. olive oil
1 can (1 lb.) tomatoes
1 cup onion, sliced
1 cup raw rice
2 tsp. salt
½ tsp. garlic salt

Brown chicken in oil in dutch oven or deep 12-inch skillet. Drain tomatoes, reserving juice. Add water to juice to make 2½ cups liquid. Add tomatoes, liquid, onion, rice, salt, and garlic salt to chicken; stir. Bring to boil. Reduce heat, cover and cook over low heat until chicken is tender and liquid is absorbed, about 40 minutes.

CHICKEN MARENGO

Serves: 8
Cooking Time: 1¾ hours

"Company will love it."

2 frying chickens, cut up
1 tsp. salt
4 tbsp. flour
¼ cup olive oil
2 medium onions, sliced
1 clove garlic, minced
½ lb. fresh mushrooms, sliced
3 tomatoes, peeled or 1-lb.
   can tomatoes
1 tbsp. tomato paste
⅓ cup Marsala or cream sherry
¾ cup chicken stock
salt to taste

Set aside necks, giblets, and wing tips of chicken; cover with 1½ cups water and ½ teaspoon salt. Boil 30 minutes to make stock, reducing liquid. Dust remaining chicken pieces with flour blended with salt. Brown in hot olive oil until crisp on all sides. Remove. Cook onion, garlic, and mushrooms in oil until tender. Add tomatoes, tomato paste, and Marsala. Simmer until well blended and smooth. Add chicken stock. Replace chicken in sauce and simmer 40 minutes longer. Serve with hot cooked rice.

CHICKEN CACCIATORE

Serves: 3 - 4
Cooking Time: 1 to 1½ hours

"Old Italian favorite."

3-4 lb. chicken, cut up
3 tbsp. olive oil
1 cup onions, chopped
¾ cup green pepper, chopped
2 cloves garlic, minced
1-1½ cups dry white wine
3 cups tomatoes (1 #2½ can)
6 oz. tomato paste
2 tsp. salt
½ tsp. pepper
1 bay leaf
½ tsp. thyme
dash cayenne pepper
½ tsp. sweet basil
1 tsp. oregano
4 oz. can mushrooms

Brown chicken in olive oil. When browned on all sides remove. Add onions, green pepper, and garlic and cook only until tender. Add remaining ingredients. Cover and simmer one hour until chicken is tender. Serve with rice. When doubling recipe, do not double tomatoes. Use one 1 pound can and one #2½ can.

PAELLA

Serves: 6
Cooking Time: 1 hour, 20 minutes

"Great buffet dish. Can be made for a crowd."

1 broiler-fryer, cut up
1 clove garlic, minced
¼ cup olive oil
6 strands saffron
1½ cups raw long grain rice
1 lb. sweet Italian sausage
1 large onion, chopped
1 green pepper, chopped
1 can (14 oz.) chicken broth
2 cans (7 oz. each) minced
   clams
1 tsp. salt
1 tsp. paprika
1 tsp. oregano
2 peppercorns
1 lb. raw shrimp, shelled
   and deveined
4 tomatoes, sliced
1 package (10 oz.) frozen peas
1 can (4 oz.) pimentos, diced

Cut sausage into one-inch thick pieces. Brown chicken with garlic in oil in large frying pan. Remove; stir in saffron and rice; sauté until rice is golden. Add sausages, onion, and green pepper; sauté 7-10 minutes longer; stir in chicken broth, clams and liquid, salt, paprika, oregano, and peppercorns. Cover and cook 10 minutes. Layer chicken, rice mixture, shrimp, tomatoes, peas, and pimentos in a 12-cup baking dish. Cover tightly. Bake in moderate oven (375°) one hour or until rice is tender and liquid is absorbed. Serve from baking dish; add a green salad and French bread.

Easy Chicken Casserole

Serves: 4
Cooking Time: 30 minutes

"If your family likes chicken soup, but is not partial to boiled chicken, try this for good results."

¼ cup butter
½ cup flour
1 cup chicken broth or 1½ chicken bouillon cubes in 1 cup hot water
1 can (14½ oz.) evaporated milk
1½ tsp. salt
2½ cups cooked diced chicken
3 cups cooked rice
1 can (3 oz.) broiled mushrooms, sliced
¼ cup chopped pimento
¼ cup chopped green pepper
½ cup slivered almonds, toasted

Melt butter, blend in flour. Gradually add broth, milk, and ½ cup water. Cook and stir over low heat till thick. Add salt, then chicken, rice, vegetables. Pour into greased 11 x 7 x 7-inch baking dish. Bake at 350° about 30 minutes. Sprinkle with almonds.

Chicken with Wild Rice Casserole

Serves: 6
Cooking Time: 45 minutes

"Can be prepared ahead and baked just before serving. Good leftover chicken recipe."

1 cup wild rice
3 tbsp. finely chopped shallots or ½ cup chopped onion
4 tbsp. butter
4 tbsp. flour
1½ cups chicken broth
1½ cups light cream
¼ tsp. nutmeg
salt to taste
freshly ground pepper to taste
¼ lb. mushrooms, thinly sliced
3 cups diced, cooked chicken
2 tbsp. finely chopped parsley
2 tbsp. grated Parmesan cheese

Preheat oven to 350°. Cook rice until tender according to package directions. Set aside. Cook shallots in half the butter, but do not brown. Sprinkle with flour and stir until blended. Add broth and cream, stirring rapidly with a whisk. When blended and smooth, simmer, stirring, about five minutes. Season with nutmeg, salt, and pepper. Sauté mushrooms in remaining butter and add to sauce with rice, chicken, and parsley. Spoon mixture into a two-quart casserole and sprinkle with cheese. Bake 25 to 30 minutes.

CHICKEN CASSEROLE

Serves: 6 - 8
Cooking Time: 40 minutes

"Good luncheon dish for leftover chicken."

½ lb. fresh sliced mushrooms
½ lb. noodles
6 tbsp. butter
6 tbsp. flour
2 cups chicken broth
salt
pepper
¼ cup sherry
½ cup heavy cream
2½ cups cooked, diced chicken
grated Parmesan cheese
butter
slivered almonds

Sauté mushrooms in butter. Cook noodles; drain and add a lump of butter. Melt six tablespoons butter and cook with flour 3 or 4 minutes. Add broth, a little at a time. Add salt, pepper, and sherry; stir. Add cream, a little at a time. Remove from heat, add mushrooms and chicken. Spoon over noodles. Sprinkle top with grated cheese and dot with butter. Top with slivered almonds. Bake in a preheated 350° oven 20 to 30 minutes.

CHICKEN AND HAM VERONIQUE

Serves: 4
Cooking Time: 20 minutes

"Lovely luncheon dish. Nice way to use leftover chicken, too!"

½ cup ham cut in 2-inch strips
1 can (2 oz.) mushroom slices, drained
¼ cup chopped onion
1 small clove garlic, minced
2 tbsp. butter
1 can condensed cream of chicken soup
½ cup milk
1 cup cubed, cooked chicken
½ cup green grapes, cut in half
4 patty shells

In sauce pan, brown ham, mushrooms, onion, and garlic in butter until onion is tender. Add soup, milk, chicken, and grapes. Heat; stir now and then. Serve in patty shells.

Chicken Breasts Smitane

Serves: 4
Cooking Time: 1 hour

"Wine and sour cream make this great."

4 large chicken breasts, split
salt
pepper
½ cup butter or margarine
2 small onions, minced
1 cup dry white wine
1 pt. sour cream
1 tbsp. lemon juice
½ lb. chopped mushrooms

Sprinkle chicken with salt and pepper and brown in butter on both sides. Cook over low heat about 40 minutes, turning occasionally. Remove chicken and keep warm on platter. Sauté onions in drippings until wilted. Add wine and boil until ½ cup remains. Stir in sour cream, lemon juice, and mushrooms. Season to taste with salt and pepper. Spoon sauce over chicken.

Stuffed Chicken Breasts

Serves: 6
Cooking Time: 1 hour

6 chicken breasts
⅛ lb. butter
½ cup Pepperidge Farm stuffing
2 eggs
1 clove garlic
½ cup chopped celery
½ lb. mushrooms, fresh
1 tsp. salt
½ cup flour
⅔ cup crumbs
½ cup water
2 beef bouillon cubes
⅓ cup sherry
½ cup sour cream

Bone and skin chicken. Then mix butter, stuffing, 1 egg, garlic, celery, chopped mushroom stems, and salt. Fill breasts. Roll. Dip in beaten egg and ⅓ cup flour, ⅔ cup bread crumbs. Fry in oil. Sear only. Add remaining flour to fat in pan and cook a few minutes. Add water with bouillon cubes and sherry. Add sautéed mushrooms and sour cream. Cool slightly. Pour on meat. Bake 15-20 minutes at 300°.

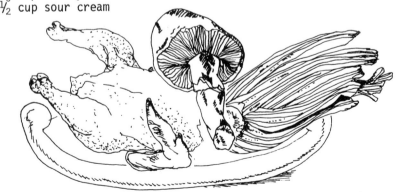

CHICKEN AND STUFFING

Serves: 6
Cooking Time: 1½ hours

"Easy as 1 - 2 - 3!"

2 sticks butter or margarine
1 medium onion, sliced
6 chicken breasts, boned
1 package prepared stuffing
  (Pepperidge Farm)
salt
pepper

Place one stick butter and onion in bottom of heavy covered casserole. Alternate layers of chicken breasts and prepared stuffing. Sprinkle with salt and pepper occasionally. Top with a second stick of butter. Cover tightly and bake at 350° for 1½ hours until done.

CHICKEN BREASTS IN FILO

Serves: 4
Cooking Time: 1 hour

"This is a very special dish, perfect for company.
Don't pass it up!"

¼ lb. butter (use for
  sautéing)
1 onion, chopped fine
½ lb. mushrooms, chopped fine
2 tbsp. minced parsley
1 clove garlic, minced
1½ tbsp. flour
⅓ cup vermouth
salt to taste
pepper to taste
2 tbsp. vegetable oil
4 boned chicken breast halves
8 filo leaves
⅓ cup melted butter
bread crumbs

In skillet, heat 3 tablespoons butter and sauté onion until golden. Set aside. Heat 3 more tablespoons butter and sauté mushrooms until juices evaporate, then add onions, parsley, and garlic and sauté a little more. Stir in flour, mixing well and add vermouth. Stir over medium heat until thickened. Season with salt and pepper. Set aside. In skillet heat remaining butter and vegetable oil and sauté breasts <u>one</u> minute on each side.

Wrap one breast in filo at a time, keeping unused sheets between damp towels. Butter one sheet of filo with <u>brush</u>, sprinkle on bread crumbs, cover with another sheet of filo, and butter again. Place chicken on leaves and put ¼ of mushroom mixture on top and roll it up like a blintze, tucking in corners. Butter outside well and bake at 350° for 35 minutes or until brown.

STUFFED CHICKEN BREASTS

Serves: 10 - 12
Cooking Time: 1 hour

"Pistachio nuts are a new twist. Good party fare."

10-12 chicken breasts, boned
   but not split

Stuffing

2 medium onions, browned in
   oil
1-lb. box Ritz crackers,
   crumbled
1 cup diced celery
1 grated carrot
2 eggs, well beaten
1 cup cold water (or more)
½ lb. shelled, salted
   pistachio nuts
chopped parsley
pepper to taste

Basting Sauce

2 cans Campbell's beef broth
½ cup Grand Marnier or
   Cointreau
1 large can frozen orange juice
½ cup honey

Break up nuts so that green shows. Combine all ingredients.
   Stuff breasts, bake 50 minutes at 350°. Baste with sauce every 10 minutes.

CHICKEN FLORENCE

Serves: 6 - 8
Cooking Time: 45 minutes

"One of our best. The gravy makes this special."

2 chickens (2½ lb. each),
   cut in serving pieces
¼ cup flour
1 tsp. salt
¼ tsp. pepper
3 tbsp. butter
3 tbsp. salad oil
3 small cloves garlic, chopped
½ bay leaf
½ tsp. marjoram
1 cup dry white wine
2 large tomatoes, peeled and
   chopped (canned can be used)
12 mushrooms (fresh)

Dredge chicken in flour, salt, and pepper. Brown quickly in butter, oil, and garlic. Add bay leaf, marjoram, wine, and tomatoes. Cover and cook slowly about 15 minutes. Add mushrooms. Cover and cook until chicken is done, about 10 minutes. Serve over rice.

CHICKEN CAPRICE

Serves: 8
Cooking Time: 30 minutes

"Can be prepared in advance and refrigerated."

4 whole chicken breasts, boned,
  skinned, and cut in half
½ lb. sweet butter
2 shallots, minced
⅛ tsp. nutmeg
½ tsp. salt
⅛ tsp. pepper
¼ cup chopped fine parsley
1 tbsp. cognac
dash Worcestershire sauce
1 or 2 bananas
1 loaf white bread, 3 or 4 days
  old, cut into cubes
1 cup flour
4 eggs, beaten
½ cup clarified butter

Have butcher skin and bone chicken breasts. Remove the filet (or under layer called supreme) under the breast. Pound chicken breasts until they are thin and also pound filet. Mix butter, shallot, nutmeg, salt, pepper, parsley, cognac, and Worcestershire sauce. Cut banana into three sections. Place one slice on each chicken breast. Divide butter mixture and spread over banana on each breast. Place filet over butter and banana and close or roll chicken breast to completely seal it. Sprinkle with a little salt and pepper. Cut crusts off white bread and dice into small cubes. Place on sheet of waxed paper. Heat a skillet with at least three to four tablespoons of clarified butter. Roll chicken first in flour then in beaten eggs, then roll in bread cubes. (Up to this point it can be made a day ahead and refrigerated.) Place into hot butter and brown for a few minutes and turn to brown all sides. Remove breasts to an oven-proof casserole and bake in a 325° oven for about 20 minutes, uncovered. Drain on paper toweling and serve.

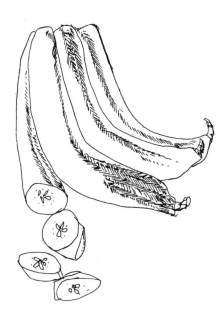

CHICKEN MAJORCA

Serves: 4 - 8
Cooking Time: 1 hour

"Complicated, but worth it."

3 oranges
3 cloves garlic, chopped
1 cup chicken broth (bouillon cube or G. Washington broth)
6 oz. mushrooms
3 tomatoes (optional)
1 or 2 chickens, cut up
¼ lb. salt butter
⅓ cup brandy or other spirits
1 tsp. meat glaze or Gravy Master
3 tsp. tomato paste
4 tsp. potato or cornstarch
½ cup cooking sherry
½ cup white wine
2 tsp. guava jelly
pepper
2 tsp. lemon juice
salt

Peel oranges with carrot scraper. Shred orange rind. Chop garlic. Prepare broth. Cut mushrooms in large pieces. Section oranges. Peel tomatoes, cut in chunks and remove seeds. Brown chicken in garlic butter (1 clove). Transfer pieces to casserole. Flame brandy and pour over chicken. Set aside and continue. Combine two ounces salt butter, orange rind, and two cloves garlic in sauce pan and cook slowly for 3 - 4 minutes. Remove pan from stove and add meat glaze, tomato paste, and potato or cornstarch. Return to stove and cook. When smooth, stir in chicken broth, sherry, white wine, guava jelly, and pepper (white preferably). Stir until mixture comes to a boil. Pour over chicken and bake on top shelf of oven 45-50 minutes, uncovered, at 350°. Baste occasionally. Melt two ounces salt butter and add mushrooms, lemon juice, salt, pepper, and pinch of sugar. Cook 3 minutes, do not overcook. Just before serving, add tomato chunks, orange sections, and mushrooms, and gently combine.

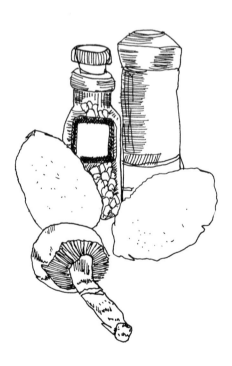

DUCK

Serves: 4
Cooking Time: 2½ hours

*"Great eating. Lazy cooks can have ducks
barbecued at poultry store."*

4-5 lb. duck
1 tsp. salt
¼ cup lemon juice
1 orange, unpeeled, ½ inch
   cut off both ends
1 apple, unpeeled, ½ inch cut
   off both ends
1 onion
1 cup orange juice
1 orange, sliced

Wash duck in cold water. Dry
well. Salt inside and out.
Sprinkle lemon juice inside and
rub skin with lemon juice. Place
orange, apple, and onion in cav-
ity of duck. These will be removed after roasting. Preheat
oven to 375°. Truss bird by
bringing cord under back and
around sides of breasts, under
tail, and then tie around legs.
Place duck on a rack in an open
roasting pan and cook for one
hour. Remove fat drippings. Set
oven up to 400° and roast 60-90
minutes more. Keep turning and
basting duck with orange juice.
(When using a rotisserie, allow
one hour and twenty minutes on
high heat. Also tie legs and
wings.) For family-style serv-
ice, cut duck into pieces. Place
duck and orange slices on an oven-
proof platter. Before serving,
broil for one minute and serve.

Montmorency Sauce (Cherry)

1 can (17 oz.) pitted dark
   cherries, drain and
   reserve juice
1 tbsp. lemon juice
2-3 tbsp. sugar
3 tbsp. port or cognac
3 tbsp. currant jelly
1 tbsp. cornstarch mixed with
   a little cherry juice

Put cherries in a bowl and pour
over lemon juice, sugar, and
cognac and let marinate at least
one hour. Heat cherry juice with
currant jelly in a sauce pan until hot. Add cornstarch mixed
with cherry juice and cook until
it thickens and becomes trans-
lucent. Add cherries to sauce
and serve with duck.

Orange Sauce

rind of 1 orange, coarsely grated
1 cup water
2 tbsp. duck fat
3 tbsp. brownulated sugar
1 cup orange juice
4 tbsp. currant jelly
2 tbsp. lemon juice
½ cup chicken broth
4 tbsp. cornstarch
3 tbsp. water

Simmer rind and water for five
minutes. Add duck fat with brown
sugar, orange juice, jelly, lemon
juice, and broth. Simmer all
gently for 2-3 minutes. Blend
cornstarch with water in a cup.
Add cornstarch slowly; if you
obtain the desired thickness before you have used it all, stop.
Serve with duck.

Duck à l'Orange

Serves: 4
Cooking Time: 2¼ hours

"An easy dish, foolproof recipe! No preparation or bother!"

1 whole duck
Lawry's seasoned salt
¼ lb. butter or margarine
1 oz. Grand Marnier (you can
  use as much of this as you
  like, the more the merrier!)
1 small can frozen orange juice
1 tbsp. orange marmalade
1 or more oranges for garnish

Remove giblets; wash off and wipe the duck. Season in and out with Lawry salt. In sauce pan, heat the butter, Grand Marnier, orange juice, and marmalade to boiling point. Pour this over duck and baste with it. Place duck in shallow pan on a rack so that fat drains off. Bake ½ hour at 400° breast down. Then bake one hour at 400° breast up. Then bake 45 minutes at 325°. Add sliced oranges to decorate.

Cornish Hens au Vin

Serves: 4
Cooking Time: 45 minutes

"Trick is to brown hens well."

2 cornish hens
butter
1 onion, diced
a few dices of bacon
¼ cup flour
1 qt. red wine
pepper
salt
1 sprig of parsley
1 cup cut up celery

Put the sweet butter with the cut-up hens in a pot (do not use an enamel pot to avoid any bad color of the wine). Cook it for a few minutes (until the sides are brown). Add the onion, bacon, and let it cook until the onion is brown. Add the flour, stir and leave it for a few minutes then add the red wine, pepper, salt, parsley, and celery. Cover and let simmer for 45 minutes. Serve hot. If the sauce is too liquid, add some flour and stir.

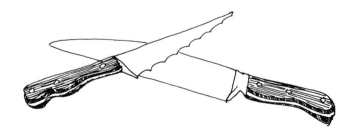

TURKEY IN WINE

Serves: 10 - 12
Cooking Time: $3\frac{1}{2}$ - 4 hours

"Different way to cook turkey."

salt
pepper
garlic powder
margarine
paprika
fresh lemon
1 turkey, 8 - 10 lb.
4 oz. white cooking wine
8 oz. orange juice
aluminum foil

Mix together salt, pepper, garlic powder, margarine, and paprika. Take fresh lemon and rub inside and outside of turkey. Then rub on mixture. Next mix wine and orange juice together. Pour a little of· this liquid mixture over turkey. Wrap turkey in aluminum foil, breast side down. Cook for one hour at 325°. After the hour, take off the foil and turn turkey, add more liquid and baste often. Cook until tender, about $3\frac{1}{2}$ hours.

CREAMED TURKEY IN POPOVERS

Serves: 6 - 8
Cooking Time: 1 hour, 15 minutes

"Good for leftover chicken too."

Creamed Turkey

1 cup or more diced cooked
    turkey or chicken
1 can cream of mushroom soup
1 can (4 oz.) mushrooms
1 tbsp. pimento
$\frac{1}{2}$ cup shredded Cheddar cheese

Combine all ingredients. Cook over medium heat until well blended.

Popovers

shortening
2 eggs
1 cup milk
1 cup flour (Gold Medal Wondra
    flour is best in this
    recipe)
$\frac{1}{2}$ tsp. salt

Grease six 5-ounce custard cups or eight muffin cups. Beat eggs slightly with fork. Add milk, flour, and salt. Beat until Smooth. DON'T OVERBEAT. Divide between cups. Bake 25 minutes at 450°. Reduce heat to 350° and bake 15 minutes longer. Remove from cups immediately. Fill with turkey mixture.

Meats

Roslyn Seasoning

"Use on roasts, steaks, pot roasts, etc."

3 tsp. salt
3 tsp. paprika
1 tsp. garlic powder
1 tsp. pepper

Mix together on wax paper and keep in shaker.

Steak Marinade

3 tbsp. scallions, cut up fine
1½ tsp. soy sauce
2 tbsp. olive oil
½ tsp. thyme
juice of ½ lemon
steak

Mix all ingredients together. Brush on both sides of uncooked meat. Marinade may be prepared beforehand and refrigerated. Steak can be either broiled or baked.

Simple Bearnaise Sauce

Serves: 8
Cooking Time: 15 minutes

2 tbsp. chopped green onion
1 tbsp. tarragon vinegar
½ cup white wine
5 egg yolks
1½ tsp. tarragon leaves
pepper
salt
½ tsp. mustard
¾ cup melted butter
pinch cayenne pepper

Simmer onions in vinegar and wine until liquid has been reduced by about two-thirds. Remove from heat and cool. Place this mixture in blender and add egg yolks, tarragon leaves, salt, pepper, and mustard. Blend at high speed for a maximum of ten seconds. Add warm, melted butter and cayenne. Quickly turn on blender again and rotate slowly until sauce thickens. Add hot water (a bit) if it gets too thick. Make ahead and keep warm in double boiler.

Barbecue Sauce

Cooking Time: 20 minutes

¼ cup salad oil
1 medium onion, cut fine
1 clove garlic, mashed
1 sprig parsley, cut fine
1 can (6 oz.) tomato paste
1½ cup water
1 tsp. vinegar
½ tsp. oregano
½ tsp. salt
1 tsp. sugar
⅛ tsp. cayenne (optional)
2 tsp. chili powder

Heat oil in heavy skillet. Add onion, garlic, parsley, and tomato paste. Simmer 3 minutes. Add water, vinegar, oregano, salt, sugar, cayenne, and chili powder. Bring to a boil, then simmer 15 minutes.

Plum Sauce

"Nice change in place of Saucy Susan."

1 cup plum jam
4 tbsp. wine vinegar
1 clove garlic, crushed
½ tsp. allspice
1 tsp. dry mustard

Combine all ingredients in blender container, and blend until smooth. May be mixed by hand.

Garlic-Lemon Sauce

Cooking Time: 2 - 3 minutes

"Good over broiled or baked chicken or fish."

¼ lb. butter
½ bunch fresh parsley,
   chopped
1 clove garlic, pressed
   or minced
juice of 1 lemon

Melt butter. Add chopped parsley and garlic. Cook 2 - 3 minutes. Add lemon juice to taste.

BAKED LONDON BROIL

Serves: 6 - 8
Cooking Time: 45 - 60 minutes

*"Prepare it the day before, marinate 24 hours ahead,
and pop in oven after a busy day."*

1 lb. mushrooms
2 green peppers
3 onions
1 small bottle (14 oz.)
   ketchup
1 small ketchup bottle
   of red wine
1 round steak, 2-3 lb.

Cut pepper in strips and onions in rings. Slice stems, leave mushrooms whole. Pour ketchup and wine over meat and vegetables. Marinate 24 hours. Bake at 425° for 45 minutes to one hour. Slice on diagonal.

LONDON BROIL

Serves: 6 - 8
Cooking Time: 30 minutes in advance
           8 minutes to broil

*"The sauce is great for london broil or steak.
Try it on leftover roast beef, too."*

1 london broil, 2-3 lb.
1 clove garlic
½ tsp. mushroom powder
2 large onions, sliced
2 tbsp. safflower oil
1 tsp. Worcestershire sauce
2 tbsp. olive oil
1 tsp. salt
½ tsp. lemon-pepper marinade

Marinate meat in mixture thirty minutes. Broil at high heat in preheated broiler approximately eight minutes. Baste with sauce once. Let meat stand for eight minutes before serving.

Party Sauce (for london broil or steak)

3 tbsp. butter
3 tbsp. flour
1 onion, finely chopped
1 can (10 oz.) beef stock
½ tsp. parsley
salt to taste
pepper to taste
¼ tsp. thyme
1 bay leaf, crumbled
¼ lb. fresh mushrooms,
   sliced or chopped

Sauté onions in butter until light brown. Add flour and blend. Cook over moderate heat until deep brown. Add stock slowly, stirring as you do. Add parsley, thyme, bay leaf, salt, and pepper. In a second pan sauté mushrooms in butter until lightly browned. Add to sauce and simmer for twenty minutes.

STEAK AND PEPPERS

Serves: 6 - 8
Cooking Time: 1 hour, 20 minutes

*"Good dish for company, with a different flavor.
Can be made in advance."*

1 large round steak cut into
   1-inch strips, 2½ lb.
1 clove garlic, diced
3 green peppers, sliced
1 package dry onion soup mix
¼ cup soy sauce
2 tbsp. sherry
3 tbsp. water
2½ tbsp. cornstarch
2 cups boiling water
4 tbsp. oil
4 tsp. sugar

Braise meat in oil and remove. Brown garlic and peppers until soft then remove peppers. Combine soup and boiling water in same pot, add soy sauce, sugar, and sherry. Stir. Combine remaining water and cornstarch; add to onion mixture, stirring until smooth. Add meat, simmer, covered, one hour. Add peppers and simmer ten minutes longer. Serve with rice.

PEPPER STEAK

Serves: 6
Cooking Time: 50 minutes

"This is an easy one and good with rice."

1½ lb. flank steak, thinly
   sliced
3 tbsp. soy sauce
1 tbsp. sugar
½ tsp. pepper
1 chicken bouillon cube,
   dissolved in ¾ cup hot
   water
1 tbsp. flour, dissolved in
   water
1 onion chopped
2 cloves garlic, chopped
4-5 scallions, chopped
1 can sliced mushrooms,
   sautéed
2 green peppers, sliced

Sear meat on both sides and remove from skillet. Add to skillet soy sauce, sugar, pepper, dissolved bouillon, and stir. Add flour and water and stir. Heat. Add onions, garlic, scallions, and mushrooms, meat and peppers. Simmer about 35 minutes.

GARLIC-PEPPER STEAK

Serves: 6
Cooking Time: 15 - 20 minutes
Marinate: 2 hours

1½ to 2 lb. flank steak
¼ cup salad oil
2 tbsp. lemon juice
2 tbsp. soy sauce
1 clove garlic, crushed
2 tbsp. chopped green onions
  or 1 tbsp. dried green
  onions
1 tsp. gound black pepper
1 tsp. celery salt

Remove any small pieces of surface fat from steak. Dry well with paper towels. In shallow baking dish, combine remaining ingredients. Place steak in marinade, at room temperature, for at least two hours. Turn frequently. (Or marinate, covered, in refrigerator six hours, turning frequently.) Drain, broil to taste. Slice meat on diagonal.

STEAK 'N' FRUIT

Serves: 6
Cooking Time: 1½ hours

"This is different and what a way to dress up a chuck steak."

2½ to 3 lb. trimmed chuck
  steak
2 tbsp. shortening
2 large onions, sliced
2-3 tsp. salt
2 tsp. brown sugar
1 tsp. pepper
1 cup grapefruit juice
  (canned)
1 large, fresh grapefruit
1 large, fresh orange
2 tbsp. cornstarch

Preheat oven to 350°. Brown meat, in shortening, on both sides. Add onions, salt, sugar, pepper, and juice. Cover and bake 1½ hours. Peel and section fresh fruit (if not available, use canned.) Add to meat last five to ten minutes of cooking time. Remove to platter, thicken gravy left in pan with two tablespoons cornstarch. Pour over meat and serve with rice (optional).

Beef Stroganoff

(BEEF IN SOUR CREAM SAUCE)

Serves: 6
Cooking Time: 30 minutes

"Serve with rice or noodles. Fine for company."

2 tbsp. oil or butter
3 medium onions
1 lb. fresh mushrooms
1 tbsp. flour
1 tsp. tomato paste
1 tsp. meat glaze or Gravy
  Master
2 lb. filet of beef
2 tbsp. butter
salt
pepper
dry mustard
1 pt. sour cream

Sauté onions in oil 3-5 minutes and transfer to casserole. Wash mushrooms thoroughly, pat dry and slice. Cook 3 - 5 minutes. Transfer to casserole. Add , thoroughly combined, flour, tomato paste, and meat glaze and set aside. Cut meat into $\frac{1}{4}$-inch slivers, about 2 inches long. Melt two tablespoons butter and quickly cook one-half of the beef and add to onions and mushrooms. Now repeat with balance of meat. Add seasonings, to taste. Add sour cream, one tablespoon at a time. Now simmer (do not boil) for 2-3 minutes. Taste for seasonings and adjust.

Easy Skillet Stroganoff

Serves: 4
Cooking Time: 30 minutes

"Serve with rice."

1½ lb. sirloin steak
2 tbsp. flour, salt, and
  pepper mixed
2 tbsp. oil
¾ cup chopped onions
½ lb. fresh mushrooms, sliced
2 tbsp. Worcestershire sauce
1 can cream of celery, chicken,
  or mushroom soup
1 cup sour cream
2 tbsp. pimento (chopped)

Cut steak into thin strips, coat with flour, salt, and pepper. Brown quickly in oil. Add onions, mushrooms, and sauté over low heat until brown. Add Worcestershire sauce, soup, sour cream, and bring to a boil. Add pimento.

SUKIAKI

Serves: 4
Cooking Time: 20 minutes

1 lb. steak
3 onions
1 bunch of scallions
½ lb. mushrooms
4 stalks celery
½ lb. spinach, cut up
1 can (8½ oz.) bamboo shoots
½ cup soy sauce
1 cup beef broth
1 tbsp. sugar

Slice meat thin and brown in oil (rapidly). Add sliced onions, scallions, mushrooms, spinach, and bamboo shoots. Cook five minutes (stir). Add soy sauce, beef broth, and sugar. Mix thoroughly. Cook uncovered for fifteen minutes. Stir a few times.

ORIENTAL BEEF WITH SNOW PEAS

Serves: 6
Cooking Time: 15 minutes
Marinate: 1½ hours

3 tbsp. sherry
2 tbsp. soy sauce
1 tsp. sugar
½ tsp. ground ginger
1 clove garlic, minced
1½ lb. sirloin steak,
     1¼ inches thick
3 tbsp. cooking oil
1 package snow pea pods
1 cup scallions cut in 1-inch
     pieces
1 cup diced celery or 2 cups
     chinese celery
1 cup fresh, sliced mushrooms
1 cup water chestnuts, drained
     and sliced
2 beef bouillon cubes
1 cup water
2 tbsp. cornstarch
salt, to taste

Combine sherry, soy sauce, sugar, ginger, garlic to make marinade. Cut partially frozen meat in very thin slices. Marinate at least 1½ hours, in refrigerator. Heat oil in wok or heavy pan and fry drained meat until gray. Then add snow peas and rest of marinade from meat and cook one more minute. Add rest of vegetables and cook about two minutes. Combine bouillon, water, cornstarch, and salt. Add to pan and cook until sauce is thickened. Serve with rice.

STUFFED BEEF TENDERLOIN

Serves: 6
Cooking Time: 1 hour, 10 minutes

"Good company dish to be prepared early in day and popped in oven while enjoying cocktails."

¼ cup butter
1 medium onion, chopped
½ cup diced celery
1 can (4 oz.) sliced mushrooms,
    drained well
2 cups soft bread crumbs
½ to 1 tsp. salt
⅛ tsp. black pepper
½ tsp. basil leaves
⅛ tsp. parsley flakes
3 lb. beef tenderloin
4 slices bacon

Melt butter in a small skillet over low direct heat. Sauté onion, celery, and mushrooms until onion is soft and transparent, about ten minutes. Place bread crumbs in a one-quart bowl. Mix in the salt, pepper, basil leaves, and parsley flakes. Pour in the butter and onion mixture. Lightly mix until well blended. Make a lengthwise cut, three-fourths of the way through the tenderloin. Lightly place stuffing in the pocket formed by the cut. Close the pocket by fastening meat together with wooden toothpicks. Place bacon strips diagonally across the top, covering the picks and the pocket. Place stuffed meat in a three-quart Pyrex oblong baking dish. Bake, uncovered, in 350° oven for one hour (medium rare).

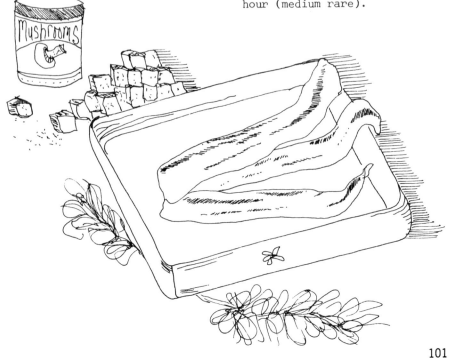

BEEF WELLINGTON

Serves: 8
Cooking Time: 1 hour

"A little extra effort required, but impressive when company is coming."

4-5 lb. filet mignon (whole)
2 tbsp. butter
1 medium onion, chopped
1½ lbs. mushrooms, chopped
1 tbsp. flour
2 tbsp. cream
2 tbsp. Madeira or port wine
1 tbsp. chopped parsley
½ tsp. salt
⅛ tsp. pepper
1 egg yolk
1 tbsp. water

Make up batch of Puff Pastry (following recipe) in advance and store in refrigerator. Season meat with Roslyn Seasoning (p. 94) and roast at 350° about 20-25 minutes; then let stand at room temperature. Sauté onions and mushrooms in butter until moisture is cooked away. Stir flour into mushrooms. Lower flame and add cream, wine, parsley, salt, and pepper and cook two minutes to thicken. Roll out pastry a little longer than filet and twice as wide. Transfer to cookie sheet. Spread mushroom mixture down center of pastry. Place filet top side down on mushrooms. Fold pastry over to enclose meat completely. Turn filet over onto another cookie sheet, so seam of dough is on the bottom. Make criss-cross design over the top with sharp knife. Slightly beat egg with water and brush over dough. Bake at 400° for 35 minutes. Serve with stuffed tomatoes.

PUFF PASTRY

½ lb. sweet butter
1¾ cups flour
½ tsp. salt
½ cup ice water

Bring butter to room temperature in a bowl. Add ¼ cup flour to butter and knead together. Turn onto waxed paper and form in rectangular block. Refrigerate 15 minutes. Place 1½ cups flour and salt in bowl. Sprinkle ice water over gradually, mixing with wooden spoon until flour is completely absorbed. Transfer to floured surface and working with hands, knead until smooth (about 5-6 minutes). Now refrigerate so dough relaxes, about 10 minutes. Roll between waxed paper to 8 x 12 inches. Place butter brick in center. Fold each end over, with open end under. Roll to 8 x 12 inches again (always rolling away from you) and fold again. Make a thumb print in dough, wrap in waxed paper and refrigerate. Repeat this procedure of rolling, folding, and refrigerating (each time increasing the number of thumb prints by one to keep track of turns) for a total of six times. (This dough can be refrigerated up to three weeks.)

Editors' Note:
   For an easier Puff Pastry recipe see page 270.

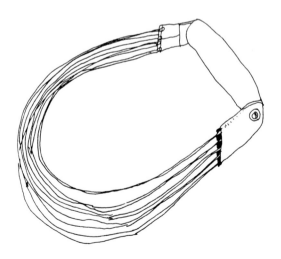

Oven Ragout or "Easy Stew"

Serves: 6 - 8
Cooking Time: 3½ hours

"Gourmet cooking without work!"

1 cup red wine (not sherry)
1 can cream of mushroom soup, undiluted
1 package dry onion soup
3 lb. beef cubes (stew beef or chuck or 1 or 2 oxtails, plus proportionate amount of beef cubes)
carrots, cut up
whole small onions
flour or cornstarch
Gravy Master

In a large, heavy casserole with tight cover combine wine, cream of mushroom soup, and onion soup. Mix well. Add meat. Bake, covered, at 325° for 2½ hours. Put in refrigerator in order to congeal and then take off excess fat. About one hour before serving, return to oven, having added carrots and onions. (If canned carrots and onions are used, then one-half hour will do.) If gravy seems too thin, thicken with flour or cornstarch. If gravy seems too pale, darken with Gravy Master. Can be made days ahead. Freezes well. Serve with noodle "twists" or spaetzle.

Beef Dinner in a Pot

Serves: 3 - 4
Cooking Time: 2½ hours

1½ lb. beef, cubed
2 tbsp. shortening
1 can (10 oz.) Campbell's beef broth
½ cup water
¼ cup ketchup
1 tbsp. prepared mustard
1 large clove garlic, minced
dash Tabasco
½ tsp. salt
generous dash pepper
2 large onions, quartered
1 small green pepper, cut up
1½ cups sliced mushrooms (¼ lb.)
2 tbsp. flour

Brown beef in shortening. Pour off fat. Add soup, water, ketchup, mustard, garlic, Tabasco, and seasonings. Cover, simmer 1½ hours. Add onions, cook 40 minutes more. Add green pepper and mushrooms; cook 20 minutes longer. Gradually blend ¼ cup water into flour until smooth. Slowly stir stew. Cook, stirring until thickened.

GOULASH

2 lb. beef (chuck) cut in
   1-inch cubes
1 cup chopped onions
2 tbsp. cooking oil
1 tsp. flour
1 tsp. salt
1 tsp. paprika
1 can (8 oz.) tomato sauce
1 can (12 oz.) tomatoes
1 clove garlic, diced (or
   garlic powder)
1 bay leaf
1 stalk celery ⎫ _ in piece of
1 tsp. parsley ⎭   cheesecloth

Brown meat and onions in hot oil. Lightly stir in flour, salt, and paprika; cook about 5 minutes. Add remaining ingredients; heat until boiling. Cover and bake in a 350° oven until meat is tender, approximately 1½ hours. Remove bay leaf, celery, and parsley. Serve with hot noodles. These may be mixed with beef before you serve.

BEEF BURGUNDY

Serves: 4 - 6
Cooking Time: 2½ hours

"Tastes even better made in advance and reheated."

3 onions, sliced
oil
2½ lb. cubed beef chuck
flour
salt
1 cup burgundy wine
1 cup prepared gravy
1 small can sliced mushrooms
   or ½ lb. fresh sautéed
1 package frozen peas and
   carrots
1 large can small whole potatoes

Lightly sauté in oil in large skillet sliced onions and set aside. Dredge meat in flour and brown on all sides with salt. Add wine and gravy, cover and simmer for two hours. Add mushrooms and onions. Simmer for ½ hour. Add peas and carrots, potatoes for last 15 minutes. If potatoes are omitted, this dish can be served over hot noodles or browned rice. Serve with salad and hot garlic bread.

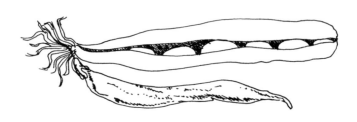

BEEF WITH WINE AND COGNAC

Serves: 6 - 8
Cooking Time: 3½ to 4½ hours

"Great company dish! Can be doubled, tripled, etc., and done ahead. Time consuming but worth it! Improves when reheated. Freeze what you can't serve."

3 lb. chuck or stewing beef cut in 1½-inch cubes
1½ cups red wine
¼ cup cognac
2 tbsp. peanut oil
salt
fresh ground pepper
½ tsp. thyme
1 bay leaf
1 large onion, diced
2 garlic cloves, diced
2 cups thinly sliced carrots, raw
½ cup diced celery
½ lb. sliced lean bacon (cut slices in ⅓)
all-purpose flour
2½ cups canned Italian-style plum tomatoes
2 cups thinly sliced fresh mushrooms
2 cups boiling water
3 packages beef broth (MBT)

Place beef in large mixing bowl. Add wine, cognac, oil, salt, and pepper to taste, thyme, bay leaf, onion, garlic, carrots, and celery. Cover and refrigerate three hours or more. Preheat oven to 350°. Place cut-up bacon in frying pan and partially cook; drain. Line a heat-proof casserole with six pieces of bacon. (The heavier the pot the better.) Drain beef and reserve marinade. Place flour in bag and dredge each cube of beef with flour and remove excess flour. Arrange a layer of beef in casserole. Add layer of marinated vegetables, ⅓ of tomatoes, ⅓ sliced raw mushrooms. Continue making layers until all ingredients are used, end with vegetables and bacon. Sprinkle with salt and pepper. Dissolve MBT broth in hot water. Add beef broth and enough marinade to cover. Cover casserole and bring liquid to boil on top of stove. Place in oven and bake for 15 minutes. Reduce heat to 300° so that casserole barely simmers. Cook 3-4 hours until meat is fork tender. Skim fat and serve with rice or noodles.

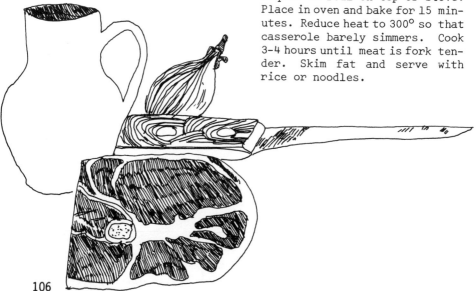

DAUBE PROVENÇALE

Serves: 8 - 10
Cooking Time: 3½ hours

"This dish is best when it is prepared one day in advance so that seasonings may fully penetrate the meat. It can be reheated several times with the flavor improving with each reheating."

4 lb. brisket of beef, trimmed, or lean stewing beef
1 lb. lean bacon (optional)
salt
freshly ground pepper
4 large onions, quartered
2 whole heads of garlic, at least 20 cloves*
1 strip of orange peel
1 bay leaf
2 springs fresh thyme or 1 tsp. dried
red wine to cover

*Do not be concerned about the large quantity of garlic required in this recipe. The long and slow cooking of this French stew will neutralize the garlic.

Cut meat into large cubes, 1½ to 2 inches. In a Dutch oven or any deep, heavy casserole, cook the bacon until it has rendered its fat. Remove bacon from Dutch oven and set aside. Cook the cubes of meat, adding a few pieces at a time, until it is lightly browned all over. (If bacon is not used, any cooking oil or good olive oil will do.) Sprinkle the meat in the Dutch oven with salt and pepper to taste. Add to this the onion quarters. Crumble and add bacon. Separate and peel garlic cloves and add whole to pot. Add remaining ingredients with enough wine to barely cover contents of pot. Add more salt and pepper to taste. Cover loosely and simmer very slowly for three hours or until meat is tender.

Let pot cool still covered. Refrigerate. Skim fat from surface when it is cool. Reheat the daube to the boiling point before serving.

SUGAR-CURED CORNED BEEF

Serves: 4
Cooking Time: 2½ hours

"Good for buffets. Leftovers make nice sandwiches."

first-cut corned beef
boiling water
cranberry-orange relish
1 can sliced pineapple
½ cup orange juice

Cook corned beef in boiling water 1½ hours or until soft. Cool and slice thin. Put back together and cover with remaining ingredients. Bake at 350° for one hour.

BRISKET

Serves: 6 - 8
Cooking Time: 3 hours

"A famous caterer's recipe."

1 brisket, 4 lb., well trimmed
paprika
salt
pepper
1 onion
4 tbsp. ketchup
¼ cup water
½ cup cooking wine
2 cloves garlic, cut up
½ tsp. basil
parsley

Sprinkle paprika on brisket. Brown for thirty minutes on each side in a 450° oven. Lower heat to 350° and add salt, pepper, and onion. In a bowl, combine remaining ingredients. Pour over meat. Cover and cook two hours.

SAUERBRATEN

Serves: 8 - 10
Cooking Time: 3 - 4 hours
Marinate: 3 - 4 days

"Try serving potato pancakes with this."

4-5 lb. beef roast, top or
    bottom round
2 cups water
2 cups vinegar
1 tbsp. salt
½ tsp. pepper
2 tbsp. sugar, white or brown
2 medium onions, sliced
1 clove garlic
6 cloves
2 bay leaves
3 or 4 celery tops
12 gingersnaps

Place meat in large earthenware or glass bowl. Heat vinegar and water, dissolve salt, pepper, and sugar. Top meat with sliced onions and pour vinegar mixture over it. Add remaining ingredients, except gingersnaps, around meat. Cover and refrigerate 3 to 4 days, turning meat daily. Remove meat and drain well. Strain liquid and reserve.

Dredge meat with flour; brown in hot fat in heavy pan. Add ½ cup of the strained liquid, cover and cook over low heat until tender (3 to 4 hours). Add more liquid as needed.

Remove meat and keep hot. To make gravy, add more strained liquid to juice in the pan to make 3 cups liquid. Bring to boil and stir to dissolve all brown drippings. Add gingersnaps (they will dissolve). Simmer and stir until gravy is thickened and smooth.

Mom's Potted Meat and Lima Beans

Serves: 6
Cooking Time: 3 hours

"Like Grandma made!"

2 large onions, diced
salt to taste
pepper to taste
garlic powder to taste
2 cans tomato sauce (8 oz.)
2 cans water
1 lb. dried lima beans
3 lb. brisket

In Dutch oven, cook all ingredients, except beans and beef until soft. Add meat and beans. Cook until tender. Cool meat, slice, and then return to heat. Serve sliced meat, surrounded by the beans.

Short Ribs Supreme

Serves: 4 - 6
Cooking Time: 2½ hours

"A family favorite for informal meals."

4 lb. short ribs
2 tsp. salt
½ cup water
½ cup chopped onions
1 clove garlic, minced
1 can (8 oz.) tomato sauce
1 cup ketchup
¾ cup brown sugar
½ cup white vinegar
2 tbsp. prepared mustard

Brown ribs in large skillet in own fat. Cover and cook one hour. Meanwhile, mix remaining ingredients and allow to stand, covered. When ribs are done, pour off drippings. Spread ribs in large casserole (9 x 13 inches) pour mixture over ribs. Bake in 300° oven, covered, for one hour. Take off cover and bake another thirty minutes.

Flanken Sweet and Sour

Serves: 4
Cooking Time: 2 hours

1 small can (8 oz.) tomato sauce
1 can (10½ oz.) marinara sauce
1 tsp. sour salt, more or less,
  to taste
2 tsp. brown sugar, more or
  less, to taste
1 bay leaf
2 onions
½ cup water
breast flanken, four slices, or
  short ribs

Sauté onions and flanken. Add all ingredients and cook for two hours over small flame. Refrigerate and remove fat from top before reheating.

ANITA'S MEATBALLS

Serves: 3
Cooking Time: 40 minutes

"Rich, but what a flavor. Don't miss this one. Serve as an hors d'oeuvre or as a main dish over noodles."

1 lb. chopped beef
1 tsp. Accent
¾ tsp. salt
1 tbsp. chopped onions
½ cup soft bread crumbs
¼ cup milk
flour
2 tbsp. butter

Sauce:

½ cup unsulphered molasses
  or Karo syrup
½ cup sherry or vinegar
½ cup ketchup
½ tsp. Tabasco
½ tsp. oregano

Mix beef, Accent, salt, onions, bread crumbs, and milk. Form into balls and roll in flour. Brown in butter. Combine all Sauce ingredients and add to browned meatballs. Simmer 8 to 10 minutes. Double Sauce when using over noodles.

SWEET AND SOUR MEATBALLS

Serves: 6 - 8
Cooking Time: 1 hour

"Serve with rice."

1½ lb. chopped meat,
  preferably round
1 egg
⅓ cup cornflake crumbs
1 cup almonds, blanched
¼ cup sugar
¼ cup firmly packed brown
  sugar
¼ cup cornstarch
1 can (1 lb., 4 oz.) pineapple
  chunks, drained, juice
  reserved
1½ cups pineapple juice
4-6 tbsp. cider vinegar
1 tbsp. soy sauce
cherries, pitted (optional)
pickles (optional)
carrots (fancy cut) (optional)

Mix together chopped meat, egg, and cornflakes. Form 1-inch meatballs and sauté until done. To make sauce: Mix together almonds, sugar, brown sugar, cornstarch. Gradually add, stirring constantly, reserved pineapple syrup, pineapple juice, vinegar, and soy sauce. Bring to a boil. Add meatballs and pineapple chunks (optional ingredients can be added at this time).

CHINESE MEATBALLS

Serves: 4
Cooking Time: 30 minutes

¼ cup fine dry bread crumbs
½ cup milk
1 lb. ground beef
½ tsp. salt
¼ tsp. pepper
½ tsp. celery salt
dash garlic salt
flour
3 tbsp. margarine
2 large green peppers or
   more, sliced
2 onions or more, sliced
2 cups beef bouillon
2 tbsp. soy sauce

Soak crumbs in milk. Mix with meat, salt, pepper, celery salt, and garlic salt. Shape into 12 balls. Roll in flour and brown in margarine in large skillet. Push meatballs to side, add green pepper and onions and brown lightly. Add bouillon and soy sauce; cover and simmer about 15 minutes. Thicken liquid with flour mixed with a little water. Simmer a few minutes. Serve with rice.

HUNGARIAN POTTED MEATBALLS

Serves: 3
Cooking Time: 1½ hours

"Great basic meatball recipe. Can be used for hamburgers, meat loaf, etc."

2 slices white bread, broken up
¼ to ½ cup cold milk
1 lb. chopped meat
½ grated onion
1 can (15 oz.) tomato sauce
1 tsp. salt
¼ tsp. pepper
¼ tsp. garlic powder

Mix bread well with milk. Add rest of ingredients, except tomato sauce. Shape meatballs. Heat tomato sauce, add meatballs. Cover, cook one hour.
Optional: Cut up raw potatoes (quartered) and add to pot ½ hour before meatballs are done.

111

BEEF AND MUSHROOMS

Serves: 4
Cooking Time: 30 minutes

"Meatballs going continental."

1 lb. ground beef
2 tbsp. bread crumbs
2 tbsp. chopped onions
2 tbsp. chopped parsley
½ tsp. salt
1 egg, slightly beaten
3 tbsp. Burgundy
2 tbsp. butter
1 can (8 oz.) sliced mushrooms
1 small onion, sliced
1 can (13¾ oz.) beef broth
¼ cup water
2 tbsp. flour

Combine first six ingredients and one tablespoon wine. Shape into balls and brown in butter. Push to one side of pan. Add mushrooms and onion, cook until onion is tender. Add soup and remaining wine, heat. Add mixture of flour and water and cook 15 minutes. Stir often. Serve with rice or noodles.

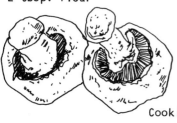

CHILI

Serves: 8
Cooking Time: 3 - 5 hours

"Hot and good. The longer it cooks, the better it is."

6 tbsp. oil
2 large onions, minced
4 cloves garlic, minced
2 lb. chopped meat
2⅔ cups whole tomatoes, drained
6 cups water (with drained juice)
2 green peppers minced
1 tsp. celery seed
½ tsp. cayenne pepper
2 tsp. cumin seed, crushed
2 small bay leaves
4 tbsp. chili powder
¼ tsp. basil
3 tsp. salt
kidney beans

Heat oil in skillet, add onions and garlic, sauté until golden. Add meat and brown. Transfer to large sauce pan, add remaining ingredients (except the beans). Bring to boil, reduce heat, and simmer uncovered until as thick as desired. About 3-5 hours or more. Just before serving add one or more cans kidney beans. Can be frozen and reheated.

Editors' Note:
Stuffed cabbage seems to be a favorite recipe of many cool have included a number of them — each a little different fr other, but all of them good. Try them all and pick your own favc. .... It is extremely versatile and is appropriately served as an hors d'oeuvre, an appetizer, or as a main dish. It can be prepared in large quantities with little extra effort and freezes well in tinfoil pans. Partially defrost the stuffed cabbage to be reheated. Place covered in 400° oven for approximately one hour or until hot. Then heat uncovered for ten minutes to lightly brown.

Unstuffed Stuffed Cabbage and Cabbage Soup

Serves: 4
Cooking Time: 2 hours, 50 minutes

"Lazy man's way, but flavor can't be beat."

2 lb. head green cabbage
1 can (1 lb.) stewed tomatoes
1 cup tomato sauce*
½ cup vinegar
¾ cup light brown sugar
2 tbsp. lemon juice
1½ cups water
1 apple, cored, pared, and cut
   into chunks
1 small package (1½ oz.)
   seedless raisins
1 lb. chopped chuck
1 egg
¼ lb. raw rice
¼ tsp. salt

*If you wish to prepare cabbage soup instead, decrease the tomato sauce to ¾ cup.

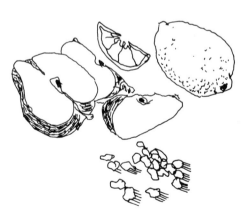

Cut cabbage into quarters, then cut quarters into chunks, shreds, strips, or whatever. Place cabbage into a six-quart pot. Add tomatoes, tomato sauce, vinegar, brown sugar, lemon juice, water, and apple. (If you are making soup, your preparations are over now. Just cover the pot and simmer for 2½ hours, adding the raisins 45 minutes before it's done.) If you are cooking this as a main dish, cover and cook over medium-high heat while you prepare the meat mixture. (This will give the cabbage a chance to get slightly soft, so that you can push it down and make room for the meat to float on top of the sauce.)

Mix chopped chuck with egg, raw rice, and salt. Form into meatballs; put meatballs on top of sauce. Cover pot, lower heat, and simmer very gently for 2½ hours, stirring occasionally. About 45 minutes before the end of the cooking time, add raisins. Before serving: Place covered pot on top of stove and cook over low heat for 15 to 20 minutes. If made with meat, this is excellent to serve over rice.

STUFFED CABBAGE

Serves: 6 - 8
Cooking Time: 1½ hours

"Pork, veal, and beef make this one different."

1 head cabbage (3 lb.)
1 onion, chopped
½ lb. pork, ground
½ lb. veal, ground
1 lb. beef, ground
½ tsp. pepper
1 tbsp. salt
1 cup rice
1 can (1 lb., 4 oz.) tomatoes

Cut around core of cabbage to loosen leaves. Boil cabbage about five minutes. Take leaves apart and set aside. Fry onion in shortening until golden. Add ground meats, salt, and pepper and fry slowly about 15 minutes. Wash rice. Drain and add to meat mixture. Mix well. Place tablespoon of meat and rice mixture in center of cabbage leaf and roll, tucking in sides. Place extra leaves in bottom of kettle and place rolled leaves side by side. Pour tomatoes over and add water to cover. Cook slowly 1½ hours.

STUFFED CABBAGE

Serves: 6
Cooking Time: 3 hours

1 head cabbage
2 lb. chopped meat
½ cup Minute Rice
1 egg
1 raw carrot, grated
1 raw potato, grated (optional)
1 slice stale white bread, wet
  and crumbled
1 tbsp. ketchup
1 tsp. sugar
salt to taste
1 onion, diced
raisins (optional)
3 small cans (8 oz. each)
  Delmonte Tomato Sauce
1 tomato sauce can of water
1 cup brown sugar
2 tbsp. lemon juice

Remove outer leaves and place cabbage in boiling water for 20 minutes. Separate leaves; cut away hard veins. Mix meat with rice, egg, carrot, potato, bread, ketchup, sugar, and salt. Roll into cabbage leaves. In large pot, place onion and raisins. Put in rolled cabbage. Mix together three small cans tomato sauce and water, pour over cabbage. Bring to a slow boil, then simmer one hour. Add brown sugar and lemon juice to taste. Add more of either if needed. Simmer 1½ hours.

114

STUFFED CABBAGE

Serves: 4 - 6
Cooking Time: 1½ hours

"Made with onion soup mix; not sweet not sour!"

¾ cup rice
1¼ lb. chopped meat
1 onion, diced
salt to taste
1 egg
1 large head cabbage
1 onion, chopped
1 green pepper, chopped
1 cup water
1 package dry onion soup mix
1 can (8 oz.) tomato sauce

Precook rice and wash and drain. Mix the rice with the chopped meat, add onion, salt, and egg. Wilt cabbage leaves in boiling water. Wrap the meat mix with the rice in leaf, three large heaping tablespoons in each leaf. Make a bed of chopped cabbage, onion and green pepper. Put the stuffed cabbage in the bed. Combine water, onion soup mix, and tomato sauce. Pour over stuffed cabbage and bake at 375° for about 1½ hours.

SWEET AND SOUR STUFFED CABBAGE

(HUNGARIAN STYLE)

Serves: 6 - 8
Cooking Time: 2 hours

3 to 3½ lb. cabbage
2 onions, chopped
2 tbsp. oil
1½ lb. chopped meat
⅓ to ¼ cup rice
1 to 2 eggs
1 tbsp. salt
½ tsp. pepper
½ tsp. paprika
1 can (#2) tomatoes
1 can (#2) sauerkraut
1 buffet can (8 oz.) tomato
  sauce
2 tbsp. lemon juice
2 tbsp. brown sugar

Gently boil cabbage until leaves are tender. Drain. Separate leaves. Sauté chopped onions in oil. To prepare meat: combine rice, eggs, ½ of the onions, salt, pepper, and paprika with meat. Remove tough center vein of cabbage leaf. Place heaping tablespoon of meat mixture in cup of leaf and roll envelope-fashion, tuck in ends. Add tomatoes to remaining onions. Add cabbage rolls, largest ones first. Add shredded cabbage (if any is left), sauerkraut, tomato sauce, lemon juice, and brown sugar. Cover, bring to a boil. Reduce heat and simmer 1½ to 2 hours. Adjust lemon juice and brown sugar for sweet and sour taste.

Apricot Stuffed Cabbage

Serves: 5 - 6
Cooking Time: 4 hours

"Sweet and sour style."

1 large head cabbage
2 lb. chopped chuck
1 egg
½ cup milk
3 tbsp. raw rice
2 large onions, diced
2 tbsp. oil
12 dried apricots

Sauce:

1 can tomato soup
2 cans (15 oz.) tomato sauce
1 tsp. salt
dash pepper
¾ cup brown sugar
1 tsp. sour salt

Core the cabbage and steam in boiling salted water until leaves are soft and pliable. Remove from water. Combine the meat, egg, milk, and rice and stuff each leaf, forming the leaves into small packages. Sauté onions in oil in a heavy pot. Layer six apricots and half the cabbage rolls, then six apricots and the remaining cabbage rolls. Combine the sauce ingredients and pour over all. Simmer, covered, for four hours.

Hungarian Stuffed Peppers

Serves: 6
Cooking Time: 2 hours

"Infallible. Freezes well."

2 slices white bread
4 generous tbsp. ketchup
4 heaping tbsp. Minute Rice
2 lb. chopped round or neck
   and tenderloin
½ tsp. salt
fresh ground pepper
6 green peppers
2 cans Campbell's tomato soup
water

Soak bread in ketchup and enough water to make bread soggy. Add soaked bread and juices with rice to meat. Add seasonings. Work in with hands. Slice tops off peppers and wash. Stuff with meat mixture. Heat soup and two cans water. And stuffed peppers and additional meatballs to use up all the meat. Cook on medium low flame covered for one hour, then cook uncovered for an additional hour. Freezes well. (Can also be cooked in oven at 350° for 1½ hours uncovered. Two large cans of tomato sauce can be substituted for soup and water.)

STUFFED PEPPERS

Serves: 6
Cooking Time: 45 minutes

"Cheddar cheese gives this a new twist."

6 medium green peppers
1 lb. chopped meat
1/3 cup chopped onion
1 tbsp. fat or oil
1/4 cup precooked rice, cold
2 cups stewed tomatoes
2 tbsp. Worcestershire sauce
salt, to taste
pepper, to taste
1 cup shredded sharp Cheddar
   cheese

Cut off tops of green peppers, clean. Brown meat and onion in fat. Add rice, tomatoes, Worcestershire sauce, salt, and pepper. Cover and simmer five minutes. Stuff peppers and stand upright in baking dish. Bake uncovered at 350° for 25 minutes. Sprinkle with cheese.

RICE STUFFED PEPPERS

Serves: 6
Cooking Time: 1 hour

"May be made in advance and baked when ready to use."

1/2 cup celery, diced
1 small onion, diced
1/2 lb. chopped meat (optional)
1 package Rice-a-Roni wild rice
1 can (4 oz.) mushrooms
1 tsp. soy sauce
6 peppers, cored

Sauté celery, onion, and chopped meat (if desired), in large fry pan. Brown wild rice as directed on package in same pan. Add water as directed on package and seasoning packet. Add mushrooms and soy sauce. Simmer until water is absorbed. Parboil peppers five minutes and let cool. Stuff peppers with rice mixture and wrap each pepper in foil. Bake at 400° for 35 minutes. Or grill: grill 3-4 inches from hot coals for 30-40 minutes, turning occasionally.

117

BLENDER MEAT LOAF

Serves: 6 - 8
Cooking Time: 1½ hours

"Juicy, meal-in-one!"

2 slices bread
2 eggs
1 small potato
1 small carrot
1 small onion
½ green pepper (optional)
1 cup tomato purée or
  vegetable juice
2 lb. ground chuck
2 tbsp. wheat germ
1½ tsp. Accent (optional)
few sprigs parsley (optional)
salt to taste
pepper to taste

Place bread in blender to make crumbs. Transfer to bowl. Place eggs in blender jar, add vegetables, juice and blend one minute. Mix well with meat, crumbs, and seasonings. Pour into bread pan and bake at 350° for 1½ hours.

WORLD'S GREATEST MEAT LOAF

Serves: 6 - 8
Cooking Time: 1 hour to 1 hour, 10 minutes

"Cheese is the unusual ingredient."

1 egg
1 tsp. salt
¼ tsp. pepper
½ tsp. dried leaf basil
½ tsp. dried leaf thyme
¼ cup ketchup
2 tsp. prepared mustard
1½ cups soft bread crumbs
1 cup undiluted can beef
  bouillon soup
½ cup finely chopped celery
½ cup finely chopped onion
1 cup shredded cheddar or
  Swiss cheese
2 lb. ground beef chuck

Beat egg lightly in medium bowl. Add salt, pepper, basil, thyme, ketchup, mustard, bread crumbs. Warm bouillon soup, add and mix until well blended. Mix in celery, onion, and cheese. Break up ground beef and add to bowl. Mix lightly but thoroughly with fork. Form into roll 12 to 14 inches long. Slide onto baking sheet or shallow baking pan. For moister meat loaf, press into loaf pan. Bake uncovered in 375° oven for one hour to one hour, ten minutes.

HERBED MEAT LOAF

Serves: 3
Cooking Time: 1 hour

"Delicious, but a little spicy for children's tastes."

½ cup soft bread crumbs
½ cup milk
1 lb. ground beef
1 egg, slightly beaten
2 tbsp. grated onion
2 tbsp. finely chopped parsley
1 clove garlic, finely chopped
⅛ tsp. dried rosemary
¼ tsp. dried oregano
¼ tsp. basil
1 tsp. salt
½ tsp. paprika
¼ tsp. pepper

Soak the bread crumbs in the milk until soft. Combine all ingredients. Shape into a loaf in loaf pan. Bake at 350° for one hour. Double quantity if desired.

AUTHENTIC BRITISH COTTAGE PIE

Serves: 4
Cooking Time: 30 minutes

"All British children grow up on this one."

1 lb. chopped meat
1 small onion, chopped
1 can (8 oz.) tomato sauce
1 lb. potatoes
2 tbsp. margarine or butter
salt to taste
pepper to taste
½ cup water
1 beef cube

Brown meat and onion in sauce pan, add salt and pepper and beef cube dissolved in ½ cup water. Cook for about 20 minutes. Then add the tomato sauce; bring to a full boil. Precook the potatoes until soft, mash with butter. Add salt and pepper to taste. Put meat mixture into baking dish. Spread potatoes over meat with a fork. Bake at 400° for 25 to 30 minutes or until golden brown.

QUICK MEAT AND VEGETABLE PIE

Serves: 6
Cooking Time: 1 hour

1½ lb. ground beef
5 medium potatoes, cooked
1 can concentrated vegetable
  soup
3 tbsp. butter or margarine

Mash potatoes and add shortening until potatoes are moistened. Put aside. Brown meat enough to pour off excess fat. Place in bowl. Add can of undiluted vegetable soup to the meat and mix. Pour into baking dish. Placed mashed potatoes on top and bake at 325° for one hour.

MEAT PIE

Serves: 4 - 6
Cooking Time: 40 minutes

"Good family dish."

4 tbsp. chopped onion
1 tbsp. butter
1 lb. chopped meat
1 can tomato soup
½ tsp. salt
½ cup flavored bread crumbs
1 egg
2 pie crusts

Sauté onion in the butter, add meat, and brown lightly. Pour off fat. Blend in remaining ingredients. Line pan with one pie crust, add mixture, top with second crust. Bake at 400° for 40 minutes.

SWISS CASSEROLE

Serves: 4
Cooking Time: 45 minutes

"Bon appetit!"

5 or 6 medium potatoes
1 small onion
1 lb. ground beef
¼ tsp. pepper
½ tsp. salt
1 can creamed corn
butter
¼ cup milk

Boil potatoes. Brown onion and meat. Add salt and pepper. Drain excess fat. Place in baking dish. Add creamed corn. Mash potatoes, adding milk and butter, salt to your taste. Top preparation with mashed potatoes. Bake at 350° for 30 minutes. Can be frozen.

Slavic Casserole

Serves: 6 - 8
Cooking Time: 30 - 35 minutes

1 small onion, minced
2 tbsp. butter or margarine
1 can (3 oz.) chopped
   mushrooms, drained
3 cups diced cooked meat (ham,
   chicken, beef, or veal,
   alone or in combination)
1 cup diced cooked potato
1 dill pickle, diced
½ cup chopped olives
salt
pepper
1½ cups dairy sour cream
2 hard boiled eggs, chopped
2 tomatoes, peeled and sliced
½ cup grated cheddar cheese

Cook onion in butter about 2-3 minutes. Add mushrooms, cook 2 minutes longer. Add to meats, potato, pickle, and olives and mix well. Season with salt and pepper and stir in sour cream. Put in shallow two-quart baking dish and sprinkle with eggs. Put tomato slices around edge and sprinkle cheese over top. Bake at 350° for 25-30 minutes.

Bar-B-Q Beef

Serves: 12
Cooking Time: 1½ - 2 hours
(Make 1 day ahead)

"Nice to serve on buns — kids love it."

1 beef roast (4-6 lb.)
2 bottles (26 oz. each) ketchup
1 tbsp. vinegar
1 tbsp. sugar
3 cups beef bouillon
1 tbsp. dry mustard
½ tsp. Tabasco
garlic powder to taste
salt to taste
pepper to taste

Roast beef, slice thin. Combine all other ingredients and bring to boil. Pour over sliced meat and refrigerate overnight. Heat and serve.

MOUSSAKA

Serves: 4
Cooking Time: 2 hours

"Eggplant and meat casserole."

2 medium onions, chopped
vegetable oil
1½ lb. ground beef
1 can (6 oz.) tomato paste
½ cup cold water
½ cup red wine
¼ cup dried parsley
½ tsp. paprika
salt to taste
pepper to taste
¾ cup bread crumbs
2 large eggplants
¼ cup + 1 tbsp. butter
¼ cup flour
2 cups milk
2 eggs, lightly beaten
¼ cup bread crumbs
½ cup grated Parmesan cheese

Sauté onion in two tablespoons oil for five minutes. Add beef and cook until brown. Pour off fat and spoon in tomato paste, water, wine, parsley, paprika, salt, and pepper. Cook, covered, 10 minutes. Stir in bread crumbs, mixing well, and set aside. Slice the unpeeled eggplants thinly, lengthwise. Fry in heated oil and drain on paper. (Eggplant must be thin and limp.) In a large casserole (three quarts or more) alternate layers of meat sauce and eggplant, starting with meat sauce and ending with eggplant on top. Melt ¼ cup butter and stir in flour slowly. Add milk and cook until thickened, stirring constantly. Season with salt and pepper. Remove from heat and add eggs, mixing well. Pour onto casserole so that it filters down. Sprinkle top with ¼ cup crumbs and Parmesan cheese and dot with 1 tablespoon butter. Bake at 350° uncovered, thirty minutes. Cool slightly before serving. Casserole can be put together in advance. However, the cream sauce and finishing up should be done just before serving.

GLAZED LEG OF LAMB

Serves: 6 - 8
Cooking Time: 2½ - 3 hours

leg of lamb, 7-8 lb.
Lawry's seasoned salt
garlic powder
1 cup water
1 cup orange juice
1 jar peach or
   apricot preserves

Season lamb all over with seasoned salt and garlic powder. Put in roasting pan in oven preheated to 325°. After 20 minutes, add ½ cup water and ½ cup orange juice. After another 20-30 minutes, spread ½ of the jar of peach preserves over the lamb. Baste frequently with drippings. Add, according to need, additional orange juice and peach preserves. Cook until lamb is done. Approximately an additional two hours.

BARBECUED LEG OF LAMB

Serves: 6 - 8
Cooking Time: 40 minutes
Marinate: 24 hours

*"Tired of ordinary barbecues? Try this — a great change
and a different way to serve lamb!"*

7 lb. leg of lamb, boned
½ cup olive oil
½ cup dry red wine
1 bay leaf, crushed
¼ tsp. thyme
½ tbsp. rosemary
8 juniper berries, crushed
¼ tsp. ground ginger
¼ tsp. cayenne pepper
¼ tsp. nutmeg
1 tsp. confectioner's sugar
salt
freshly ground black pepper
1 clove garlic, slivered

Have butcher bone leg of lamb. Combine all ingredients except garlic to make marinade. Marinate lamb in refrigerator 24 hours, turning occasionally. When ready to cook, insert garlic between fat and meat of lamb. Barbecue or broil on hot barbecue or preheated broiler approximately 20 minutes on each side. Should be served slightly pink. Slice thin and serve.

GLAZED PORK RIB ROAST

Serves: 6 - 8
Cooking Time: 3½ hours

"Great dress up for a pork roast."

4-5 lb. loin center or rib
  cut of pork
1 tsp. salt
½ tsp. cinnamon
¼ tsp. allspice

Spicy Plums and Sauce:

1 can (1 lb., 14 oz.) purple
  plums
2 tbsp. cornstarch
½ tsp. salt
¼ tsp. cinnamon
⅛ tsp. allspice
2 tbsp. lemon juice
1 tbsp. butter or margarine

Preheat oven to 325°. Rub pork with salt, cinnamon, and allspice. Roast in oven 35-45 minutes per pound. While pork is in oven, drain syrup from plums into sauce pan. Reserve plums. Combine cornstarch and spices with 2 tablespoons syrup; stir into sauce pan. Cook until boiled three minutes. Stir in lemon juice and butter. Measure out ¾ cup sauce for glazing pork. Pour remainder over plums in bowl to be served warm with roast. When pork is about half done, brush with sauce to glaze, rebasting with sauce from pan every 30 minutes.

PORK CHOPS

Serves: 6
Cooking Time: 1½ hours

"Quick and easy! Can be prepared ahead and just bake and serve."

6 pork chops, 1 inch thick
salt
pepper
garlic powder
sliced onion
1 can condensed tomato soup
½ can Chablis wine
½ can water
1 or 2 tsp. Worcestershire sauce

Brown chops in fry pan on both sides. Heat oven to 350°. Place chops in baking dish with seasonings and onion. Pour over a mixture of remaining ingredients. Bake 1 to 1½ hours, uncovered.

Spare Ribs, Chinese Style

Serves: 4
Cooking Time: 2½ hours

3 lb. spare ribs
1 cup water
3 tbsp. brown sugar
3 tbsp. ketchup
1 tbsp. spare rib sauce
1 tsp. garlic salt
salt to taste
lemon juice to taste
dry mustard to taste

Bake ribs in oven till fat runs out, about one hour at 350°. Combine remaining ingredients and bring to boil. Pour over ribs and cook 1½ hours more. Keep basting until there is no more sauce.

Barbecue Spare Ribs

Serves: 6 - 8
Cooking Time: 1½ hours

"Can be made ahead and heated."

6-8 lb. spare ribs
2 lemons, sliced
2 large onions, sliced
1 cup ketchup
⅓ cup Worcestershire sauce
1 tsp. chili powder
1 tsp. salt
2-3 drops Tabasco
2 cups water
4 tbsp. brown sugar
4 tbsp. apricot jam

Preheat oven to 450°. Place ribs in shallow pan, meaty side up. Put slices of lemon and onions over meat. Roast in oven for 30 minutes. Meanwhile, combine next 5 ingredients in a sauce pan, bring to a boil, and set aside. Pour off excessive fat of ribs; discard lemon and onion slices. Bring mixture to a boil again, stir well and pour over ribs. Continue baking for 40 minutes at 400°, basting every 15 minutes. (Can be done ahead to this point.) Remove ribs, separate sauce. Add brown sugar and apricot jam to sauce. Place ribs back and pour sauce over ribs. Bake 20 minutes, basting every five minutes.

Spring Veal Savory with Asparagus

Serves: 6
Cooking Time: 45 minutes

"Different and easy to prepare."

1½ lb. thinly sliced veal
   cutlet
2 tbsp. shortening
1 package dry onion soup mix
2 tbsp. flour
1 cup water
¾ cup tomato juice
1 tbsp. Marsala wine
1 large clove garlic, minced
2 lb. fresh asparagus, cut in
   2-inch pieces

Cut veal into serving-size pieces. Pound with meat hammer or edge of heavy saucer. In skillet, brown veal in shortening; pour off fat. Add soup mix and flour; gradually stir in water, tomato juice, and wine. Add garlic and asparagus. Cover; cook over low heat for 30 minutes or until tender, stirring now and then.

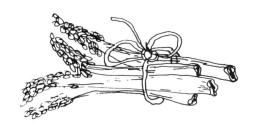

Barbecued Veal

Serves: 3
Cooking Time: 30 minutes
Marinate: Several hours

*"Different — a great company dish! You've never had
anything like this."*

1 lb. veal scaloppine, cut in
   small pieces
¼ cup salad oil
dash garlic powder
3 tbsp. soy sauce
2 tbsp. ketchup
1 tbsp. vinegar
¼ tsp. pepper

Combine all ingredients, except veal. Marinate veal in this mixture several hours. Sauté veal and marinade in one tablespoon oil in uncovered skillet for 30 minutes. Serve over rice.

VEAL BRAISED À LA MARSALA

Serves: 4 - 6
Cooking Time: 1 hour

*"Can be made ahead and frozen. Heat and serve
when company comes."*

2 lb. veal scaloppine
5 tbsp. corn oil
salt
pepper
½ lb. fresh mushrooms
1 Bermuda onion
1 clove garlic, crushed
½ bay leaf, crumbled
1 tbsp. tomato paste
¼ tsp. oregano
¼ tsp. powdered savory
½ tsp. salt
⅛ tsp. pepper
1 tsp. flour
1 can (13¾ oz.) chicken stock
1 cup Marsala wine
2 tbsp. chopped parsley

Brown veal in corn oil. Place aside in clean pan. Salt and pepper veal. Place sliced mushrooms and sliced onion in pot and sauté in two tablespoons corn oil. Add chopped garlic. Sprinkle bay leaf and then mix contents with fork. Add tomato paste, oregano, savory powder, ½ teaspoon salt, ⅛ teaspoon pepper, and flour. Add chicken stock and wine. Simmer five minutes. Pour mixture over veal. Sprinkle with parsley. Cover dish with aluminum foil to freeze or bake in oven to heat. When frozen, bake in a 375° oven for 30 minutes.

VEAL MARSALA

Serves: 4 - 6
Cooking Time: 25 minutes

"Quick and easy way."

1 to 1½ lb. veal, sliced thin
¼ cup flour
1 tsp. salt
dash of pepper
¼ lb. butter
½ lb. mushrooms, sliced
½ cup canned consommé
¼ cup dry Marsala wine

Flour veal lightly, season, brown quickly in butter on both sides. Push to side of pan. Add mushrooms and brown. Add additional butter if necessary. Stir in consommé and wine. Cover pan and simmer 10-15 minutes.

FRENCH VEAL

Serves: 6 - 8
Cooking Time: 1¾ hours

"Rich sour cream sauce is oh la la!"

3 lb. veal, flat
2 tbsp. butter
¼ cup onions, chopped
¼ lb. mushrooms, sliced
1 clove garlic, minced
1 tbsp. flour
½ cup water
1 tbsp. paprika
salt
pepper
2 cups sour cream

Cut veal into 2-inch pieces. Preheat oven to 350°. Heat butter in frying pan over medium heat. When bubbling, add veal and brown on all sides. Remove browned veal and place in a two-quart baking dish or casserole. Add onions, mushrooms, and garlic to butter remaining in frying pan. Push mushrooms aside, stir flour into butter, slowly add water. Whip with spoon and add paprika, salt, and pepper. Cook until thickened (one minute). Spread mixture over veal. Add sour cream last. <u>Cover.</u> Bake 1½ hours.

VEAL PICCATA

Serves: 3
Cooking Time: 30 minutes

"An old standby."

2 tbsp. flour
½ tsp. salt
¼ tsp. pepper
1 lb. veal scaloppine
½ cup butter
¼ cup dry white wine
1 lemon, thinly sliced
¼ cup chopped parsley, fresh

Sauce:

1 tbsp. butter
1 egg yolk
¼ cup wine

Combine flour, salt, and pepper to coat veal. In hot butter, sauté veal until well browned. Add wine, lemon, and parsley and simmer, covered, ten minutes. Remove veal to serving platter and keep warm. Discard lemon. Make sauce: Slowly heat butter in same skillet. Beat egg yolk with wine. Slowly add to butter in skillet, stirring constantly. Cook over low heat stirring until sauce is thickened and hot. Pour over veal.

Veal Cardinal

Serves: 2
Cooking Time: 25 minutes

flour
6 very thin slices of veal
olive oil
1 small can (4 oz.) of pimentos
6 oz. mozzarella
1 cup white wine
3 oz. butter, melted
fresh parsley

Flour veal and sauté in olive oil. Place veal in pan. Put a piece of pimento on each slice. Then add one ounce of mozzarella on top of the pimentos. Pour in wine and butter. Place in pre-heated oven (375°) for 15 minutes. Sprinkle with parsley and serve.

Veal Cordon Bleu

Serves: 6
Cooking Time: 15 minutes

"Can be partially cooked ahead of time and frozen."

12 slices veal, Italian-style, pounded very thin
½ tsp. salt
¼ tsp. pepper
6 slices Swiss cheese
6 slices prosciutto or boiled ham
2 eggs, beaten with 4 tbsp. cold water
½ cup flour
1 cup fresh bread crumbs (plain)
3 tbsp. olive oil
3 tbsp. butter

Season veal with salt and pepper. Place one slice of cheese and ham on six slices of veal. Cover each with remaining veal. Beat eggs with the cold water. Dredge each veal sandwich first in flour, then egg, and bread crumbs, making sure that all parts are covered with crumb mixture. Place in freezer or refrigerator until ready to use. Preheat oven to 375°. Heat skillet with olive oil and butter and brown veal on both sides; about two minutes on each side. Transfer to flat baking pan and bake for ten minutes at 375°. Can be served with the following sauce.

Sauce:

1 cup chicken or beef broth
1 tsp. Bovril
1 tsp. tomato paste
½ cup Marsala or Madeira wine
1 tbsp. cornstarch
2 tbsp. water

Combine broth, Bovril, tomato paste, and wine in sauce pan, bring to boil. Blend cornstarch with water. Lower flame under sauce. Add cornstarch, stirring constantly, and allow to thicken. Sauce can be prepared one hour in advance.

Veal Roast

Serves: 8
Cooking Time: 3 hours

*"A nice change for veal with an interesting flavor.
Great combination of spices make this different."*

4-5 lb. veal rump or
   shoulder roast
1 clove garlic
¼ cup flour
1 tsp. salt
⅛ tsp. pepper
¼ tsp. allspice
½ tsp. thyme
½ tsp. sage
2 bay leaves, crushed
oil for browning
1 onion, minced
4 carrots, sliced
2 stalks celery, diced
1 cup boiling water

Rub meat with a small piece of garlic. Dredge meat with the flour, salt, pepper, and spice mixture. Brown meat in a deep heavy kettle (similar to a Dutch oven). When well browned, remove from kettle and brown the vegetables in the same kettle. (The vegetables won't get real brown, so just stir them around the pot until onions are transparent.) Put meat back into pot, add boiling water, cover, and cook slowly until tender (2 to 2½ hours). Thicken juice for gravy.

Veal Francesca

Serves: 3 - 4
Cooking Time: 50 minutes

"Sauce is also good over chicken or fish."

1 lb. veal, sliced thin
1 egg
plain bread crumbs
oil and margarine, enough
   to sauté veal

Season veal, dip in beaten egg and plain bread crumbs. Fry in oil and margarine until lightly browned. Place veal in flat baking dish and pour over sauce. Bake in preheated 375° oven for 20 minutes.

Sauce:

¼ lb. butter
½ bunch fresh parsley,
   chopped
1 clove garlic, pressed
   or minced
juice of 1 lemon

Melt butter. Add chopped parsley and garlic. Cook 2-3 minutes. Add lemon juice to taste.

Veal Sauté with Peppers "For Dieters"

Serves: 3 - 4
Cooking Time: 40 minutes

¼ cup sliced onions
½ cup sliced mushrooms
2 tbsp. oil
1 lb. veal, cubed
2 green peppers, sliced
paprika
garlic salt
1½ cups chicken broth

Brown onions and mushrooms in oil. Add veal and brown. Add green peppers and season everything with paprika and garlic salt to taste. Pour in chicken broth and cover. Allow to simmer until meat is tender. Serve over rice.

Veal Fayot

Serves: 6
Cooking Time: 1 hour, 20 minutes

2 cups sliced onions
2 tbsp. butter
6 veal cutlets
salt
ground black pepper
1 cup grated Gruyère cheese
½ cup fine dry bread crumbs
4 tbsp. butter
½ cup dry white wine
¾ cup beef stock

Cook onions in butter until transparent. Place half in the bottom of a baking pan. Sprinkle cutlets with salt and pepper, and put on top. Cover with remaining onions. Mix cheese with bread crumbs and sprinkle over the onions. Dot with butter. Combine wine and stock and pour over the top. Bake at 325° for one hour.

VEAL AND PEPPERS

Serves: 6
Cooking Time: 1 hour

*"An old favorite of the family and company loves it.
Can be made ahead."*

¼ cup olive oil
2 cloves garlic, sliced thin
2 lb. veal, cubed as for stew
3½ cups (#2½ can) tomato purée
1 tsp. oregano
1 tsp. salt
½ tsp. pepper
1 tsp. chopped parsley
3 green peppers, sliced in
   strips

Heat oil in heavy skillet or casserole. Add garlic, cook until lightly brown. Add veal and slowly brown on both sides. Meanwhile, combine tomato purée with spices and slowly add to browned veal. Cover and cook slowly for 45 minutes or until meat is tender. Last 15 minutes of cooking add green peppers. May be served with any pasta as sauce is very good. As with most stews flavor improves when made day before.

COWBOY SUPPER

Serves: 6 - 8
Cooking Time: 30 minutes

"Frankfurters served a little differently on rice or mashed potatoes!"

4 hard-boiled eggs
½ cup green pepper
½ cup chopped onion
2 tbsp. oil
12 frankfurters
2 cups chopped fresh tomatoes
salt to taste
pepper to taste
paprika to taste
½ tsp. caraway seeds
1 bay leaf

Prepare eggs in advance. Steam green pepper and onions until tender in about two tablespoons oil. Combine remaining ingredients. Cover and steam entire mixture over low heat for 15 minutes. Add hard-boiled eggs, quartered.

SAUSAGE AND PEPPERS

Serves: 4 - 6
Cooking Time: 55 - 60 minutes

2 lb. sausage
2 large onions, sliced or chopped
2 jars (6 oz.) pepper piccalilli

Cut up sausages in 1-inch pieces. Fry with sliced onion, about 45 minutes. Add pepper piccalilli and cook for ten minutes. Serve with French bread.

Mrs. E. Savauce, Bethpage, New York

TONGUE IN APRICOT-RAISIN SAUCE

Serves: 4 - 6
Marinate: 3 hours

"Mashed potatoes go nicely with this."

pickled tongue
medium can (12 oz.) of apricot nectar
½ cup white raisins

Cook pickled tongue until tender. Cool and slice. Take a can of apricot nectar and the white raisins and bring to a boil. Let tongue marinate in this sauce a couple of hours. May be used as hors d'oeuvre or main course.

SWEETBREADS

Serves: 3
Cooking Time: 45 minutes

1 lb. sweetbreads
ice water
2 tsp. lemon juice
½ tsp. salt
2 sautéed onions

Wash and soak sweetbreads in ice water one hour. Drain, cover with water, lemon juice, and salt. Bring to a boil and cook slowly 15 minutes. Drain, cover with cold water and let cool. Drain and remove membranes, tubes and connective tissue. Cut up and add to sautéed onions. Bake 20-30 minutes.

SPANISH CHICKEN LIVERS IN WINE

Serves: 3
Cooking Time: 35 minutes

"For excellent results, serve immediately."

1 lb. chicken livers
4 tbsp. butter
½ cup chopped green onions
   (scallions)
1 clove garlic
1 tbsp. flour
¾ cup chicken stock (fresh or canned)
1 tbsp. chopped parsley
1 tbsp. vegetable oil
salt to taste
pepper to taste
¼ cup dry Madeira or dry sherry
½ tsp. lemon juice

Trim and cut chicken livers in half, towel dry. Sauté onions and garlic in two tablespoons butter about five minutes (do not brown). Stir in flour and simmer a few seconds. Add stock, all at once. Boil over high heat, stirring constantly, until thick. Add parsley, lower heat, and simmer, uncovered, about ten minutes. Set aside. Heat two tablespoons butter and oil in heavy skillet until lightly brown. Add livers, sprinkle liberally with salt and pepper. Sauté briskly turning constantly until brown, and pink on inside. Remove livers. Add wine to pan drippings and juices. Boil briskly 2-3 minutes. Pour in juices that came from livers. Add sauce that was set aside. Bring to a boil. Add livers, lemon juice, taste for salt. Serve immediately! Serve over rice.

Eggs and Cheese

EGG 'N THE EYE

Serves: 1
Cooking Time: 5 minutes

"Also called 'Rocky Mountain Toast.'"

1 slice white bread
1 egg
butter for frying

With a glass turned upside down, press out a hole in center of bread. Save middle. Lightly fry bread in butter on both sides. Drop egg in center of bread while still frying. Cook egg till done on both sides. Fry center of bread separately and place on center of egg and bread when done. Serve hot.

EGG SOUFFLÉ

Serves: 8
Cooking Time: 1½ hours
Chill: 8 hours

"Breakfast, brunch, or light supper."

12 slices of bread, without
   crusts
9 slices of American cheese
6 eggs, well beaten
3 cups milk

Make six sandwiches using 1½ slices of cheese in each sandwich. Butter one side of bread. Press sandwich flat and cut into nine pieces. Place beaten eggs and milk into greased baking dish with room for rising. Then put all the pieces of sandwiches into the same dish. Let it stand in refrigerator overnight, or if you plan to serve in the evening, you can prepare it in the morning. Bake at 350° for 1½ hours.

CHEWY CHEESE EGG

Serves: 1
Cooking Time: 5 minutes

2 eggs, beaten
2 tsp. mozzarella cheese,
   cut up
salt
pepper

Mix all ingredients together and make an omelet. Good for sandwiches also.

LUNCHEON PUFF-UPS

Serves: 4
Cooking Time: 45 - 60 minutes
Chill: 1 hour

"This is nice, because it can be baking while you are cocktailing!"

8 slices white bread, without
   crusts
4 slices Swiss cheese
4 slices yellow cheese
2 eggs
1½ cups milk or half and half
salt
pepper
dry mustard
garlic salt
minced onion
Parmesan cheese
paprika

Put together bread and cheeses in sandwich fashion. Chopped ham or corned beef may be substituted for yellow cheese. Beat eggs lightly, add, still beating, milk or half and half, and seasonings to taste. Put sandwiches in a 9-inch square pan, preferably teflon lined. Important: Do not use a larger pan, or liquid will thin. Pour egg-milk mixture over sandwiches and let stand one hour or more in refrigerator, turning over once to make sure sandwiches are well soaked. Sprinkle with Parmesan cheese and paprika. Bake at 325° for 45 minutes to one hour, until custard is set and top is puffed and a bit brown. Cut into individual squares (one sandwich per serving).

PUFFED CHEESE CASSEROLE

Serves: 2 - 4
Cooking Time: 1 hour

2 slices bread
2 oz. processed cheese
1 egg, beaten
2 large pinches salt
1 pinch paprika
⅔ cup milk
⅓ tsp. grated onion (optional)
1 tsp. parsley or chives
   (optional)
large pinch dry mustard
   (optional)

Cut bread in half on the bias, and then in half again. Place half of the pieces in greased, oven-proof bowl. Place cheese, sliced, on top of bread. Add rest of bread; do not overlap. Mix egg, salt, paprika, milk, onion, parsley or chives, and dry mustard. Pour liquid over bread. Let stand one hour or overnight. Bake at 350° about one hour or until brown. Serve hot.

BLINTZES

Serves: 16 - 20
Cooking Time: 1 hour

"Marvelous light meal."

¼ cup butter, melted
2 eggs
dash salt
1 cup flour
1½ cups milk

Melt butter. Put eggs, salt, flour, and milk into blender. Add melted butter. Grease small frying pan lightly and make sure it is hot. Pour spoonful of batter into pan, should be set in about two minutes. Turn onto towel to cool. After pan is hot, turn to medium flame.

Filling:

8 oz. farmer cheese
lump butter
egg yolk.
1 tbsp. sugar
dash salt

Mix together all ingredients. Place teaspoon of filling on each pancake. Fold and fry in butter until brown. Serve with cherry preserves and sour cream.

MOCK BLINTZES

Serves: 4
Cooking Time: 10 - 15 minutes

"Can be frozen, thawed for 10 minutes, and baked."

8 slices white bread
1 package (8 oz.) cream cheese
⅛ tsp. vanilla
1 egg yolk
2 tbsp. sugar
¼ lb. sweet butter, melted
1 cup sugar
1 tsp. cinnamon

Remove crust from bread and roll thin. Blend together cream cheese, vanilla, egg yolk, and two tablespoons sugar. Spread mixture onto bread, roll diagonally. Dip blintzes in butter and roll in sugar and cinnamon. Bake in preheated 350° oven. Cut in half.

BASIC CRÊPE BATTER

Yield: 24
Cooking Time: 1 hour

"May be made in advance."

3 eggs
¾ cup flour
⅛ tsp. salt
1 tsp. sugar
1 cup milk
2 tbsp. melted butter

Put all ingredients into blender, except melted butter. Blend all for about one minute. Then add melted butter and blend again. Have batter ready. Line the top of your counter with paper toweling. Heat skillet slowly over medium heat. Skillet is ready when a bit of butter sizzles immediately upon touching pan. Use one teaspoon butter for each pancake. Pour in ¼ cup of batter. Holding the handle of pan, roll batter around the pan so that it just covers the entire bottom of pan and dries almost immediately. If there seems to be too much wet batter on the pan, tilt pan over bowl of batter and pour back excess. When pancake is delicately browned on the underside, turn it over and brown on the other side. Holding the handle of the skillet, quickly turn it over onto absorbent paper. Pancake should fall put. (May be made day in advance.)

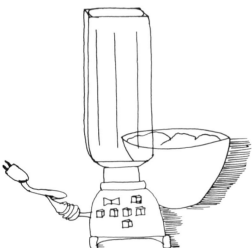

Les Cheffettes, Great Neck, New York

CRÊPES FROMAGE

Yield: 24
Cooking Time: 1 hour, 10 minutes

"May be served as appetizer, luncheon, or light supper dish."

Basic Crêpe Batter, see above
4 oz. Swiss cheese, grated
4 oz. sharp Cheddar cheese, grated
4 tbsp. Parmesan cheese, grated
2 tbsp. parsley, chopped
1 tbsp. chives, chopped
1 tsp. Worcestershire sauce
⅛ tsp. pepper
cheese
butter

Prepare Basic Crêpe Batter. Mix cheeses and seasonings well. Place a full tablespoon on each crêpe and roll up tight. Place on a buttered baking sheet. Sprinkle with cheese and dot with butter. Bake at 400° for ten minutes.

Les Cheffettes, Great Neck, New York

APPLE PANCAKES

Serves: 1
Cooking Time: 5 - 10 minutes

Basic Crêpe Batter, see page 139
1 McIntosh apple
2 tbsp. butter
1 tbsp. sugar
cinnamon

Prepare crêpe batter. Peel and slice apple, very thin. Heat a 10-inch skillet and turn on your broiler. Drop butter into skillet. It should sizzle immediately. Pour in about three tablespoons batter just to cover bottom. Place thin apple slices all over pancake. Pour a little more batter over apples. Sprinkle with sugar and some cinnamon. Wait for pancake to dry and set all over. Set skillet under broiler until pancake puffs, about one minute. Serve immediately.

NORWEGIAN PANCAKES

Serves: 4 - 5
Cooking Time: 5 minutes

"Variety of fillings makes this fun to serve."

1 cup dairy sour cream
1 cup small curd cottage
   cheese
4 eggs
¾ cup sifted flour
1 tbsp. salt

Combine sour cream and cheese. Add other ingredients and beat with mixer or blender until well mixed. Bake on hot greased griddle until bubbles break on surface. Turn and bake until golden brown. Serve with butter and syrup. Makes approximately 24 4-inch pancakes.
Variations: To batter add, for Blueberry Norwegian Pancakes, one cup blueberries, fresh or drained canned or frozen.

FONDUE AMERICAN

Serves: 10
Cooking Time: 1 hour, 15 minutes
Chill: Overnight

"Fun to serve at any informal gathering."

½ cup butter or margarine
1 small clove garlic, minced
½ tsp. dry mustard
12 slices white bread without
   crusts
2 cups grated sharp Cheddar
   cheese
2 tbsp. grated onion
1 tsp. salt
½ tsp. Worcestershire sauce
⅛ tsp. pepper
dash cayenne
4 eggs
2⅓ cups milk
⅔ cup dry white wine

In small bowl combine butter, garlic, and mustard and beat. Spread mixture on bread. Line bottom of long flat Pyrex dish with half the bread — butter side down. Reserve the rest. In large bowl, toss cheese, onion, salt, Worcestershire sauce, pepper, and cayenne. Sprinkle cheese mixture over bread. Cover with rest of bread slices — butter side up. In medium-size bowl, beat eggs. Add 1½ cups milk and all the wine. Beat well and pour evenly over bread. Let stand 30 minutes. Pour rest of milk over bread. Cover. Refrigerate overnight or until needed. Bake at 350° for one hour, 15 minutes. Let stand. Cut up in finger-size pieces and serve on hot tray.

FONDUE

Cooking Time: 10 minutes

1 clove garlic, mashed
1 cup Rhine, Chablis, or
   Reisling wine
½ lb. Swiss cheese, grated
1½ tbsp. flour

Rub pot with clove of mashed garlic. Heat wine over very low heat. Grate Swiss cheese into a bowl and add flour. When wine is bubbly, add cheese by handfuls. Melt completely before adding more. Season with salt and pepper. Serve with cubed crusty bread.

Spinach Cheese Roll

Serves: 8 - 10
Cooking Time: 30 minutes

"This is Greek inspired; it is an excellent appetizer, luncheon dish, buffet supper — in short, it is most versatile. Freezes well!"

1 onion, diced
2 tbsp. butter or oil
1 package (10 oz.) frozen, chopped spinach, thawed and squeezed dry
$\frac{1}{2}$ lb. feta cheese
1 pt. pot cheese
2 eggs, beaten
salt
pepper
nutmeg
10 sheets of filo pastry
$\frac{1}{4}$ cup bread crumbs
$\frac{1}{4}$ lb. melted butter
additional bread crumbs

Sauté onion in butter until golden (3 to 5) minutes). Add spinach and simmer with onion until moisture is evaporated. Crumble feta cheese into bowl. Add pot cheese and eggs. Mix well. Stir in spinach mixture. Season with salt, pepper, and nutmeg to taste.

Place one sheet of filo on a jelly roll pan. Brush with butter and cover with second sheet. Repeat until five sheets are used. Sprinkle bread crumbs all over. Place half of spinach-cheese mixture down the middle lengthwise. Turn in ends of pastry and roll ends over to enclose like a jelly roll. Brush top with melted butter. Repeat for second roll. Brush with melted butter. Sprinkle with bread crumbs, if desired. Bake at 375° for 30 minutes. Let cool slightly. Cut into slices.

Cheese Strata

Serves: 4 - 6
Cooking Time: 1$\frac{1}{4}$ hours
Chill: Overnight

12 slices white bread
$\frac{1}{2}$ lb. grated Cheddar cheese
2$\frac{2}{3}$ cups milk
2 eggs
salt
pepper
minced onion

Butter casserole dish. Cut crusts from bread and line pan with six slices, cover with $\frac{3}{4}$ of the cheese. Put rest of bread on top and sprinkle with cheese. Pour milk, mixed with beaten eggs and seasonings, over all. Cover and leave in refrigerator overnight. Bake at 400° for 1 to 1$\frac{1}{4}$ hours or until brown.

Editors' Note:

Since quiche is such a popular and versatile dish, we have included a number of them. Use them as hors d'oeuvres, lunches, and as suppers served with a salad. Prepare several at a time and freeze them for future use. Try Orinoke frozen pie crusts to use with the fillings when in a hurry.

QUICHE LORRAINE

Serves: 6
Cooking Time: 1 hour

*"This quiche pastry does not have to be prebaked.
Seasoning is a little different."*

1½ cups (6 oz.) grated Swiss
   cheese
8 slices crisp bacon, crumbled
pastry for 9-inch pie crust,
   unbaked
3 eggs
1 cup heavy cream
½ cup milk
½ tsp. salt
¼ tsp. pepper
½ tsp. cayenne
½ tsp. powdered mustard

Crust:

1¼ cups sifted flour
½ tsp. salt
½ cup Crisco shortening
3 tbsp. ice water

Combine flour, salt, Crisco together. Add ice water. Form into ball and roll out between wax paper. Fit into 9-inch pie shell. Sprinkle cheese and bacon into pastry-lined pie pan. Mix remaining ingredients together and pour over cheese. Bake in preheated oven at 375° for 45 minutes or until firm and brown. Cut into wedges. Can be served hot or cold.

QUICHE LORRAINE

Serves: 6 - 8
Cooking Time: 55 minutes

9-inch unbaked pie shell, chilled
1 tbsp. soft butter or margarine
12 slices bacon
½ cup sautéed onions (if desired)
4 eggs
2 cups heavy cream
¾ tsp. salt
pinch nutmeg
pinch sugar
⅛ tsp. pepper
¼ lb. natural Swiss cheese grated (1 cup)

Heat oven to 425°. Rub butter on pie shell. Fry bacon and crumble into pieces. Combine eggs, cream, salt, nutmeg, sugar, pepper, with hand beater just enough to mix well. Sprinkle pie shell with bacon, cheese, and sautéed onions. Pour in cream mixture. Bake at 425° for 15 minutes. Reduce heat to 300° and bake 40 minutes longer or until knife comes out clean.

QUICHE LORRAINE WITH BACON AND ASPARAGUS

Serves: 6 - 8
Cooking Time: 40 minutes

9-inch pie crust, unbaked
½ lb. Swiss cheese, sliced small
½ package (10 oz.) asparagus tips, drained*
½ lb. bacon pieces fried crisp and drained*
4 eggs
1 tbsp. flour
½ tsp. salt
dash cayenne
dash nutmeg
2 cups milk
1 tbsp. butter

*Prepare in advance.

Line 9-inch pie pan with pastry. Cover with cheese, asparagus, and bacon. Beat eggs with flour, salt, cayenne, nutmeg, milk, and melted butter. Pour custard over bacon, asparagus and cheese. Bake at 375° for 40 minutes until set. Cut into wedges. Serve warm as an hors d'oeuvre.

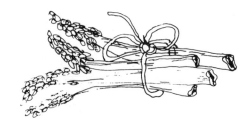

Quiche Fromage

Serves: 8
Cooking Time: 35 minutes

Basic Pie Pastry:

¼ lb. sweet butter
½ cup vegetable shortening
2½ cups all-purpose flour,
    sifted
½ tsp. salt
1 tsp. sugar
5-6 tbsp. water

Place all ingredients in big mixing bowl, except water. Rub all together with fingers or pastry blender into small pieces. Add water and blend with one hand. Press dough firmly into a rough ball. It should just hold together and be pliable, but not damp and sticky. Place on lightly floured cloth or board and knead with heel of hand. Form into ball again, sprinkle lightly with flour and wrap in wax paper and refrigerate for about one hour. Roll out dough and fill a 10-inch quiche pan or 9-inch pie plate.

Cheese Filling:

8 oz. sharp Cheddar cheese,
    grated
1 tbsp. flour
3 eggs
1 cup light or heavy cream
½ tsp. salt
¼ tsp. pepper
¼ tsp. nutmeg

Preheat oven to 400°. Stir flour into grated cheese. Beat eggs. Stir cream and seasonings into eggs. Line bottom of pastry shell with cheese. Pour in eggs and cream. Bake at 400° for 35 minutes.

Mushroom and Onion Quiche

Serves: 6
Cooking Time: 1 hour

½ lb. mushrooms
1 large onion
9-inch uncooked pie crust
½ lb. Swiss cheese, grated
3 eggs
½ pt. heavy sweet cream
½ pt. milk
¼ cup butter

Stew mushrooms and onions in butter. Place in bottom of pie shell. Put grated cheese on top of mixture. Beat eggs, add heavy cream, milk, salt, and pepper, stirring gently. Pour over entire pie shell. Sprinkle nutmeg on top. Bake at 375° for approximately 45-50 minutes.

CRAB MEAT QUICHE

Serves: 6 - 10
Cooking Time: 45 minutes
Chill: 1 hour

1½ cups crab meat, fresh or
   canned
1 tbsp. chopped celery
1 tbsp. chopped onion
2 tbsp. chopped parsley
2 tbsp. sherry
4 eggs, slightly beaten
1 cup milk
1 cup cream
¼ tsp. nutmeg
½ tsp. salt
¼ tsp. white pepper
pastry for one-crust 9-inch pie

Pick over crab meat to remove bits of cartilage and shell. Combine the crab meat, celery, onion, parsley, sherry and refrigerate at least one hour. Sprinkle the inside of a partly baked pastry shell with the crab meat mixture. Combine eggs, milk, cream, nutmeg, salt, and pepper in blender three seconds and pour in pie shell. Bake 15 minutes at 450° then reduce the oven temperature to moderate 350° and bake until a knife inserted one inch from the pastry edge comes out clean. Serve immediately.

SHRIMP QUICHE

Serves: 4 - 6
Cooking Time: 40 minutes

2 tbsp. onion, minced
2 tbsp. butter
½ lb. shrimp, cooked
¼ tsp. salt
2 tbsp. dry white wine
3 eggs
1 cup milk
1 tbsp. cocktail sauce
½ tsp. salt
dash pepper
¼ cup Swiss cheese, grated
8-inch pastry shell, baked

Cook onion in butter over low heat until tender (about 1 - 2 minutes). Add shrimp and stir gently for 2 minutes. Season with ¼ teaspoon salt and add wine. Simmer for about 1 minute. Cool. Beat eggs, milk, cocktail sauce, ½ teaspoon salt and a dash of pepper. Gradually add shrimp. Pour mixture into 8-inch pie shell. Sprinkle cheese over all and bake 25-30 minutes.
Note: For richer quiche, use half and half or heavy cream instead of milk.

SEAFOOD QUICHE

Serves: 8 - 12
Cooking Time: 45 minutes

*"Great for company! Great to freeze! A tried and tried recipe.
Easy to make! Delicious! Needs some preparation."*

1 package of 2 (9-inch) frozen pie shells (the ambitious can make the shells themselves)
1 package (6 oz.) frozen king crab meat, thawed and drained
1½ cups chopped, cooked, shelled, deveined shrimp (or use canned shrimp)
1 package (8 oz.) natural Swiss cheese, chopped
½ cup finely chopped celery
½ cup finely chopped scallions
1 cup mayonnaise
2 tbsp. flour
1 cup dry white wine
4 eggs, slightly beaten

Separate frozen pie shells. Combine dry ingredients of crab meat, shrimp, cheese, celery, scallions. Mix together and divide equally into each pie shell. Combine mayonnaise, flour, white wine, and eggs. Pour equally over each pie. Fill shells up almost to top. (There will be extra liquid, this can be frozen for future use.) Bake in preheated 350° oven for 45 minutes or until a silver knife inserted in center comes out clean. (Cooking time varies with oven type.) Cool, cover with plastic wrap and refrigerate (if to be used soon) or freeze. If you are freezing them, wrap in aluminum foil instead of plastic.
To Serve: If refrigerated let stand one hour to get to room temperature and reheat in 300° oven for 20 minutes. If frozen, unwrap pie and bake frozen in preheated 350° oven for one hour. Cut into pie wedges and serve. Great with a salad as a light meal and wine, of course. Great as an appetizer.

CRAB MEAT QUICKIE

Serves: 6
Cooking Time: 45 minutes

8- or 9-inch pie shell
½ cup mayonnaise
2 eggs, slightly beaten
½ cup milk
7 oz. drained and flaked crab meat
8 oz. Swiss cheese, diced
½ cup scallions
bread crumbs
Parmesan cheese

Mix all of the ingredients except the last two. Pat the bottom of pie shell with little dabs of butter before putting in the ingredients. Pour ingredients into unbaked pie shell and sprinkle bread crumbs and Parmesan cheese on top. Bake at 350° for 45 minutes.

Potatoes, Rice, and Pasta

Approximate Measure:

Noodles:

12 oz. = 9 cups uncooked = 6 cups cooked
8 oz. = 6 cups uncooked = 4 cups cooked
6 oz. = 4½ cups uncooked = 3 cups cooked

Spaghetti:

1 lb. = 6½ cups cooked
8 oz. = 3¼ cups cooked

Rice:

Raw = 1 cup (½ lb.) = 3 cups cooked
Precooked = 1 cup = 2 cups cooked

Potatoes:

1 lb. (3 potatoes) = 2½ cups sliced or diced = 2 cups mashed

Potatoes Savoyard

Serves: 6 - 8
Cooking Time: 60 minutes

*"Very rich, but very nice with lamb or any relatively
bland meat or fish."*

1¼ cups boiling water
2 packages beef broth
2½ lb. potatoes
6 tbsp. butter
2 tbsp. fresh parsley, chopped
1 tsp. salt
⅛ tsp. black pepper
1 cup grated Swiss cheese
   (¼ lb.)

Preheat oven to 425°. Dissolve beef broth in boiling water. Peel potatoes, slice thinly and place in cold water to cover until ready to use. Using two tablespoons butter, generously butter shallow two-quart pan. Drain potatoes well between absorbent toweling. Layer half of potatoes, overlapping them in pan. Dot with two tablespoons butter. Sprinkle on half of parsley, salt, pepper, and cheese. Repeat for next layer. Dot with remaining butter. Pour on boiling broth and bake 55-60 minutes until potatoes are tender, top browned, and broth absorbed.

POTATO PANCAKES

Serves: 4
Cooking Time: 5 minutes

"Serve with apple sauce, sour cream."

4 medium potatoes
1 egg
½ tsp. salt
dash pepper
2 rounded tbsp. flour
1 medium onion, grated

Peel potatoes. Wash well. Grate them. Add beaten egg, salt, and pepper. Mix well. Add flour and mix well again. Drop heaping tablespoons of mixture onto hot griddle or frying pan, which contains oil or shortening. Makes approximately 12 pancakes.

POTATO PUDDING

Serves: 8
Cooking Time: 1 hour

"Delicious. Nice side dish when you're serving pot roast."

6 medium to large potatoes
3 medium onions
4 eggs
3 tbsp. Nabisco cracker meal
1 or 2 tbsp. coarse salt, to taste fairly salty
½ tsp. black pepper
1 heaping tbsp. chicken fat
4 tbsp. salad oil

By hand, grate potatoes and onions into a large bowl. (Don't drain.) Add eggs, cracker meal, salt, and pepper. Mix chicken fat and oil in large Pyrex pan (9 x 13 inches) and heat 1-2 minutes in oven to blend. Pour ⅓ of oils into potato batter and mix well. Pour potato batter into Pyrex dish which is coated with remaining oil and fat. Bake in preheated 350° oven for 1 hour.

POTATO CROQUETTES, ITALIAN

Serves: 4
Cooking Time: 20 minutes

"Great for leftover potatoes."

4 potatoes, peeled, cooked,
   diced
2 eggs, well beaten
⅛ tsp. salt
½ tsp. pepper
½ cup bread crumbs
1 clove garlic, minced
1 tsp. minced parsley
1 tbsp. grated Parmesan cheese
3 slices salami, minced
oil for frying

Wash and cook potatoes. In bowl mash and add the eggs, salt, pepper, bread crumbs, garlic, parsley, and cheese. Beat until well blended. Fold in minced salami. Roll in hands to desired shape. Heat the oil and brown the croquettes on all sides. Serve hot.

POTATO CASSEROLE

Serves: 5
Cooking Time: 1 hour

"Easy 1 - 2 - 3."

5 medium Idaho potatoes
1 package (8 oz.) American
   cheese
1 can cream of mushroom soup

Peel and slice potatoes. Butter casserole thoroughly. Place a layer of potatoes, a layer of cheese and repeat until the casserole is full. Pour can of soup over it and bake at 350° for one hour.

SWEET POTATO PUFFS

Serves: 4
Cooking Time: 30 minutes

*"If you want to be fancy, serve on a piece of sliced pineapple.
Can be prepared ahead."*

2 cups cooked sweet potatoes,
   mashed
salt
1 cup pineapple tidbits
½ cup crushed cornflakes
4 slices pineapple (optional)
margarine

Form potatoes into four balls and press pineapple in center. Dip in crushed cornflakes and fry in margarine.

APRICOT SWEET POTATO

Serves: 12
Cooking Time: 40 minutes

"Made easily with canned potatoes but looks and tastes professional."

2 cans (1 lb., 1 oz.) sweet
   potatoes, vacuum packed
2½ cups brown sugar
3 tbsp. cornstarch
2 tsp. grated orange peel
½ tsp. salt
¼ tsp. cinnamon
2 cans (1 lb., 1 oz.) apricot
   halves
4 tsp. butter or margarine
1 cup pecan halves

Arrange potatoes in a lightly greased baking dish. Combine sugar, cornstarch, grated orange peel, salt, and cinnamon. Drain apricots and reserve two cups syrup. Add syrup to sugar mixture. Cook and stir over medium heat. Simmer three minutes. Add apricots, butter, and pecans. Bring to a boil. Boil for 2 minutes. Pour over potatoes. Bake uncovered at 375° for 25 minutes.

ORANGE SWEET POTATOES

Serves: 6
Cooking Time: 30 - 40 minutes

"Very different flavor."

6 medium sweet potatoes,
   cooked, peeled, and sliced
½ cup brown sugar
5 tbsp. butter
2 medium oranges, sliced thin,
   unpeeled
¼ cup honey
½ cup orange juice
¼ cup bread or cornflake
   crumbs

Build up following layers in a medium-size, buttered casserole: potatoes, sprinkled with brown sugar then dotted with butter, and then orange slices. Repeat until potatoes and oranges are used up. Heat honey (enough to make it liquid) and mix with orange juice. Pour over casserole. Combine crumbs with whatever butter and sugar are left and spread over top. Cover and bake 30-40 minutes in 350° oven. Remove cover after 15 minutes.

SWEET POTATO PIE

Serves: 6
Cooking Time: 40 minutes

"May be used warm as side dish or cold as a dessert."

1 large can (40 oz.) sweet
  potatoes
2 eggs
1 tbsp. brown sugar (or more)
2 oz. crème de cacao
8-inch prepared graham cracker
  crust
pecan halves

Mash potatoes and mix with remaining ingredients, except pecans. Pour into pie crust and sprinkle with additional brown sugar and place whole pecans on top. Bake at 350° for 40 minutes, or until the brown sugar is bubbly.

SWEET POTATOES AND APPLES

Serves: 8 - 10
Cooking Time: 45 - 60 minutes

*"Very good! May be made ahead and stored in
refrigerator for several days."*

1 large can (40 oz.) yams
2 cans Comstock apple pie
  filling
cinnamon

Slice yams into bite-sized pieces and place in lightly greased casserole. Add apple pie filling; mix lightly. Sprinkle cinnamon on top and bake uncovered, 45 minutes to one hour at 350°.

SOUTHERN YAM PUDDING

Serves: 8
Cooking Time: 15 minutes

"Very traditional."

2 large cans (40 oz. each) yams
¼ cup dark brown sugar
¼ cup butter
dash salt
dash cinnamon
¼ cup (a little more) milk, hot
½ cup chopped pecans
marshmallows

Boil potatoes in their syrup, drain and mash. Add sugar, butter, salt, and mix well with cinnamon and nuts. Pour in mixer, beat, add hot milk to soften. Grease and put into baking dish. Heat at 300° for 15 minutes. Just before serving, put marshmallows on top, broil five second.

SOUTHERN SWEET POTATO PIE

Serves: 6
Cooking Time: 2 hours

"Meringue makes this very festive. Can be made ahead up to last one-half hour."

3 medium sweet potatoes
⅓ stick butter
4 eggs, separated
2½ cups sugar
pinch salt
grated rind and juice of 1
  lemon
grated rind and juice of 1
  orange
2 cups scalded milk
dash nutmeg
dash cinnamon
¼ tsp. lemon extract
½ cup sherry or bourbon
10-inch unbaked pie crust

Meringue:

4 egg whites
8 tbsp. sugar

Cook sweet potatoes; mash while warm adding butter. Separate eggs, beat yolks lightly, adding sugar, salt, lemon, and orange. Add milk with sweet potatoes to egg mixture. Beat well, adding nutmeg and cinnamon, lemon extract and sherry or bourbon. Pour into unbaked crust, brown in oven at 450° for ten minutes, reduce heat to 275° and bake one hour or until custard is set.

Beat egg whites until peaked, add sugar gradually and beat until stiff and glossy. Spread on pie. Bake at 200° for 30 minutes.

SOUTHERN PECAN THANKSGIVING STUFFING

Serves: 8 - 12
Cooking Time: 40 minutes

"Don't wait 'til Thanksgiving to try."

2 onions
4 large stalks celery
½ green pepper (optional)
1 lb. hamburger
pecans
½ lb. chopped mushrooms
  (optional)
garlic
½ can (2 oz.) rubbed sage
  (optional)
1 large can (40 oz.) College
  Inn consommé
1 package (16 oz.) prepared
  stuffing, cube style
1 package prepared corn bread
  stuffing

Dice onions, celery, and green pepper. Mix with hamburger and fry with pecan pieces, mushrooms, and garlic, add sage. Combine with consommé and stuffing mixes and put in baking dish. Heat in a 350° oven for 30 minutes. Baste with turkey drippings while cooking and before serving.

Seasoned Rice

Serves: 4
Cooking Time: 15 minutes

"Very good side dish."

1 cup Carolina rice
1 large onion, diced
½ green pepper, diced
salad oil
1 tbsp. soy sauce
2 cups water

Cook rice in water for 12 minutes. Sauté onion and green pepper in a little salad oil until cooked, not brown. Mix with rice and put in a pan. Add soy sauce and cook for a few minutes.

Rice Torte

Serves: 10
Cooking Time: 30 minutes

"Can also be used as side dish."

bread crumbs
1 cup minced onion
½ cup margarine
1 cup raw rice, boiled
4 eggs
1 cup Romano cheese
salt, to taste
pepper, to taste

Prepare baking pan by greasing bottom and sides. Cover pan with bread crumbs to make crust. Sauté onion until soft in margarine. Add to cooked rice three beaten eggs and cheese, salt, and pepper to taste. Spread into baking pan evenly. Beat remaining egg and pour over rice for shiny top. Bake at 350° for 30 minutes. Serve warm or cold.

Rice Pilaf Ring

Serves: 8 - 10
Cooking Time: 60 minutes

"Great for company. Can be prepared in advance."

4 cups chicken broth
6 tbsp. butter
2 cups Uncle Ben's converted rice
3 onions, diced and sautéed
1 green pepper, diced and sautéed
½ cup boiled ham, diced and sautéed
½ tsp. salt
¼ tsp. pepper

Heat stock. Melt butter in a large skillet. Add rice and brown, stirring constantly. When rice is evenly browned, pour stock into rice. Cover and cook over low heat for 20 to 25 minutes. Sauté onions, green pepper, and boiled ham. When rice has absorbed all liquid, add sautéed onion, pepper, ham, and seasonings. Pack rice into a 1½-quart ring mold that has been buttered. If you prefer, this can be prepared in advance and reheated by setting the ring mold covered with tin foil in a pan of hot water and baking at 350° for 30 minutes or heated on top of the stove in a pan of water.

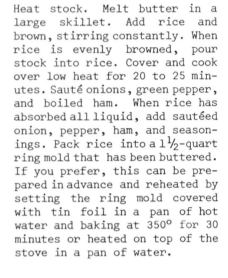

Ginger Rice Ring

Serves: 8 - 10
Cooking Time: 30 minutes

"A perky new twist for rice."

2 tbsp. butter
4 stalks celery, cut up
2 cups cooked rice
1 can (10½ oz.) chicken consommé
2 tbsp. chopped crystallized ginger
2 egg whites

Sauté celery in butter. Mix all remaining ingredients (except egg whites) together. Beat egg whites stiff. Blend all together. Pour into greased, 2-quart mold. Cook in pan of water, covered, in preheated 350° oven until hot. Note: Two tablespoons of either orange or lemon rind may be mixed to above for additional flavor.

Rice Pilaf

Serves: 4
Cooking Time: 1¼ hours

2 cups liquid, well seasoned
1 cup long grain rice
2½ tbsp. butter
½ cup parsley, finely chopped
½ cup carrots, finely chopped
½ cup celery, finely chopped
½ cup onions, finely chpped
½ cup pine nuts (pignoli)

Liquid must be boiling hot. Casserole must be hot. Put empty casserole into oven set at 375°. Have stock (chicken, beef, or just highly seasoned liquid) boiling then start the rice. Do not wash the rice. Put the butter in a large pan with a high heat. When the butter is hot put in the rice and stir constantly until rice is well coated and hot to the touch. In about five minutes the rice will be golden brown. Remove from heat. Pour rice into casserole. Pour boiling stock (carefully) over rice. Cover and place in oven for 30 minutes. Add vegetables and nuts, mixing through with a fork. Cover and return to oven for 30 minutes longer. Can be frozen and reheated.

Easy Rice Pilaf

Serves: 4 - 6
Cooking Time: 45 minutes

"Easy and tastier than prepared, expensive mixes!"

1 medium onion, diced
1 clove garlic, minced
1 stalk celery, diced
¼ cup butter or margarine
1 cup long grain rice, uncooked
2 cups chicken broth or wine
salt
pepper

Sauté onion, garlic, and celery in shortening until onion is limp. Add rice, stirring often until rice is golden. Add chicken broth, cover, and simmer until rice is tender, stirring occasionally. Add salt and pepper to taste.

Rice Balls

Serves: 12
Preparation Time: 1 hour

"Different luncheon or supper dish served with salad."

1 lb. rice
1 lb. margarine
4 egg yolks
1 lb. ground beef
1 can (6 oz.) tomato paste
salt
pepper
4 tbsp. bread crumbs
4 tbsp. Parmesan cheese
4 egg whites
bread crumbs
flour
oil for frying

Cook rice until dry, add salt to taste. Add margarine, stirring until melted. Beat egg yolks and add to rice, stirring all the time. Let cool. Brown ground beef, add tomato paste and three cans water, salt and pepper to taste. Cook slowly till meat gets dry. Add four tablespoons bread crumbs and cheese. Let cool. Form rice into a ball and make pocket. Fill with beef mixture, cover with rice forming ball the size of a snowball. Using three individual dishes—one for beaten egg white, one for bread crumbs, and one for flour, dip balls into flour, egg white, bread crumbs, and then deep fry.

Mexican Beef and Rice Casserole

Serves: 4
Cooking Time: 40 minutes

3 tbsp. oil
½ cup raw rice
1 onion, thinly sliced
1 clove garlic, minced
1 lb. ground meat
2 tsp. salt
2 tsp. chili powder
⅓ cup ketchup
1 can (14 oz.) tomatoes, stewed
1 cup water
½ cup raisins (optional)

Brown rice. Add onion, garlic, and meat. Cook until meat is browned. Put in salt, chili powder, ketchup, tomatoes, water, and raisins. Cover. Stirring once in a while, cook 25 minutes until rice is tender.

Noodle Pudding Soufflé

Serves: 6 - 8
Cooking Time: 1 hour

1 pt. sour cream
½ lb. cottage cheese
6 eggs
½ cup sugar
½ tsp. salt
4 oz. broad noodles
cinnamon to taste
butter

In bowl, beat sour cream and cheese, add one egg at a time and beat. Add sugar and salt. Cook noodles and drain. Add noodles to beaten ingredients. Grease casserole, pour ingredients into pan. Sprinkle with cinnamon and dot with butter. Bake first 30 minutes at 400°. Bake second 30 minutes at 325°.

Noodle Pudding

Serves: 4 - 6
Cooking Time: 1 hour

"Make the day before serving."

½ lb. medium noodles
3 eggs
¾ cup sugar
1 lb. cottage cheese
½ pt. sour cream
1 tbsp. vanilla
¼ cup butter
½ cup raisins
cornflakes
cinnamon

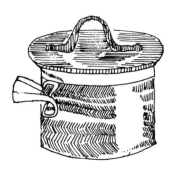

Boil noodles and drain in cold water. In bowl, beat together eggs and sugar. Then add cottage cheese, sour cream, and vanilla. Melt butter and use one-half of amount in mixture (save rest). Fold in noodles and raisins to mixture. In 9 x 13-inch pan put rest of melted butter on bottom and sprinkle cornflakes over butter. Fold in noodle mixture. On top put cornflakes and sprinkle on cinnamon. Bake at 350° for one hour or until brown.

APRICOT NOODLE PUDDING

Serves: 8 - 10
Cooking Time: 45 - 60 minutes

1 package (8 oz.) medium
  noodles
½ lb. cottage cheese, creamed
8 oz. sour cream
2 eggs
¼ cup butter
½ cup raisins
½ cup sugar
1 jar (12 oz.) apricot jam,
  heated to loosen

Cook noodles. Mix all ingredients into noodles. Pour into two-quart, greased Pyrex dish and bake at 350° 45 minutes to one hour.

CHERRY NOODLE PUDDING SUPREME

Serves: 10 - 12
Cooking Time: 1 hour

"Very versatile. Can be used as side dish, dessert, or buffet."

½ lb. medium noodles
¼ lb. cream cheese
½ cup sugar
⅓ cup milk
1 lb. cottage cheese
1 pt. sour cream
1½ tsp. vanilla
½ tsp. cinnamon
3 eggs
1 can (21 oz.) cherries used
  in pie filling

Boil noodles. Rinse in cold water. Mash cream cheese and add all other ingredients, except eggs and cherries. Beat eggs one at a time and stir into the noodle mixture. Bake in buttered pan (9 x 13 inches) in moderate oven (350°) for one-half hour. Remove from oven and spread cherries over the top and bake another one-half hour.

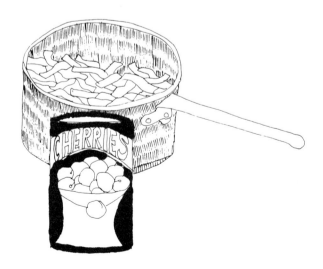

PINEAPPLE NOODLE PUDDING

Serves: 16 - 18
Cooking Time: 45 minutes

"Better if baked day before serving."

1 lb. noodles
1 jar (1 lb.) apple sauce
1 dozen eggs
8 oz. orange juice
3 tbsp. sugar
6 tbsp. margarine
1 large can (20 oz.) crushed
  pineapple, drained
1 tsp. lemon rind
½ tsp. orange rind
1 tsp. vanilla

Partially boil noodles, drain. Mix all ingredients together. Grease pan. Bake at 400° for 45 minutes.

RAISIN NOODLE PUDDING

Serves: 10 - 12
Cooking Time: 30 minutes

1 package (12 oz.) broad
  noodles
½ cup sweet butter
½ cup milk
½ cup sugar
16 oz. cottage cheese,
  creamed
16 oz. sour cream
2 eggs
1 tbsp. vanilla
½ cup raisins
¼ cup brownulated sugar
¼ cup Kellogg's cornflake
  crumbs

Cook noodles according to directions on package. When cooked, combine butter with noodles. Mix all other ingredients, except sugar and cornflake crumbs, in 9 x 13-inch Pyrex baking dish, then add noodles. Mix brown sugar and cornflake crumbs and sprinkle over complete dish. Bake at 450° for 30 minutes or until done.

MIXED-FRUIT NOODLE PUDDING

Serves: 6 - 8
Cooking Time: 1 hour

"Coconut and fruit cocktail make this dish different. May be doubled. Excellent starch to be served with chicken, lamb, beef, or pork."

4 oz. broad egg noodles
2 packages (3 oz. each) cream cheese
½ pt. sour cream
¼ cup sugar
2 eggs, well beaten
raisins
coconut
1 tsp. vanilla
1 can (1 lb.) fruit cocktail, drained

Boil, rinse, and drain noodles. Mash cream cheese with sour cream. Add sugar and eggs, raisins, coconut, vanilla, and fruit cocktail. Add to noodles and bake at 350° for one hour. Serve warm or at room temperature. Note: If freezing, bake ½ noted time, cool and freeze. Bake remaining time before serving.

NOODLE PUDDING WITH SPINACH

Serves: 6
Cooking Time: 45 minutes

"This is very good with broiled fish or chicken as a substitute for potatoes and green vegetable."

1 package (8 oz.) broad noodles
1 onion, diced
½ cup butter or margarine, melted
3 eggs, slightly beaten
2 packages (10 oz.) chopped spinach, thawed and drained
1 cup sour cream

Cook noodles till barely tender. Sauté onion in a little of the butter or margarine till slightly brown. Add to cooked noodles. Fold in eggs, spinach, sour cream, and rest of melted butter. Mix and place in baking dish. Put dish in pan of water and bake in 350° oven for about 45 minutes. Double recipe for 12. You can put this into a greased ring mold, bake, and unmold when done.

NOODLES LORRAINE

Serves: 10 - 12
Cooking Time: 45 minutes

1 package (8 oz.) broad egg
   noodles
2 tbsp. butter or margarine
1 large onion, chopped
2 eggs, beaten
1 tsp. salt
½ tsp. nutmeg
8 slices bacon, crisp cooked
   and crumbled
2 cups Swiss cheese, diced
½ cup grated Parmesan cheese

Cook noodles according to package directions; drain. Melt butter and cook onion until transparent. In large bowl, combine eggs, salt, and nutmeg. Add noodles, butter, onion, bacon, and cheeses. Place in two-quart baking dish. Bake in a preheated 375° oven for 45 minutes.

NOODLE AND BEEF CASSEROLE

Serves: 8
Cooking Time: 1½ hours

"Good way to stretch a pound of beef."

1 large box (1 lb.) broad
   noodles
1 large or 2 small onions
2 tsp. oil or margarine
1 lb. ground beef
garlic powder
salt
pepper
oregano
2 cans tomato soup, undiluted

Parboil noodles. Brown onions, diced fine, in oil. Add meat, cook until all particles are brown. Add seasonings to taste and mix well. In a two-quart casserole, alternate layers of noodles, soup, meat, ending with noodles and soup. Bake for one hour at 350°. This freezes very well.

CASSEROLE HAMBURGER DELIGHT

Serves: 5 - 6
Cooking Time: 45 minutes

1 lb. ground beef
2 tsp. oil
1 large onion, sliced
3 green peppers, diced
2 cloves garlic, minced
1 lb. broad noodles, cooked
1 qt. Buitoni spaghetti or
   marinara sauce

Brown meat in oil. Remove meat from pan with slotted spoon. Sauté onions and peppers. Mix all remaining ingredients together. Bake in casserole for 45 minutes in preheated 375° oven.

Fettucine Alfredo

(PASTA IN BUTTER SAUCE)

Serves: 4 - 6
Cooking Time: 15 minutes

1 lb. fettucine
1½ sticks sweet butter
½ pt. heavy cream
¼ to ½ cup mild Parmesan
  cheese
fresh black pepper

Cook fettucine *al dente*, seven minutes. Rinse in colander with hot water. Transfer to covered casserole. Melt butter, then mix thoroughly with noodles, to coat. Place on heating tray or in oven to heat thoroughly. Whip cream until stiff. Toss together with cheese, black pepper, and noodles. Serve immediately.

Linguine with White Clam and Shrimp Sauce

Serves: 4 - 6
Cooking Time: 20 minutes

6 tbsp. olive oil
3 cloves garlic, sliced thin
3 tbsp. parsley flakes
3 tbsp. oregano
1 can (8 oz.) minced clams
6-8 boiled shrimp, chopped
1 bottle (8 oz.) clam broth
1 tsp. black pepper
1 lb. thin linguine, cooked

In a large skillet heat olive oil, add garlic, and cook over low light for five minutes (do not brown garlic). Add parsley and oregano. Cook for ten minutes stirring frequently. Add clams, shrimp, and broth. Heat for two minutes, add black pepper. Pour mixture over a platter of linguine. Toss at table. Serve with green salad, garlic bread, and white wine.

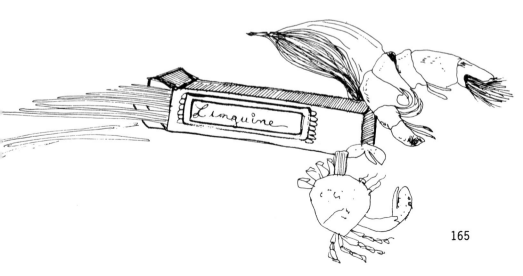

BACON SAUCE AND SPAGHETTI

Serves: 4 - 6
Cooking Time: 30 minutes

"Especially good for bacon lovers!"

½ lb. lean bacon slices
(hickory smoked, if you
like), cut into 1½-inch
pieces
1 large onion, diced
1 can (#2½) tomatoes, plum
style
salt, to taste
pepper, to taste
basil or garlic powder
(optional)
1 lb. spaghetti, cooked
grated Parmesan cheese

In heavy skillet, cook bacon until crisp. Add onions and sauté until soft and golden. Add tomatoes and break up with back of spoon. Add seasonings. Cook uncovered over medium high flame about 30 minutes, until slightly thickened, stirring once or twice. Serve over cooked spaghetti. Sprinkle on Parmesan cheese, if desired.

SPAGHETTI-BROCCOLI-ANCHOVY MIX À LA CASA VOLPE

Serves: 6 - 8
Cooking Time: 15 minutes

1 lb. spaghetti, no. 8 or 9
2 packages (9 oz. each) frozen
broccoli spears
2 small tins flat anchovies
½ cup olive oil
2 small cloves garlic
dash hot red crushed pepper
salt, to taste
pepper, to taste

Boil pasta and broccoli according to directions—however, omit salt in boiling water. In the meantime, empty the anchovies into small frying pan, add olive oil, press the garlic cloves into mixture, add hot pepper flakes. Sauté all together gently until anchovies disintegrate (about 2 or 3 minutes). Set aside until pasta and vegetables are done then mix all three together in serving bowl, add salt and pepper, and serve immediately. Mixture should be slightly moist, add some of the cooking water if necessary. Can be used with roast pork or fish.

PEAS AND MACARONI

Serves: 6
Cooking Time: 20 minutes

1 small onion
6 strips bacon, diced
1 can (17 oz) or 1 package
  (9 oz.) frozen peas
1 lb. small shell macaroni
grating cheese
salt
pepper

Sauté onion and diced bacon until tender. Drain peas and add to onions and bacon. Mix well and turn off heat. Boil macaroni. Drain, reserving one cup of water from macaroni. Toss macaroni with pea mixture. Add salt and pepper. Serve hot with grating cheese. If it dries out, add reserved water.

BAKED MACARONI

Serves: 3 or 4 as a main course
6 - 8 as a side dish
Cooking Time: 1 hour

"One of the best. Never fails."

2 tbsp. butter
2 tbsp. flour
$\frac{1}{2}$ tsp. salt
$\frac{1}{8}$ tsp. pepper
$\frac{1}{4}$ tsp. paprika
$2\frac{1}{2}$ cups milk
$1\frac{1}{2}$ cups grated cheese, sharp
  Cheddar preferably
8 oz. macaroni
$\frac{1}{2}$ cup buttered bread crumbs
  (I use Pepperidge Farm
  stuffing to make bread
  crumbs)
1 can (7 oz.) tuna, drained
  (optional)

Melt butter. Blend in flour and seasonings. Add milk and cook, stirring constantly until thick (like a medium white sauce). Add one cup cheese and melt. Cook macaroni according to package directions. Combine macaroni and sauce and pour into greased baking pan. Top with remaining cheese and crumbs and bake at 375° for 40-60 minutes.
Note: Recipe, when doubled, fits a three-quart Pyrex baking dish.

SHRIMP CLAM CASSEROLE

Serves: 10 - 12
Cooking Time: 30 - 40 minutes

¼ cup olive oil
¼ cup margarine
1 large can (10 oz.) minced
  clams, with juice
1 small can (8 oz.) minced
  clams, with juice
2 cans (15 oz. each) Buitoni
  marinara sauce
3 tbsp. Parmesan cheese
4-5 cloves garlic, pressed
⅓ cup parsley
1½ tbsp. oregano
3 tbsp. basil
2½ lb. cooked cleaned shrimp
1 lb. (#22) macaroni shells,
  cooked

Melt margarine with olive oil. Add clams with juice, marinara sauce, Parmesan cheese, garlic, parsley, oregano, and basil. Blend together. Cook for ten minutes, stirring occasionally. Remove from heat. Add shrimp and cooked macaroni to sauce. Pour into casserole and bake in preheated 350° oven for 20-30 minutes.

WINTER CASSEROLE

Serves: 6
Cooking Time: 1 hour

"A little different with a slightly sweet flavor."

2 tbsp. corn oil
¼ cup finely chopped onion
¼ cup finely chopped green
  pepper
1 lb. ground beef
1 can (1 lb., 12 oz.) tomatoes,
  reserve liquid
½ cup Karo all-purpose syrup
½ tsp. salt
½ tsp. chili powder
¼ tsp. pepper
1 bay leaf
2 tbsp. cornstarch
¼ cup tomato liquid
3 cups cooked macaroni or rice
  (macaroni shells are nicest)
1 cup shredded Cheddar cheese

Heat corn oil in skillet. Add onion and green pepper. Cook until tender. Add ground beef; brown, stirring often. Pour out and save ¼ cup liquid from tomatoes. Add remainder of tomatoes, Karo syrup, salt, chili powder, pepper, and bay leaf to meat mixture. Bring to boil, cover, simmer 15 minutes. Blend cornstarch with tomato liquid, stir into meat mixture. Bring to boil, stirring. Add macaroni or rice; pour into two-quart casserole. Sprinkle with cheese. Can be made ahead to this point. Bake at 350° about 30 minutes.

BAKED ZITI CASSEROLE

Serves: 8 - 10
Cooking Time: 1 hour, 45 minutes

Sauce:

¼ cup olive or salad oil
1 cup onion, finely chopped
1 clove garlic, crushed
1 can (2 lb., 3 oz.) Italian
   tomatoes
1 can (6 oz.) tomato paste
2 tbsp. chopped parsley
1 tbsp. salt
1 tbsp. sugar
1 tsp. oregano
½ tsp. dried basil leaves
¼ tsp. pepper
1 lb. ziti
3 tbsp. grated Parmesan cheese

In a six-quart kettle, add hot oil, sauté onion and garlic until golden brown. Add undrained tomatoes, tomato paste, 1½ cups water, parsley, salt, sugar, oregano, basil, and pepper. Mix well, mashing tomatoes with fork. Bring to boil. Reduce heat and simmer, covered, stirring occasionally, one hour.

Cheese Filling:

2 containers (15 oz. each)
   ricotta cheese
1 package (8 oz.) mozzarella
   cheese, diced
⅓ cup grated Parmesan cheese
2 eggs
1 tbsp. chopped parsley
1 tsp. salt
¼ tsp. pepper

Preheat oven to 350°. Cook ziti as package directs. In large bowl combine the cheeses, eggs, parsley, salt, and pepper. Beat with wooden spoon until blended. Spoon a little tomato sauce into a 5-quart casserole. Layer a third of the ziti, cheese mixture, sauce, sprinkle with a little Parmesan cheese, repeat twice. Bake uncovered 45 minutes or until bubbling in center.
Note: If desired, make casserole ahead and refrigerate. Remove from refrigerator while preheating oven. Bake 60 minutes or until heated through.

Baked Ziti Quick Style

Serves: 8
Cooking Time: 30 minutes

1 package (1 lb.) ziti
1 lb. ricotta cheese (part skim)
salt
pepper
oregano
garlic powder
1 large jar (29 oz.) marinara
  sauce
1 large can (28 oz.) peeled
  tomatoes
1 lb. mozzarella cheese,
  shredded

Cook package of ziti according to directions. Drain well and place in large casserole. Add ricotta cheese and mix with noodles. Add salt, pepper, oregano, garlic powder, to taste. Use large jar prepared marinara sauce and add slowly to noodle mixture, taking care that consistency does not get too watery. Place on top the tomatoes (slightly mashed) and shredded mozzarella cheese. Bake at 350° for about 30 minutes, or until bubbly.

Lasagna

Serves: 10
Cooking Time: $1\frac{1}{2}$ hours

1 lb. lasagna noodles
2 tbsp. oil
1 clove garlic, minced
1 medium onion, chopped
$1\frac{1}{2}$ lb. chopped meat
$\frac{1}{2}$ lb. sweet sausage (optional)
2 tsp. salt
$\frac{1}{4}$ tsp. pepper
$\frac{1}{2}$ tsp. basil (optional)
2 cans (6 oz. each) tomato paste
$1\frac{1}{2}$ cups hot water
$\frac{1}{2}$ lb. ricotta or cottage cheese
$\frac{1}{2}$ lb. mozzarella cheese, sliced

Cook and drain noodles. In hot oil, using a heavy pan, cook garlic and onions until soft. Add beef, sausage, and seasonings and cook until crumbly. Mix in tomato paste and hot water. Simmer five minutes. In a shallow baking dish (9 x 13 x 2 inches) put a thin layer of sauce, half the noodles, all of the ricotta and half the mozzarella cheese. Repeat with half the remaining sauce, the noodles, remainder of sauce and mozzarella cheese on top. Bake in moderate oven, 350° for 35 minutes. Let stand ten minutes before cutting.

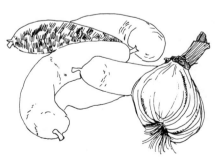

LASAGNA ROLL-UPS

Yield: 12 rolls
Cooking Time: 1½ hours

½ package (1 lb.) lasagna
noodles
¼ cup oil

Filling:

1 lb. cream cheese
½ lb. cottage cheese
½ lb. ricotta cheese
½ tsp. crushed garlic
¼ cup sour cream
salt
pepper

Meat Sauce:

1 tsp. crushed garlic
1½ cups onions, chopped
2½ oz. salt butter
¼ cup olive oil
2 tbsp. tomato paste
salt
pepper
1 large can tomatoes
1½ lb. lean chopped meat

Topping:

mozzarella cheese
Parmesan cheese
butter

Cook noodles in boiling salted water and add oil. Strain, rinse, and spread noodles on towels. Pat dry. Crush garlic; chop onions. Butter platter and slice mozzarella cheese. Mix cheese filling and spread ¼ inch on each noodle, then roll up and arrange on buttered platter. Cook onion and garlic slowly for 3-4 minutes in butter and olive oil. Add tomato paste. Add tomatoes, salt, and pepper and cook 2-3 minutes. Add chopped meat and simmer 10 minutes. Spoon sauce over rolls, reserving a little for topping. Place one slice mozzarella cheese on each roll. Spoon over balance of sauce. Sprinkle with Parmesan and dot with butter. Just before serving, brown under broiler.

ORZO

Serves: 6
Cooking Time: 40 minutes

"Nice side dish. Can be made ahead."

1 box Orzo (Ronzoni macaroni
product)
2 envelopes George Washington
beef seasoning
sliced mushrooms, to taste
green peppers, to taste
onions, to taste
margarine
soy sauce, to taste

Cook Orzo as directed on package, adding beef seasoning to water. Sauté mushrooms, green pepper, and onions in margarine. Drain Orzo and mix vegetable mixture and macaroni together. Add soy sauce. Bake 20 minutes at 400°. Can be frozen.

BARLEY BAKE

Serves: 4
Cooking Time: 15 minutes

"Nice side dish. Try with fish."

1 package (8 oz.) Goodman's
   egg barley
¼ lb. margarine
1 package dry onion soup mix
1 large can (8 oz.) sliced
   mushrooms or Progresso
   whole baby clams (10 oz.)

Boil barley for eight minutes. Drain. Add ¼ pound margarine, dry onion soup mix, and mushrooms (or clams). Place in casserole, bake at 300 to 325° for 15 minutes, uncovered.

MATZO PUDDING

Serves: 12 or more
Cooking Time: 50 minutes

"Can be served as side dish or as dessert with coffee."

12 matzos
9 eggs, well beaten
1½ tsp. salt
1½ cups sugar
¾ cup oil
3 tsp. cinnamon
1½ cups chopped walnuts
6 large apples, cored,
   peeled, and sliced
1½ cups raisins

Break matzos into pieces and soak in water until soft. Drain. Beat eggs with salt, sugar, oil, and cinnamon. Add to drained matzos and stir in nuts, apples, and raisins. Bake in 350° preheated oven for 50 minutes. Can be served with meat or serve with coffee.

Vegetables

String Bean Casserole

Serves: 6
Cooking Time: 35 - 40 minutes

"Easy to prepare and attractive to serve."

1 large can (16 oz.) French-
  style string beans
1 can cream of mushroom soup
  (undiluted)
4 or 5 onion rings
grated cheese (optional)

Drain liquid from beans and put in covered baking dish. Add soup and mix well. Place onion rings on top. Grated cheese may be added if you so desire. Bake at 350° for 35-40 minutes.

Green Beans Scandia

Serves: 4
Cooking Time: 15 minutes

"This is an old family recipe that is a new combination for many of us."

1 can (1 lb.) cut green beans
  or 1 lb. fresh cooked
  string beans
2 chicken bouillon cubes
2 tbsp. butter or margarine
1 tbsp. sugar
dash of pepper
1 tbsp. cornstarch
1 tbsp. cold water
3 to 4 tbsp. vinegar
2 to 2½ cups chopped cabbage

If using fresh string beans, cook in 1½ cups water. Drain liquid from beans into sauce pan. Add next four ingredients. Heat to boiling, stirring constantly. Stir in cornstarch which has been mixed with one tablespoon cold water. Cook, stirring until mixture thickens and is clear. Add vinegar. Stir in cabbage. Bring to boil. Simmer, covered, about five minutes. Add beans. Reheat.

LIMA BEAN CASSEROLE

Serves: 14 - 16
Cooking Time: 2 hours

"If the children never liked beans before, they might like them after this."

6 cans (13½ oz. each) large butter beans, reserve liquid
½ box (16 oz.) dark brown sugar
1 box (2½ oz.) dried onion flakes
1 large can (29 oz.) pear halves
dark Karo syrup
several tbsp. ketchup
1 cup bean liquid

In large casserole, alternate layers of beans, onions, and brown sugar. Mix bean liquid and ketchup. Pour over beans. Cover with pear halves, round side up. Drizzle with syrup. Bake uncovered at 375° about two hours.

BAKED LIMA BEANS

Serves: 10 - 12
Cooking Time: Approximately 2½ hours

"This is not for the dieter, but A-1 for the lima bean lover."

1 lb. dried baby limas
salted water
¼ cup diced green pepper
¼ cup diced onions
¼ cup diced celery
1 tsp. salt
¼ cup dark molasses
3 tbsp. prepared mustard
1 lb. can whole tomatoes, with juice
cubes of bacon or chicken fat

Soak beans in salted water overnight. Drain soaked beans. Add all ingredients except bacon or chicken fat. Top mixture with bacon or chicken fat. Cover and bake at 325° until beans are tender, approximately 2½ hours.

Broccoli Casserole

Serves: 6
Cooking Time: 25 minutes

"String beans or cauliflower substitute well for broccoli."

2 packages frozen, chopped
  broccoli
2 cans Campbell's cream of
  mushroom soup (condensed)
1 package Pepperidge Farm
  seasoned stuffing mix
  (crumbs)—(you won't need
  entire package)
1 can French fried onion rings

Cook broccoli and drain. In a casserole, spread a layer of broccoli, then a layer of cream of mushroom soup, then a layer of stuffing crumbs. Repeat same layers. Bake in a 350° oven until hot and bubbly. Add fried onion rings to top layer and bake until crisp and golden brown.

Broccoli and Cheese Casserole

Serves: 6 - 8
Cooking Time: 50 minutes

"Delicious."

3 packages frozen broccoli
2 onions, diced
2 tbsp. butter
2 tbsp. flour
½ cup liquid from broccoli
1 jar (8 oz.) Cheese Whiz
3 eggs, beaten
1½ cups Ritz crackers,
  crushed

Cook broccoli and drain, reserving ½ cup of liquid. Sauté onions in the butter. Add all ingredients together except Ritz crackers. Put in greased dish. Sprinkle crushed crackers on top of casserole and dot with butter. Bake at 350° for 40-45 minutes.

COMPANY VEGETABLES

Serves: 6
Cooking Time: 40 minutes

"Try this one with cauliflower also."

2 packages (10 oz. each) frozen, chopped broccoli
1 cup diced American cheese
1 can cream of mushroom soup
⅔ cup evaporated milk
3½ oz. can French fried onion rings

Cook broccoli as directed on package for four minutes. Drain, pour into two-quart baking dish. Sprinkle with diced cheese. Mix evaporated milk with soup and pour mixture over broccoli and cheese. Bake at 350° for 25 minutes. Top with onion rings and bake for an additional 8-10 minutes.

CARROT MOLD

Serves 6 - 8
Cooking Time: 1 hour
Preparation and Setting: 2 hours, 30 minutes
Refrigerate: Overnight

"Very pretty for a dinner party."

1 package (raw) carrots grated fine (2 cups)
¾ cup oil
1 egg
½ cup brown sugar
1 tbsp. water
½ tsp. salt
1 tbsp. lemon juice
1½ cups flour
1 tsp. baking powder
1 tsp. baking soda
½ tsp. pepper
1 tsp. cinnamon

Blend all ingredients. Grease Bundt pan well. Set in refrigerator overnight. Remove from refrigerator two hours before baking. Bake at 350° for one hour.
Note: Serve with green peas.

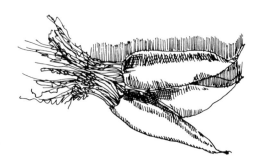

STEAMED CARROT PUDDING

Serves: 12
Cooking Time: 3 hours

"What a way to eat carrots! Based upon old traditional ethnic recipe."

2 tbsp. butter
1 cup brown sugar
2 eggs
½ cup milk
½ cup flour
½ cup raisins
½ tsp. salt
¾ cup matzo meal
2 cans (16 oz. each) shoe-string carrots, drained (available at Waldbaums)
½ tsp. cinnamon
½ tsp. baking soda
½ tsp. baking powder
½ tsp. nutmeg
1 small jar currant jelly

Cream together the butter and sugar. Add all ingredients, except jelly. Grease a mold well. Melt jelly over hot water and pour into bottom of mold. Add carrot mixture. Cover mold (use large piece of foil tied down with string). Place mold into pot filled halfway with water and steam for three hours.

CORN FRITTERS

Serves: 4 - 6
Cooking Time: 15 - 20 minutes

"These are special! They can be used as a side dish at dinner or as an unusual hors d'oeuvre. Watch out for kitchen raiders!"

1 egg, well beaten
½ cup milk
1 cup pancake mix
1 tsp. sugar
¾ cup raisins
1 cup whole-kernel corn, drained
vegetable oil

Blend together milk and egg. Add gradually to pancake mix. Stir in sugar. Stir in corn and raisins. Heat enough vegetable oil in deep fry pan to float corn fritters. Drop batter from tablespoon into hot oil. Do not crowd. Fry fritters 3-5 minutes and drain on paper toweling.

CORN PUDDING

Serves: 6
Cooking Time: 1 hour

"Try this one when you're serving a roast."

1 can creamed corn
1 can corn niblets
1 egg, slightly beaten
1/3 cup dry bread crumbs
1/2 cup sour cream
1/2 tsp. salt
1/8 tsp. pepper

Mix all ingredients together. Butter a 1½ quart casserole. Pour in mixture. Bake at 350° for one hour or until firm.

EGGPLANT À LA PROVENÇALE

Serves: 4 - 6
Cooking Time: 30 - 40 minutes

"Great served with fish."

1 medium onion, sliced
1 clove garlic, minced fine
1 green pepper, cut up
1 large or 2 small eggplants
2 peeled tomatoes, cut up
tomato juice
salt to taste
pepper to taste

Sauté onion, garlic, and green pepper until soft. Add peeled and cubed eggplant, tomatoes, and, if necessary, some tomato juice. Cook and cover until eggplant is soft and well cooked. Add the seasonings just before serving.

MARINATED EGGPLANT

Serves: 6
Cooking Time: 20 minutes
Refrigerate: 2 days

"Nice and spicy."

1 eggplant
1/2 cup chopped celery
1/2 cup chopped pimento
1 clove garlic
2 tbsp. chopped capers
2 tbsp. parsley
1/8 tsp. powdered dill
1/4 tsp. oregano
1/2 tsp. salt
1/8 tsp. pepper
1/2 cup salad oil

Cook eggplant in salted water, to cover, for 20 minutes or until tender. Cool and cut into 2-inch pieces. Combine rest of ingredients, add eggplant. Refrigerate for two days.

EGGPLANT

(RUMANIAN STYLE)

Serves: 4 - 6
Cooking Time: 20 minutes

"Served cold — as hors d'oeuvre, appetizer, or relish."

eggplant
1 onion, sliced into rings
1 bell pepper, sliced
salt to taste
2-3 tbsp. salad oil
tomato (optional
olives

Select eggplant light in weight for its size. Bake on barbecue or potato baker at high heat until fork tender. Cool. Peel. Place in chopping bowl with onions and pepper. Chop fine. Add salt to taste, salad oil. Some people add a tomato. Serve chilled as an appetizer or as an hors d'oeuvre with olives or crackers.

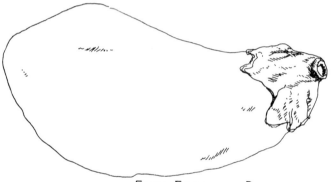

EASY EGGPLANT PARMIGIANA

Serves: 6
Cooking Time: 40 minutes

"Good meat substitute. A meal in itself."

1 medium eggplant
2 eggs
2 cups flour
Wesson oil
1 lb. mozzarella
Parmesan cheese
1 qt. Ragu meat sauce

Peel eggplant. Slice $\frac{1}{8}$-inch thick. Dip in beaten eggs, then put in flour on both sides. Fry in $\frac{1}{2}$-inch oil until golden brown. Drain on brown paper or paper toweling. Layer eggplant with thin slices of mozzarella and dash of Parmesan cheese and Ragu sauce in casserole. Continue layering until all ingredients are used. Bake in oven at 375° for 25 minutes.

Camille's Grandma Madeline's Eggplant Parmigiana

Serves: 6 - 8
Cooking Time: 15 - 30 minutes

*"Many years of doing have perfected this excellent recipe.
Can be a side dish or good, filling main dish
for a meatless meal."*

1 large eggplant or
  2 small ones
1 cup oil for frying
3 eggs
dash salt
3 tbsp. grated Parmesan cheese
1¼ cups tomato sauce

Tomato Sauce:

1 can (8 oz.) Del Monte tomato
  sauce
1 can water
1 whole clove garlic
sprinkle of oregano
salt
pepper

Combine sauce ingredients. Bring to boil and simmer for 10 minutes.

Wash and peel eggplant, leaving a small amount of brown skin. Slice eggplant ¼-inch thick, into round slices. Heat oil in frying pan. Beat eggs thick, add salt. Dip eggplant slice in egg, making sure entire slice is coated. Place coated eggplant in frying pan and brown on both sides. Remove, continue browning eggplant slices until none remain. You may need more than three eggs, plus you may have to add more oil to the frying pan. Remove garlic from tomato sauce. Put tomato sauce at bottom of casserole, add a layer of eggplant, sprinkle some Parmesan cheese, more tomato sauce, and continue making layers until all ingredients are used. Bake at 350° for 15 to 30 minutes.

Variations: You may dip eggplant into egg and then bread crumbs before frying. You may use ½ pound mozzarella cheese (sliced thin) plus Parmesan cheese when making layers in casserole. In that case, bake at 400° for 15 minutes. You may use your own leftover tomato sauce, preferably meat sauce.

Camille Lubeski, Merrick, New York

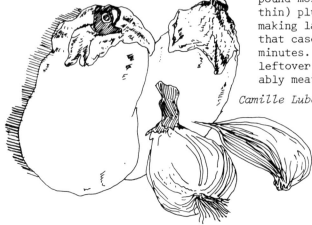

Father Capon's Ratatouille Niçoise

Serves: 6-8
Cooking Time: 1 hour

"Perfect casserole to take when asked to bring a dish!"

1 large eggplant, peeled and
    cubed
3-4 summer squash or zucchini,
    cubed
1 large onion, sliced
4 fresh tomatoes, peeled and
    chopped
2-3 cloves garlic, crushed
2 tbsp. olive oil
salt
pepper, freshly ground
1 bay leaf
grated Parmesan cheese

In as little water as possible gently boil eggplant, squash, and/or zucchini for 10 minutes. Sauté onion and garlic in oil until golden. Add to eggplant mixture. Add all ingredients except cheese, and simmer 30 minutes, covered. Put in large casserole (if there is too much liquid, pour some off). Cover generously with cheese. Bake at 350° until nicely browned.

Ratatouille Niçoise

Serves: 6
Cooking Time: 1 hour, 20 minutes

"Anyone who's traveled through the south of France has had the opportunity to enjoy Ratatouille. This recipe is an excellent one given to me by a French Canadian. Can be made ahead."

½ cup salad or olive oil
    (I use French olive oil)
2 large onions, thinly sliced
2-3 minced garlic cloves
1 small eggplant, peeled and
    diced
4 large beefsteak tomatoes or
    1 large can (1 lb., 12 oz.)
    California-style tomatoes
4 zucchini
2 green peppers, cleaned and
    diced
½ tsp. basil
½ tsp. thyme
salt to taste
pepper to taste

Heat oil in heavy sauce pan (when possible use enameled, cast iron one). Add onions and garlic, brown quickly over high heat. Add eggplant and tomatoes and mix, crushing mixture with back of wooden spoon. Add zucchini and green peppers and mix well. Add seasonings and cook 2-3 minutes over high heat, stirring most of the time. Cover and simmer about 1 hour, stirring once or twice, until sauce is thick and creamy. This ratatouille can be served hot or cold, as an hors d'oeuvre, salad, or hot as a vegetable. Easily doubled and will keep 10-15 days refrigerated.

MUSHROOMS SAUTÉ

Serves: 8 - 10
Cooking Time: 15 minutes

"Great with roast beef or sliced steak."

2 lb. mushrooms, sliced
  thin
½ lb. butter or margarine
4 large onions, chopped
6 tbsp. soy sauce

Clean mushrooms thoroughly and slice thin. In large skillet, melt butter, add onions, and then mushrooms. Allow to simmer for five minutes, add soy sauce. Continue to simmer for another 15 minutes (do not overcook).

MUSHROOM PARMIGIANA

Serves: 12
Cooking Time: 25 - 30 minutes

2 lb. fresh mushrooms
3 large cans (16 oz. each)
  tomato sauce with onions
1 tsp. salt
¼ tsp. pepper
1 clove garlic, crushed
¼ cup unsaturated oil
1 cup grated Parmesan cheese

Clean mushrooms, removing stems. In large bowl, combine all ingredients, except cheese. (Line baking pans with foil for easier cleaning.) Pour mixture of sauce and mushrooms into baking pans. Make sure each mushroom is exposed with brown side up. Spoon mixture from bottom of pan over each mushroom. Top with cheese. Bake at 325° for 25-30 minutes or until tender. Can be made ahead and heated.

ONION KUCHEN

Serves: 8
Cooking Time: 30 minutes

"Try this one with pot roast."

2 medium onions, sliced in
  rings
1 package buttermilk biscuits
1 egg
1 cup sour cream
½ tsp. salt
1 tsp. poppy seeds
3 tbsp. butter

Sauté onions in butter. Separate biscuits and place in ungreased 8-inch cake pan. Spoon onion on top. Beat egg, add sour cream and salt. Spoon over onions. Sprinkle on poppy seeds and bake at 375° for 30 minutes.

Vegetables à la Casalingo

Serves: 6
Cooking Time: 1 hour, 15 minutes

"This dish compliments any meat, fish, or fowl."

2 lb. mushrooms
4 fresh hearts of artichokes
¼ cup olive oil
1 clove garlic, finely minced
½ tsp. salt
dash of pepper
dash of oregano
1 package (8 or 9 oz.) frozen green peas

Preheat oven to 375°. Place all the mushrooms and artichokes in a deep baking dish, after they have been properly cut (artichokes in quarters, mushrooms in half). Add to these vegetables, olive oil, garlic, ¼ teaspoon salt, pepper, and oregano. Mix well and put in oven for about one hour. Just before mixture is about to come out of the oven, prepare the peas according to package directions. Drain and add to the artichokes and mushrooms that have finished baking. Replace baking pan in oven for about 15 minutes.

French Fried Green Peppers

Serves: 6
Cooking Time: 15 minutes

"Chill one hour before frying."

1 lb. green peppers
¾ cup bread crumbs
1 tbsp. salt
½ tsp. oregano
¼ tsp. pepper
⅔ cup Parmesan cheese
2 eggs
¼ cup water
oil

Cut peppers into ½-inch-thick rings. Cut rings in halves or thirds depending on size. Combine crumbs, salt, oregano, pepper, and cheese in a small bowl. Beat eggs and water together in another small bowl. Dip pepper strips in eggs, then crumbs. Chill one hour. Fry in ½-inch hot oil until brown and tender.

Green Pepper Italian

Serves: 4
Cooking Time: 30 minutes

"It's our family favorite with a garden dinner."

6 large green peppers
3 tbsp. olive oil
4 peeled, fresh or canned
  tomatoes, chopped
1 tsp. basil or oregano
1 tsp. sugar
2 tbsp. capers (optional)

Cut the green peppers in half, remove the insides, and cut the skin into quarters or eighths. Heat the oil in a deep frying pan, add the pepper and stir over high heat until they're blistered in places. Add the chopped tomatoes, basil or oregano, sugar, and capers. Stir until mixture comes to a boil. Simmer 25 minutes, uncovered, and season to taste.

Squash Marinara

Serves: 4
Cooking Time: 35 minutes

"Easy."

1 medium yellow squash
1 egg
Italian bread crumbs
Ragu marinara sauce, small
mozzarella cheese
oregano

Peel and slice squash in thin slices and dip in beaten egg and then in Italian bread crumbs. Sauté. In a casserole layer squash, marinara sauce, cheese, and sprinkle a little oregano. Top with cheese. Bake at 350° for 20 minutes. Same recipe can be made with shrimp.

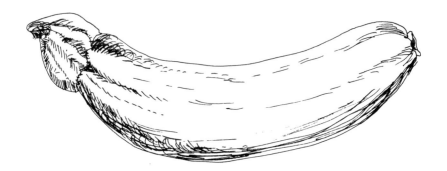

BOILED SUMMER SQUASH

Serves: 4 - 6
Cooking Time: 10 minutes

"From the farm to the pot."

4 young summer squash
1 cup boiling water
1 tsp. salt
⅛ tsp. pepper
¼ cup butter

Wash squash, but do not peel. Cut into cubes or slices. Cook in boiling water with ½ teaspoon salt until barely tender, 5 to 10 minutes. Drain. Season with ½ teaspoon salt, pepper and butter.

SAVORY SPINACH

Serves: 6 - 8
Cooking Time: 30 minutes

"Good creamed spinach variation."

3 packages (10 oz. each)
   frozen spinach
1 cup sour cream
1 package dry onion soup mix
slivered almonds (optional)

Cook spinach until thawed. Drain. In large bowl, mix spinach with sour cream and onion soup mix. Put in greased casserole, add almonds, if desired, and bake at 350° for 30 minutes.

SPINACH SIDE DISH

Serves: 3 - 4
Cooking Time: 40 minutes

1 package (10 oz.) frozen
   chopped spinach
1 cup flavored bread crumbs
3 eggs
½ cup butter
1 tsp. salt

Boil and salt spinach. Drain and mix with all ingredients. Put into greased cake pan and bake ½ hour at 300°. Can be topped (before baking) with Velveeta or mozzarella cheese.

"PASSOVER" SPINACH SQUARE

Serves: 12
Cooking Time: 1 hour

"You don't have to be Jewish to try this one."

1 lb. spinach, fresh or
   frozen
5 squares matzos
5 eggs, separated
1 lb. cottage cheese
3 tbsp. sour cream
½ lb. sliced Edam cheese
salt to taste

Preheat oven to 350°. Cook spinach about 10 minutes in a pot on top of stove. In bowl, break up matzos, place cooked spinach in a colander and let juice moisten matzos. Spill off excess water. Mix in spinach. In another bowl, mix egg yolks with cottage cheese, sour cream, and salt. Fold in stiffly beaten egg whites. In a 9-inch square glass baking pan, spread ¼-inch of egg mixture. Top with two slices Edam cheese and then a layer of spinach mixture. Repeat layers until all ingredients are used. Bake 45 minutes or until firm.

SPINACH PIE

Serves: 6
Cooking Time: 1 hour, 10 minutes

"Compliments a spicy main dish."

8 oz. cottage cheese
⅓ bar farmer cheese
2 packages (10 oz. each) frozen
   chopped spinach
2 eggs, beaten well
½ bunch dill, chop the leaves
salt to taste
matzo meal

Put cottage cheese and farmer cheese through Foley food mill. Cook spinach and drain. Combine all ingredients except matzo meal. Heavily grease a 9-inch pie pan or 8 x 8-inch square pan, sprinkle with matzo meal and heat well. Pour in spinach mixture. Bake one hour at 350°. Serve with a dollop of sour cream on top.

SPINACH CASSEROLE

Serves: 6
Cooking Time: 25 minutes

"Can also be used as a stuffing for chicken."

2 packages (10 oz.) frozen
    chopped spinach, cooked
salt to taste
pepper to taste
grated Parmesan cheese
2 eggs
1 clove garlic, chopped
1 package (3 oz.) cream cheese
buttered bread crumbs

Mix all ingredients except buttered bread crumbs. Mixture should hold its shape. Put in casserole, add bread crumbs on top. Bake at 350° until hot and bubbly.

SPINACH AND CORN

Serves: 6
Cooking Time: 25 minutes

"Try this with a chicken or fish course."

¼ cup minced onion
2 tbsp. butter or margarine
1 can (16 oz.) cream style corn
1 package (10 oz.) frozen
    chopped spinach, cooked and
    drained
1 tbsp. white vinegar
½ tsp. salt
¼ tsp. pepper
¼ cup fine white bread crumbs
2 tbsp. Parmesan cheese

Sauté onions slightly in butter. Combine corn, spinach, onions, vinegar, salt, pepper; put in greased casserole. Take bread crumbs, Parmesan cheese, and two tablespoons butter, mix together and sprinkle on top. Bake at 400° for 25 minutes or until bubbly.

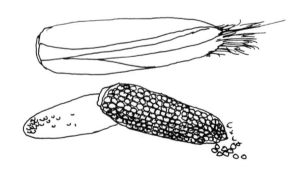

BROILED TOMATOES

Serves: 4
Cooking Time: 10 minutes

"Nice side dish for steak. Broils right along with meat."

2 tomatoes
pepper
pinch of sugar
crushed garlic, with salt
onion, sliced thin (optional)
bread crumbs
grated Parmesan cheese
butter

Cut tomatoes in half. Sprinkle with pepper, sugar, and garlic crushed with salt. Add onion. Sprinkle with bread crumbs and cheese. Dot with butter and brown under broiler.

TOMATO AND ARTICHOKE CASSEROLE

Serves: 6
Cooking Time: 25 minutes

"Good to use in winter when fresh vegetables are limited."

1 can (2 lb., 3 oz.) plum
  tomatoes
1 can (14 oz.) artichoke hearts
¾ cup diced onion
¼ lb. butter
½ tsp. basil
2 tbsp. sugar
salt to taste
pepper to taste

Preheat oven to 325°. Grease heavy shallow casserole. Drain tomatoes. Rinse artichokes in cold water and drain; cut in half. Sauté onions in butter until tender. Add tomatoes, artichokes, and basil; heat five minutes, stirring gently. Season with sugar, salt, and pepper. Pour into casserole and bake for 15 minutes or until hot.

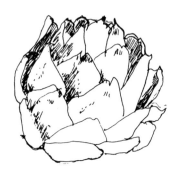

FRENCH FRIED ZUCCHINI

Serves: 4 - 5
Cooking Time: 20 minutes

"A best seller. Even children will eat their vegetables prepared this way."

3 cups zucchini, thinly sliced
1½ cups 4C* bread crumbs
2 eggs, well beaten
vegetable oil

*The 4C brand of bread crumbs is an Italian flavored, definitely spiced crumb that requires no further seasoning.

Into large plastic bag add one cup bread crumbs and zucchini slices. Shake bag well to evenly coat zucchini with crumbs. Remove coated zucchini from bag and dip each slice in beaten egg. Pour remaining ½ cup of bread crumbs into the plastic bag and singly recoat each zucchini slice. Drop gently one by one into preheated hot vegetable oil and fry for five minutes or until golden brown. Remove and drain on paper toweling.

ZUCCHINI

Serves: 6
Cooking Time: 1 hour, 15 minutes

"We really liked this one!"

olive oil
1 medium onion, finely sliced
2 cloves garlic, cut into
  pieces
1 medium can (16 oz.) plum
  tomatoes (mashed)
½ tsp. oregano
1 tsp. salt or more to taste
½ tsp. pepper or more to
  taste
4 zucchini

Brown onion with garlic in a little olive oil. Add tomatoes, oregano, salt, and pepper. Simmer for 30 minutes. While sauce is cooking, take four zucchini, peel, and cut them into quarters. Cut quarters into 1-inch pieces. After first half hour, place zucchini in sauce and cook for 40-45 minutes longer.

Salads, Relishes, and Molds

CRAB MEAT SALAD

Serves: 10 - 12

1 lb. crab meat, chopped fine
4 hard-boiled eggs, chopped
   fine
⅔ cup celery, finely chopped
¼ cup onion, minced
4 tbsp. chili sauce
4 tbsp. mayonnaise
½ tsp. salt
⅛ tsp. white pepper
rye bread, toast, or crackers

Cut crab in tiny pieces; remove shell and bone. Mix together with eggs, celery, and onion. Add chili sauce, enough mayonnaise to bind, and salt and pepper to taste. This should be a fairly thick spread.

SHRIMP AND ARTICHOKE

Serves: 4
Marinate: Overnight

"Great summer dish."

4 artichokes
24 jumbo shrimp
¼ cup wine vinegar
1 tsp. salt
1 tbsp. sugar
2 tsp. chives or fresh
   scallion tops
2 tsp. parsley
3 drops Tabasco
2 cloves garlic, pressed
fresh dill
¾ cup sour cream
¼ cup mayonnaise
juice of lemon (½ to whole)
crumbled bacon
sugar, to taste

Clean artichokes. Prepare by stripping tough outer leaves and removing stems. Boil until tender and refrigerate. Clean shrimp. Mix marinade: wine vinegar, salt, 1 tablespoon sugar, chives, parsley, Tabasco, garlic, and fresh dill. Marinate shrimp overnight. Prepare dressing: Mix together sour cream, mayonnaise, lemon juice, bacon, and sugar to taste. Separate artichoke leaves to make well in center. Fill with dressing and hang shrimp on edge.
Note: Shrimp may be served on cantaloupe with dressing.

COLD SHRIMP SALAD

Serves: 2*
Marinate: Overnight

"Very special — lobster, chicken, or turkey can be substituted."

3 tbsp. olive oil
1 tbsp. vinegar
salt to taste
pepper to taste
½ cup mayonnaise
2 tbsp. chili sauce
1 tsp. dried dill
celery, diced, to taste
Tabasco, to taste
carrot, grated, to taste
4 water chestnuts, diced
2 cups shrimp, cooked

Combine olive oil, vinegar, salt, and pepper and mix with fork. Stir in remaining ingredients and mix everything together. Pour over two cups of shrimp, lobster, chicken, or turkey, cooked. Allow to sit overnight before serving.

*Use approximately 1 cup shrimp, etc. per person. Double and triple recipe as needed.

PINEAPPLE-SHRIMP SALAD

Serves: 6
Preparation Time: 10 minutes
Chill: 2 hours

"Come for lunch. Try with chicken also."

1 cup canned pineapple
   chunks, drained
1¼ lb. cooked and cleaned
   shrimp
1 cup chopped celery
1 tsp. minced onion
½ cup mayonnaise
¼ cup Kraft French dressing
dash salt
lemon juice

Cut pineapple chunks in half and cut shrimp to approximately same size as pineapple chunks. Combine all ingredients and serve cold on lettuce leaves or inside pineapple shells.

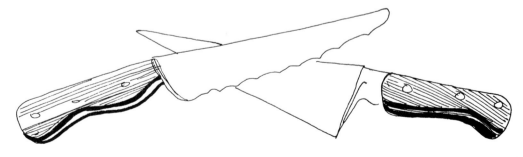

Italian Salad

Serves: 6
Preparation Time: 15 minutes

1 head lettuce
1 medium red onion
1 small package radishes
2 medium or 1 pt. cherry
   tomatoes
¼ lb. feta cheese
1 package Good Seasons
   Italian dressing

Prepare dressing as per directions on package and pour over lettuce. Add remaining ingredients.

Caesar Salad

Serves: 6 - 8

¼ lb. bacon
¾ cup croutons
2 heads romaine lettuce
2 tbsp. fresh parsley,
   chopped
2 tbsp. Parmesan cheese,
   freshly grated
2 hard-cooked eggs

Cut bacon into strips and fry or bake. Drain on paper towels. Fry croutons to golden brown in bacon fat or oil. Drain. Wash lettuce and parsley and dry carefully in a towel.

Dressing:

1 tsp. kosher salt
¾ tsp. black and white
   peppercorns
¼ tsp. dry mustard
1 tsp. Dijon mustard
1 tsp. lemon juice
¼ tsp. sugar
2 tbsp. olive oil
6 tbsp. vegetable oil
1 small raw egg
½ tsp. chopped garlic

Place all ingredients into large wooden salad bowl. Stir well with wooden spoon. Tear lettuce in pieces and place on top of dressing. Sprinkle croutons over. Now add bacon, chopped parsley, freshly grated Parmesan cheese, and hard-boiled eggs cut into sixths and place around salad.

Romaine Salad with Caesar Dressing

Serves: 8

"Dressing made in a blender is fast and neat."

1 egg
1 tbsp. lemon juice
1 tbsp. tarragon vinegar
½ tsp. dry mustard
1 clove garlic
½ tsp. salt
¼ tsp. pepper
1 can (2 oz.) anchovies,
   drained
¾ cup oil (either olive or
   corn or half and half)
½ cup Parmesan cheese,
   freshly grated
romaine lettuce (approximately
   2 large heads)

Mix first eight ingredients in blender. Then add oil slowly to make a mayonnaise consistency. Add to lettuce and toss well. Sprinkle on cheese.

Homemade Croutons:

Freeze thinly sliced Arnold bread. Trim edges and cut into uniform square cubes. Sprinkle lightly with powdered garlic. Fry in medium hot oil until golden. Drain on paper toweling.

Salad Monblason

Serves: 4 - 6

"A bit of gourmet from the blender when you're tired of a green salad."

Dressing:

4 shallots or scallions,
   green and white part
4 cloves garlic, peeled
¾ tbsp. salt
¼ tbsp. pepper
1 tbsp. sugar
½ tbsp. mustard (Dijon if
   possible)
1 tbsp. water
⅓ cup tarragon vinegar
2 cups olive oil and corn
   oil, combined

In your blender, blend the first eight ingredients for about 30 seconds, or until shallots and garlic are minced. Add oil, a little at a time, until blended. This dressing can be stored in your refrigerator for about a month.

Salad:

1 cup shredded beets
½ cup vinegar
2 tbsp. sugar
1 lb. endive

Marinate beets in vinegar, plus sugar about one hour. Slice endive in half and separate leaves. Cut in smaller pieces if necessary. Strain beets. Toss beets and endive with ½ cup of dressing when ready to serve.

WALDORF SALAD

Serves: 4

"This goes very well with fowl."

4 apples, cut in chunks but
   not peeled
1 stalk celery, cut up fine
¼ cup coarsely chopped walnuts
mayonnaise
sour cream

To make dressing, combine 2 to 1
mayonnaise and sour cream. Use
2 to 3 tablespoons of mixture
for dressing.

ISRAELI SALAD

Serves: 4 - 6

1 ripe avocado, cut in chunks
½ can pitted black olives
2 tomatoes, cut in chunks
1 medium onion, cut in rings

Gently combine all ingredients
with dressing.

Dressing:

1-2 tbsp. lemon juice
2-3 tbsp. oil
1 clove garlic, crushed
   (optional)
salt
pepper

MUSHROOM SALAD

Serves: 4
Marinate: Overnight

"Marinated mushrooms make this a very special salad."

½ cup olive oil
4 tbsp. red vinegar
4 tbsp. lemon juice
½ tsp. salt
¼ tsp. fresh ground pepper
12 large fresh mushrooms
1 bunch watercress
½ cup fresh chives, chopped

Combine first five ingredients.
Slice mushrooms paper thin, and
add them to the mixture. Marinate overnight. Just before
serving, transfer mushrooms and
marinade to salad bowl, wash and
drain watercress, add to mushrooms with ¼ cup chopped chives.
Toss, and sprinkle rest of chives
on top. Serve immediately.

German Potato Salad

Serves: 4 - 6
Cooking Time: 30 minutes

"Bring on the frankfurters."

8 medium potatoes
1 tsp. salt
$\frac{1}{4}$ cup salad oil
$\frac{1}{4}$ cup wine vinegar
$\frac{1}{4}$ cup diced onions
dash pepper
$\frac{1}{4}$ tsp. nutmeg

Boil potatoes. Peel and slice while hot. Soak in salt and $\frac{1}{4}$ cup water. Drain. Add oil, vinegar, onions, pepper, and nutmeg. Toss and chill.

Coleslaw

Serves: 4

"This goes very well with meats or fish."

$\frac{1}{4}$ head cabbage, shredded
1 carrot, shredded
1 tbsp. lemon juice
1 tbsp. sugar
2-3 tbsp. dressing
salt
pepper

Shred vegetables on grater. Then add remaining ingredients. Combine, then adjust seasoning to your taste.

Dressing:
    Two parts mayonnaise to one part sour cream.

Noodle Salad

Serves: 8 - 12
Cooking Time: 15 minutes

"Good filler for buffets and summer entertaining.
Take it on the boat too."

8 oz. medium egg noodles
2 cups sharp Cheddar cheese, finely diced
$1\frac{1}{2}$ cups peas, cooked
$\frac{1}{2}$ cup radishes, sliced
$\frac{1}{2}$ cup celery, diced
$\frac{1}{2}$ cup sweet mixed pickles
$\frac{1}{4}$ cup onion, chopped
1 tsp. salt
$\frac{1}{4}$ tsp. pepper
1 cup French salad dressing
1 cup mayonnaise

Cook and drain noodles, combine with all ingredients, except mayonnaise. Toss lightly and chill. Stir in mayonnaise.

Antipasto à la Pete T.

Serves: 6
Preparation Time: 10 minutes

"Bon Appetite!"

2 cans (2 oz. each) anchovies,
   flat
1 jar (5½ oz.) roast peppers
1 tbsp. oregano
½ tsp. dried basil
4 tbsp. olive oil
2 tbsp. wine vinegar
hot crushed peppers to taste

Take round platter and arrange in design so it resembles a flower, alternating one anchovy and one cut roast pepper (same size as anchovy) in a circle. Put oil from can of anchovies (adds to flavor) on anchovies. After arranging sprinkle oregano and dried basil on top. Put olive oil and vinegar in jar and shake to mix. Sprinkle on top of anchovies and roast peppers. Add hot crushed pepper to taste. Eat with garlic bread or hot French or Italian bread.

Greek Salad or Health Salad

Serves: A crowd
Marinate: 3 days

"Three days marinating makes a super salad."

1 large cabbage, sliced
2 peeled cucumbers, tined and
   sliced thin
2 green peppers, sliced thin
2 carrots, sliced thin
1 medium onion, sliced thin

Dressing:

1½ cups sugar
2 cups white vinegar
⅔ cup water
1¼ cups salad oil
¼ cup salt

Pour dressing over salad. Marinate three days in a tightly covered container. Stir every day.

Cold Side Dish

(ONIONS AND TOMATOES)

Serves: 4 - 6
Marinate: 2 hours

"Onions and tomatoes with a Spanish flair."

¼ cup salad or olive oil
2 tbsp. wine vinegar (or more
   to taste)
salt
pepper
1 large Spanish or Bermuda
   onion, sliced very thin
3 or 4 fresh tomatoes, sliced
   not too thin

Mix oil, vinegar, salt, and pepper. Pour over sliced tomatoes and onions. Let marinate for two hours. Serve cold.

Cucumber Salad with Dill

Serves: 4
Preparation Time: 15 minutes

2 cucumbers, sliced very thin
⅓ cup white vinegar
1 tsp. salt
3 tbsp. sugar
1 large onion, sliced thin
fresh dill

Combine all ingredients except dill, making sure juices are mixed well. Garnish with dill. Chill.

Mother's Bean Salad

Serves: 6
Marinate: Overnight

"Delicious!"

¼ cup salad oil
½ cup vinegar
½ cup sugar
1 can (16 oz.) cut string
   beans, drained
1 can (16 oz.) cut wax beans,
   drained
1 can (16 oz.) red kidney
   beans, drained
1 onion, sliced

Combine oil, vinegar, and sugar. Pour over beans and onions. Marinate overnight.

Green Bean Salad – Hot or Cold

Serves: 8 - 12
Cooking Time: 1 hour

"Great for boats, picnics, buffets, etc.!"

½ white onion, sliced
⅓ cup olive oil
2 cans (16 oz. each) green
  beans, any style
1 can (16 oz.) Del Monte
  stewed tomatoes
2 tbsp. tomato purée
2 tbsp. sugar

Sauté onion in olive oil in sauce pan. Add all ingredients, stir, then simmer for one hour to "marry," stirring occasionally. Refrigerate or leave at room temperature. If serving hot, omit sugar.

Honey Dressing

Yield: 1¾ cups
Cooking Time: 3 minutes

"Sweet dressings should be served more often."

½ cup vinegar
¼ cup sugar
¼ cup honey
1 tsp. dry mustard
1 tsp. paprika
1 tsp. celery seeds
1 tsp. celery salt
1 tsp. onion juice
1 cup vegetable or salad oil

Mix vinegar, sugar, honey, mustard, and paprika in small sauce pan and boil three minutes, cool. Add remaining ingredients and beat or shake vigorously. Serve with any fruit salads or on greens, if you like a sweet dressing.

Whipped Cream Dressing

Preparation Time: 10 minutes

"Fine dressing for shredded lettuce, coleslaw, grated beets. May be used in fruit salad."

8 tbsp. sweet cream
2 tbsp. honey
2 tbsp. lemon juice
dash of paprika

Whip cream and honey together, slowly. Add lemon juice and paprika.

CRANBERRY-ALMOND RELISH

Yield: 3 cups

"Condiments can make a meal"

1 can (1 lb.) whole cranberries
2 tbsp. orange marmalade
3 tbsp. lemon juice
⅔ cup blanched almonds

Mix all ingredients. Chill and serve.

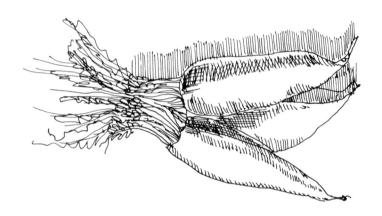

CARROT AND ONION RELISH

Serves: 6
Cooking Time: 45 minutes

"Cold cuts and this condiment!"

1 cup margarine
4 large carrots
4 medium onions
2 small cans (8 oz. each)
   Del Monte tomato sauce
1 cup water
1 tsp. sugar
¼ tsp. salt

Melt margarine in skillet. Slice carrots fine and long with potato peeler. Slice onions. Add carrots and onions to melted margarine in skillet. When carrots and onions are sautéed, add tomato sauce, water, sugar, and salt. Simmer for approximately 30 minutes. Can be served with any roasts, chicken, pork, etc. Delicious with cold cuts. Serve hot.

CENTURY-OLD RECIPE FOR MUSTARD PICKLES

Yield: 5 quarts
Cooking Time: 25 minutes

"Original family recipe! Wonderful for gift giving!"

    1 qt. cucumbers, peeled and cut in chunks
    3 green peppers, cut fine
    3 red peppers, cut fine*
    1 large cauliflower, broken into flowerettes
    1 qt. small cucumbers*
    1 qt. small white onions*
    1 cup celery, cut fine

*To simplify matters, substitute three small jars pimento for the red peppers, three jars (10 oz. each) gerkins for the small cucumbers, and three jars (12 oz. each) cocktail onions for the small white onions.

Put the above in a weak brine of one cup salt to two quarts water and let stand overnight. Then scald 15 minutes in brine and drain. Cook 10 minutes in mixture of:

    6 tbsp. dry mustard
    1 tbsp. tumeric
    1 tsp. celery seed
    2 cups sugar
    ¾ cup flour
    2 qt. white vinegar

Fill sterile jars and seal.

My Mother's Recipe for Bread and Butter Pickles

Yield: 3 quarts
Cooking Time: 20 minutes

"Another recipe handed down in my family."

1 gal. cucumbers, thinly sliced
1 tsp. powdered ammonium alum (purchase in drug store)
½ cup salt

Mix and let stand for three hours in large bowl filled with ice cubes. Drain. Mix:

5 cups sugar
½ tsp. ground cloves
1½ tsp. turmeric
2 tbsp. mustard seed
1 tsp. celery seed
3 cups white vinegar

Add cucumbers and put on medium fire — scald but do not boil. Fill sterile jars and seal.

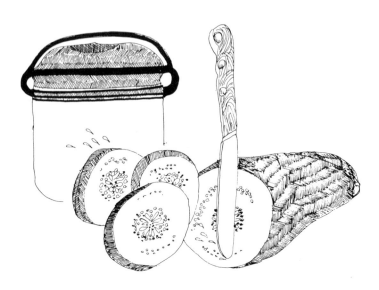

Words to the Wise:

1. Gelatin will mold more quickly in metal molds than in glass or plastic.

2. Oil mold ring lightly before pouring gelatin for easy unmolding.

3. For large molds decrease required liquid about ¼ cup for each 3 ounces of jello. The firmer consistency makes the mold less fragile and less likely to crack after unmolding.

4. Moisten top of gelatin mold as well as serving plate before un-molding so mold will slide more easily onto plate.

5. To double a recipe use two 3 ounce packages or one 6 ounce package of jello and twice the amounts of other ingredients except salt, vinegar, and lemon juice. 1½ times the amounts of these ingredients are sufficient.

Chilling Guide:

Slightly thickened ... 1 hour, 15 minutes .... may now add Dream Whip, sour cream etc.

Very thick .... 1 hour, 30 minutes .... may now add fruits or vegetables

Set but not firm ..... 2 hours .... add other layers

Firm .... 3 hours - individual mold }
4 hours - 1½ quart mold } unmold and
5 hours - 2 or 3 quart mold } serve

GEFILTE FISH MOLD

Serves: 12
Cooking Time: 15 minutes
Chill: 2 hours

"A most unusual dish."

2 packages lemon jello
2¾ cups water
½ cup fish juice
1 small jar (6 oz.) horseradish (white)
mayonnaise
1 jar gefilte fish (8 pieces)

Dissolve jello in all liquids. Add horseradish. Line fish mold with thin layer of mayonnaise. Place fish, side by side, in mold. Pour liquid over fish. Set in refrigerator. Serve cold, sliced.

BEET BORSCHT MOLD

Serves: 8
Cooking Time: 15 minutes

"Very unique."

2 packages lemon jello
1 cup boiling water
2½ cups beet borscht
    (jarred, with pieces)
4 tbsp. sour cream
cucumber, cut up (optional)
radishes, cut up (optional)
scallions, cut up (optional)

Dissolve jello with boiling water. Add beet borscht and sour cream. Beat with egg beater. Season to taste. Add cucumber, radishes, scallions, and mix. Pour into mold. Refrigerate until firm.

CUCUMBER RING

Serves: 8
Cooking Time: 45 minutes

"Nice change for a dinner salad."

Cucumber Trim Layer (Optional):

½ envelope unflavored
    gelatin (1½ tsp.)
1 tbsp. sugar
½ tsp. salt
¾ cup boiling water
2 tbsp. lemon juice
thin slices unpared cucumber

Thoroughly mix gelatin, sugar, and salt. Pour boiling water over and stir to dissolve sugar. Add lemon juice. Overlap cucumber slices in bottom of 6½ cup ring mold. Pour gelatin mixture over them. Chill till firm.

Cucumber Salad Layer:

1 envelope unflavored
    gelatin (1 tbsp.)
2 tbsp. sugar
¾ tsp. salt
⅔ cup boiling water
3 to 4 tbsp. lemon juice
6 medium cucumbers, pared
1 package (8 oz.) cream cheese
1 cup mayonnaise or salad
    dressing
¼ cup minced onion
¼ cup minced parsley

Thoroughly mix gelatin, sugar, and salt. Pour boiling water over and stir to dissolve sugar. Add lemon juice. Halve cucumbers, scrape out seeds, put through food chopper, using fine blade (measure two cups drained ground cucumber). Soften cream cheese; add cucumber, mayonnaise, onion, and parsley, mixing well. Stir in gelatin mixture. Pour over firm gelatin in mold. Unmold on greens.

TOMATO ASPIC

Serves: 10 - 14
Cooking Time: 20 minutes
Refrigerate: Overnight

"Perfect with meat. Use in place of salad."

2 cans tomato soup
3 packages (3 oz. each) cream
   cheese
2 tbsp. Knox gelatin
1 cup cold water
½ cup green pepper, diced
½ cup celery, diced
½ cup onion, diced
1 cup Hellman's mayonnaise

Heat soup. Mix in cream cheese. There can be tiny lumps. Dissolve gelatin in cold water; add gelatin and cold water to above mixture, let cool. Mix diced vegetables into mayonnaise and add to above. When very cool, grease ring mold and put in mixture. Refrigerate overnight.

COTTAGE CHEESE SALAD

Serves: 4

"Good for summer luncheon."

1 tbsp. unflavored gelatin
2½ tbsp. cold water
2½ tbsp. boiling water
2 cups cottage cheese
¼ cup mayonnaise
½ tsp. salt
¼ cup green pepper, diced
¼ cup celery, diced
¼ cup onion, minced
¼ cup cucumber, diced

Combine gelatin and cold water and let stand five minutes. Dissolve soaked gelatin in boiling water. Combine cottage cheese, mayonnaise, and salt. Combine cheese mixture with gelatin. Fold in remaining ingredients. Pour into mold and chill.

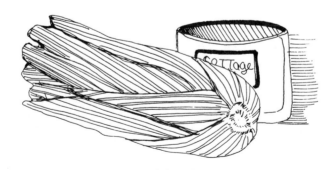

Apricot Mold

Serves: 8
Chill: 3 hours

"Sweet and delicious, but you can only buy Jello at A & P."

2 small packages apricot
  jello (A & P brand)
2 medium cans peeled whole
  apricots
6 tbsp. sour cream
2 cups juice from apricots

Prepare jello according to directions (do not add the extra water at end). Split apricots in half and remove pits. Line mold with apricot halves. Add apricot juice to jello. Pour mixture into mold, about $\frac{1}{2}$ inch to cover apricots, then place mold in refrigerator. Wait until jello is completely set. Leave remaining jello out. Mash remaining apricots, add sour cream and remaining jello, and beat until well blended. Pour into two quart mold. Let set. Unmold.

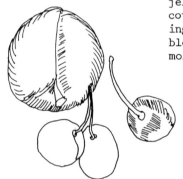

Bing Cherry Mold Dessert

Serves: 6 - 8

"Try serving this with whipped cream."

1 package cherry or black
  cherry jello
2 tbsp. sugar
dash of salt
1 cup boiling water
1 can (1 lb., 1 oz.) pitted
  dark sweet cherries
1 tbsp. lemon juice
1 package (3 oz.) cream cheese
  softened

Dissolve jello, sugar, and salt in boiling water. Drain cherries, measuring syrup; add water to make $\frac{3}{4}$ cup, if necessary. Add syrup and lemon juice to jello. Blend a little jello with the softened cream cheese. Chill remaining jello until very thick, about 1 hour, 30 minutes. Then whip until fluffy. Gradually add jello to cream cheese, blending with beater. Fold in cherries. Pour into 1 quart mold. Chill until firm. Unmold and serve.

Bing Cherry-Lime Salad

Serves: 16

2 packages cherry jello
1 can (15 oz.) pitted bing
   cherries
2 packages lime jello
¾ pt. sour cream
1 small can (8¼ oz.) crushed
   pineapple
½ cup walnuts

Make cherry jello according to directions. Add pitted bing cherries. Pour into large mold and let set. Prepare lime jello, but use only three cups water. When jello is dissolved, add sour cream, put into blender, just to mix. Add pineapple and nuts. Pour over cherry mixture and let harden.

Raspberry Fool Dessert

Serves: 8

"A double treat for raspberry fans."

2 packages raspberry jello
2 packages frozen raspberries,
   drained (save juice)
½ pt. heavy cream, unwhipped

Dissolve jello in one cup boiling water. Add raspberry liquid and enough water to make three cups. Let jello set for one hour. Add unwhipped cream and whip it together with jello. Add raspberries. Pour into sherbet glasses. Chill. Serve with additional whipped cream.

Peach Jello Mold

Serves: 8
Cooking Time: 20 minutes

"Heavenly, light."

1 large package peach jello
1 can (12 oz.) peach nectar
1 small can (8¾ oz.) peach
   halves or slices (reserve
   juice)
½ pt. sour cream
2 scant cups boiling water

Dissolve jello in hot water, add nectar and reserved peach liquid (not to exceed two cups). Place peach halves skin side down in greased ring mold. Add jello to cover. Allow to set in refrigerator while whipping sour cream. Spoon over jello. Allow to set 2-3 hours. Carefully ladle remaining jello over sour cream layer and set.

STRAWBERRY SOUR CREAM GELATIN MOLD WITH BANANAS

Serves: 10 - 12
Cooking Time: 20 minutes
Chill: 2 hours

"Fruity and good."

2 packages strawberry gelatin
1 cup boiling water
2 packages (10 oz.) strawberries
  with juices
1 can (1 lb., 4 oz.) crushed
  pineapple, drained
1 cup coarsely chopped nuts
3 medium bananas, mashed
1 pt. sour cream

Stir gelatin in water until dissolved. Add all at once: berries, pineapple, nuts, and bananas. Stir. Pour half in a dish or mold and let set in refrigerator. Then spread the sour cream over this layer. Pour remainder of mixture on top of sour cream. Let set and serve.

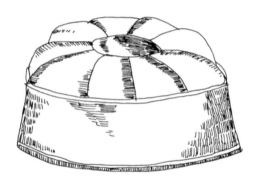

BAVARIAN MOLD

Serves: 8

"Peaches add something extra."

1 medium can (16 oz.) sliced
  peaches
1 large package raspberry jello
½ cup hot water
½ pt. heavy cream

Mash and drain peaches, reserve liquid. Dissolve jello with combination of half hot water and half peach liquid. Let jello thicken slightly. (Don't allow jello to harden too much, or it won't taste like a fluffy bavarian). Add peaches, mix through gently. Whip cream and gently fold in mixture. Pour in mold. Chill until set.

Orange-Sour Cream-Jello Mold

Serves: 16 - 20
Cooking Time: 20 minutes

"Perfect for a ladies' luncheon."

6 packages orange jello
4 cups boiling water
4 cups cold water
8 or 10 ice cubes
1 can (1 lb., 4 oz.) crushed
　pineapple
½ cup broken, shelled walnuts
4 heaping tbsp. sour cream
15 maraschino cherries,
　drained

Oil three-quart mold with hole in center. Turn upside down to drain excess oil. In very large bowl, stir jello in boiling water. Add cold water, mix thoroughly, then add ice cubes. When melted, put into refrigerator. When slightly jelled, remove from refrigerator and add all remaining ingredients at once. Stir thoroughly then pour into oiled mold.

Orange Sherbet Jello Mold

Serves: 10

2 packages orange jello
2 cups boiling water
1 qt. orange sherbet, melted
½ cup orange juice
1 small can (11 oz.) mandarin
　oranges, drained

Dissolve jello in boiling water. Let orange sherbet melt and add to jello and water. Mix in orange juice and mandarin oranges. Pour into mold and chill until firm.

Raspberry Sherbet Mold

Serves: 6 - 8
Cooking Time: 20 minutes
Chill: 6 hours

"A very different mold."

1 large package raspberry jello
2 cups water
1 can (#211) crushed pineapple,
　drained
10 maraschino cherries
1 pt. raspberry sherbet
½ cup juice from pineapple and
　cherries
crushed walnuts (optional)

Dissolve jello in two cups of boiling water. Add juice and softened sherbet. Beat until foamy. Add remaining ingredients; pour into mold. Refrigerate until firm.
Note: Lime jello and lemon-lime sherbet can be substituted.

JEWELED JELLO MOLD

Serves: 14 - 20

"Perfect for a light lunch."

5½ cups boiling water
1 package lime jello
1 package red jello
2 packages lemon jello
1 large can (20 oz.) crushed
   pineapple, reserving juice
1 pt. sour cream

Dissolve lime jello in 1¾ cups boiling water. Pour into ice tray. Dissolve red jello in 1¾ cups boiling water and pour into another ice tray. Refrigerate. Next day, dissolve lemon jello with two cups boiling water. Add juice of crushed pineapple to make three cups. Cool and set slightly. Add sour cream and crushed pineapple. Cut jello from ice trays into squares and fold into mixture. Pour into large mold. Refrigerate.

RED, WHITE, AND BLUE JELLO MOLD

Serves: 16 - 20

mayonnaise
3 packages raspberry jello
1 can (#2½) sliced peaches
1 can crushed pineapple
1 package lemon jello
1 cup sour cream
1 can blueberries (Muselman
   or White Rose)
¼ cup walnuts, chopped fine

Lightly grease a large mold pan with mayonnaise. Dissolve 1½ packages raspberry jello in one cup boiling water. Drain peaches and add juice to jello. Place peaches around bottom of mold. Pour in jello and put in refrigerator until firm.

Drain can of pineapple and heat juice in small sauce pan. Dissolve lemon jello and add enough hot water to make one cup. Let stand at room temperature at least 10 minutes. Blend in sour cream and add pineapple. Pour into mold. Let stand in refrigerator until very firm.

Dissolve 1½ packages raspberry jello in one cup boiling water. Add can of blueberries, juice, and chopped walnuts. Pour into mold and put in refrigerator until very firm. Make sure each layer is completely firm when next layer is poured on.

Rainbow Mold

Serves: 10 - 12

1 package red jello
1 package yellow jello
1 package green jello
1 package Dream Whip
1 can (20 oz.) crushed pineapple
1 pt. fresh strawberries, sliced
oil
hot water
cold water

Slightly oil a two-quart mold. Mix first layer of jello in mold, using one cup each hot water and cold water and sliced strawberries. Place in refrigerator to set. When hardened, prepare second jello layer separately and place in refrigerator until it wiggles. Fold in Dream Whip and add to mold. When firm, prepare third layer of jello adding drained crushed pineapple. Add to mold. Refrigerate until firm.

Jello Dessert

Serves: 10 - 12

3 small packages jello
  (raspberry, lemon, cherry)
3 cups hot water
1 cup peach juice
1 cup sour cream
1 small can (8¼ oz.)
  crushed pineapple
1 large can (21 oz.) blueberries
  (Comstock)

Mix together raspberry jello, one cup hot water and one cup peach juice. When it hardens, start on second box of lemon jello. Add one cup hot water, one cup sour cream and one small can crushed pineapple (which has been blended). Let set. Add the cherry jello, one cup hot water and one can blueberries. (Preferably made in a 13 x 7 x 9-inch loaf pan.)

CUBED JELLO CAKE

Serves: 16

3 packages jello (green, red, yellow)
1½ cups water (for each package)
1 envelope gelatin
¼ cup cold water
1 cup hot pineapple juice
1 pt. heavy cream
½ cup sugar
1 tsp. vanilla
graham cracker crumb crust

Place the three packages of jello in refrigerator in ice cube trays without separators to set. Dissolve one envelope gelatin in the cold water; add the hot pineapple juice and cool. Whip the heavy cream and sugar; fold in the vanilla. Fold in pineapple and gelatin mixture; fold in jello (one flavor at a time) which has been cubed. Pour mixture into spring form pan, which has been lined with graham cracker crust and refrigerate until ready to serve.

COFFEE CHIFFON MOLD

Serves: 8
Preparation Time: 35 minutes

"Coffee lovers don't miss this."

1½ cups milk
1 cup light cream
2 tbsp. instant coffee
5 eggs, separated
½ cup sugar
2 packages Knox gelatin
½ cup cold water
½ tsp. salt
⅔ cup sugar
1 pt. heavy cream (optional)

Scald the milk, light cream, and instant coffee in the top of a double boiler. Separate 5 eggs. Beat yolks until thick. Add ½ cup sugar. Add gradually to the hot coffee mixture. Cook until mixture coats spoon. Remove from heat. Stir in gelatin, softened in cold water. Chill until syrupy. Beat egg white with salt until stiff but not dry. Gradually add ⅔ cup sugar. Fold into coffee mix. Pour into two-quart mold. Chill well until set. Surround with puffs of whipped cream and chipped chocolate.

Breads

Raisin Bread

Serves: 6 - 8
Cooking Time: Approximately 2 hours

"Serve warm with cream cheese."

1 package yeast
¼ cup warm water
¾ cup milk
⅓ cup butter
6 tbsp. sugar
1 tsp. salt
3 cups flour
1 egg
1½ cups raisins
2 tbsp. butter
2 tsp. cinnamon
¼ tsp. nutmeg

Mix yeast in water. Heat milk, stir in butter, sugar, and salt and cool. Stir in yeast and beaten egg. Beat half the flour into mixture. Beat and cover and let rise, 1½ hours. Stir in rest of flour and raisins. Put dough into large bowl and let rise until doubled in bulk. Punch down and put on board. Roll out a little. Sprinkle butter, sugar, and cinnamon. Roll up and place in a large loaf pan, 9 x 5 x 3 inches. Let rise. Bake at 350° for 45-50 minutes.

Apple Sauce Nut Bread

Yield: 8 - 10 slices
Cooking Time: 50 - 60 minutes

"Almost like cake."

1 large orange
½ cup seedless raisins
1 cup applesauce
2 cups sifted all-purpose flour
2 tsp. baking powder
2 tsp. baking soda
½ tsp. salt
1 cup sugar
½ cup chopped nuts
1 egg
2 tbsp. melted butter or
  margarine

Squeeze juice of orange. Put rind through chopper with raisins. Add juice, rind, raisins to apple sauce. Sift flour, baking powder, baking soda, salt and sugar; add fruit mixture and nut meats. Mix thoroughly. Beat egg and melted butter or margarine. Pour into greased loaf pan, 8½ x 4½ x 2½ inches. Bake in moderate oven at 350° for 50 to 60 minutes. Cool on wire rack.

DATE-NUT BREAD

Serves: 6
Cooking Time: 1 hour

"Rich and chewy."

½ lb. dates, pitted
1 cup water, boiling
1 tsp. baking soda
1¾ cups flour
1 cup sugar
½ tsp. baking powder
1 tsp. salt
1 egg
½ cup walnuts, broken
   (optional)
1 tbsp. butter, melted

Cut pitted dates lengthwise into 4 or 5 pieces; soak in boiling water to which has been added baking soda; let cool. Pour remaining ingredients into a greased loaf pan. Bake mixture for about one hour at 325°.

ORANGE BREAD

Yield: 8 - 10 slices
Cooking Time: 40 - 50 minutes

2 cups flour
¼ tsp. salt
1 tsp. soda
1 cup sugar
1 tbsp. orange peel, grated
1 egg, beaten
½ cup Wesson oil
1 cup milk

Sift flour, salt, and soda into a mixing bowl; stir in sugar and orange peel. Combine eggs, Wesson oil, and milk; add all at once to flour mixture. Stir until well mixed. Pour into greased 9 x 5 x 3-inch pan. Bake at 325° approximately 40-50 minutes, or until loaf tests done.

BANANA BREAD

Serves: 8 - 10
Cooking Time: 1 hour

"Bread in the round."

¼ lb. butter, room
   temperature
1 cup sugar
3 large bananas
2 eggs
2 cups all-purpose flour
pinch of salt
1 tsp. baking soda
½ cup shelled walnuts
   (optional)

Preheat oven to 350°. Grease and flour two 32-ounce juice cans. Beat butter and sugar until creamy and set aside. Mash bananas (or put through ricer). Add eggs, flour, salt, and baking soda to butter and sugar mixture and beat at medium speed. Add bananas and beat at slow speed. Fold in nuts. Pour batter into prepared cans and bake 45 to 60 minutes. Test with tester.

BANANA QUICK BREAD

Serves: 8 - 10
Cooking Time: 60 - 70 minutes

"Can be stored for a long time, like fruit cake."

1¾ cups sifted flour
2¾ tsp. double-acting baking
   powder
½ tsp. salt
½ cup chopped nuts
⅓ cup shortening
⅔ cup sugar
2 eggs
1 cup mashed ripe bananas
1 cup mixed candied fruits and
   peels
¼ cup raisins

Blend together in bowl: flour, baking powder, salt, and chopped nuts. Cream shortening, add sugar, eggs, flour mixture and bananas and fold in fruits and raisins into a 4½ x 8½ x 3-inch loaf pan (Grease bottom only). Bake at 350° for 60 to 70 minutes.

Irish Soda Bread

Serves: 6 - 8
Cooking Time: 45 minutes

"Soft inside, crunchy outside."

3 cups flour
1 tsp. salt
¼ cup sugar
1 tsp. baking soda
2 tsp. baking powder
¼ lb. butter, melted
3 tbsp. caraway seeds
¾ cup raisins
1 egg
¾ cup buttermilk

Mix flour, salt, sugar, baking soda, and baking powder. Blend in melted butter, adding caraway seeds and raisins. Break egg into a separate dish and add ½ cup buttermilk, mix with fork. Make a well in the middle of the flour mixture. Add egg and buttermilk. Mix. Flour hands and knead lightly. Bake on a greased and floured cookie tin. Brush milk on top. Make an X on top. Bake at 350° about 45 minutes.

My Mother's Challah

(SABBATH TWIST)

Yield: 1 large twist
Cooking Time: 15 minutes - 400°
45 minutes - 350°

4 cups flour
1 tsp. salt
1 cake yeast
2 tsp. sugar
1⅛ cups lukewarm water
2 eggs
2 tbsp. oil
1 egg yolk
poppy seeds

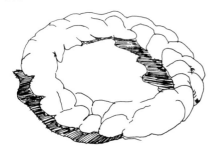

Sift three cups of flour and salt into large bowl. Make a well, break up yeast and place in center of well. Sprinkle sugar over yeast and add one cup of water. Let stand ½ hour. Add eggs, oil, remaining eighth cup water and one cup flour. Mix well. Let stand in warm place (covered), about two hours. Divide dough into three parts. Knead each one until very smooth and satiny. Roll out each about 1½ inches thick. Twist into braid. Fasten ends well. Place in greased bread pan or cookie sheet. Let stand ½ hour. Brush with beaten egg yolk and sprinkle with poppy seeds. Bake 15 minutes at 400° then 45 minutes at 350°.

Honey White Bread

Yield: 2 loaves
Cooking Time: 30 - 35 minutes

"They don't make it like this in the bakeries. It is always a treat to have homemade bread."

¼ cup very warm water
butter or margarine
1½ cups evaporated milk
2 heaping tbsp. honey
3 tbsp. oil
1 tbsp. salt
6 cups unbleached white flour
2 tbsp. wheat germ (optional)
1 package dry yeast

In small bowl, mix yeast and warm water. Set aside. Heat the milk to scalding. In large bowl, mix honey, oil, salt, milk (cool until luke warm). Add yeast mix. Add flour (one cup at a time), mixing after each addition, up to five cups. (Add wheat germ.) Add sixth cup by kneading in (only until dough feels smooth and looks satiny), about eight minutes. Oil bowl and place dough in and cover with cloth. Let rise two hours. Punch down dough and cover, letting it rise ½ hour. Shape into loaves and place in two well-greased loaf pans. Brush top with butter or margarine. Cover and let rise for 1½ hours. Bake in preheated 350° oven for 30-35 minutes.

Baking Powder Biscuits

Yield: 12
Cooking Time: 12 - 15 minutes

"Good for Sunday morning breakfast."

2 cups sifted flour
1 tsp. salt
3 tsp. baking powder
⅓ cup Crisco
¾ cup milk

Mix dry ingredients. Cut in Crisco, mix well. Add milk and mix well. Knead lightly. Roll out and cut. Bake at 425° for 12-15 minutes.

POPOVERS

Serves: 8
Cooking Time: 40 minutes

"Complements roast beef or any other beef meal."

1 cup flour
½ tsp. salt
2 eggs
1 cup milk
1 tbsp. melted butter or oil

Preheat oven to 425°. Grease six to eight popover or muffin pans. Sift flour into a bowl, add salt, eggs, milk, and melted butter or oil. Beat with a rotary beater or wooden spoon until the mixture is very smooth. Pour batter into pans until they are ⅔ full. Bake 40 minutes or until well puffed and golden. Pierce during last five minutes of baking to allow steam to escape.

PHILADELPHIA CINNAMON BUNS

Yield: 3 - 4 dozen
Cooking Time: 20 minutes

1 batch dough for
   Refrigerator Rolls, see
   page 223
½ cup butter
1 cup brown sugar
2 tsp. cinnamon

Use the recipe for Refrigerator Rolls. Turn the dough out on a well-floured, cloth-covered board. Roll into a rectangle, 12 x 9 inches. Spread with butter, sprinkle with cinnamon and brown sugar—one teaspoon cinnamon to ½ cup brown sugar. Beginning at the wide side, roll up. Pinch edge into a roll. Cut into 12 pieces. Place in a greased 9-inch square pan, the bottom of which has been covered with ¼ cup of melted butter and ½ cup of brown sugar. Let rise in a warm place until double in bulk, about one hour. Heat oven to 400°. Bake for 20 minutes. Turn upside down on the plate immediately.

CINNAMON BUNS

Serves: Approximately 12
Cooking Time: 25 minutes

¼ lb. butter
4 tbsp sugar
2 cups flour
½ tsp. baking powder
½ tsp. baking soda
salt
1 cup sour cream
2 oz. butter, melted
1 tsp. cinnamon
2 tbsp. sugar
4 oz. nuts, chopped

Cream ¼ pound butter, sugar. Add flour, baking powder, baking soda, salt, and sour cream. Roll out. Sprinkle melted butter, cinnamon, sugar, nuts on top. Roll up and cut in 1½-inch slices, put cut side down in buttered muffin pans. Bake in 350° oven for 15 minutes, brush with milk and put back in oven for 10 minutes more.

SCOTCH SHORTBREAD

Yield: 2 loaves
Cooking Time: 1 hour

"Nonrising bread similar to rye bread in texture."

5 cups flour
1 cup superfine sugar
½ lb. butter
½ lb. margarine
2 tbsp. shortening

Knead ingredients together on board. When dough forms, shape into two pieces. Bake one hour at 350°.

ONION PLETZL

Yield: 2 boards or 2 dozen rolls

"This recipe will produce either onion rolls or onion board. Choose your fancy. To make an onion board, merely roll out dough into a square and sprinkle onion and poppy seeds on top."

¾ cup oil
4 eggs
4 cups flour
1 tsp. salt
½ tsp. pepper
4 full tbsp. poppy seeds
3 tsp. baking powder
2 tbsp. sugar
½ cup cold water
3 large onions, chopped

Beat eggs, add oil and rest of ingredients. Sauté onions in some oil until soft. Add onions. Knead and make rolls about 1½ inches in width and cut slices about one inch. Bake on a greased cookie sheet at 350°.

REFRIGERATOR ROLLS

Yield: 3 - 4 dozen
Cooking Time: 12 - 15 minutes

"Done in three stages over the period of a day."

1 cup boiling water
1 cup shortening (butter,
    Spry or oleo)
$\frac{2}{3}$ cup sugar
1$\frac{1}{2}$ tsp. salt
2 eggs, beaten
2 packages dried yeast
1 cup cold water
6 cups unsifted flour

Pour boiling water over shortening, sugar, and salt. Blend and cool. Add eggs. Let yeast stand in cold water for five minutes, then stir and add to mixture. Add flour, blend well, cover, and place in refrigerator for at least four hours. Dough must be in large bowl as it rises. It will keep a week or ten days. About three hours before using, roll the dough in desired shapes, using enough flour to make them easy to handle. Place in greased pans and allow them to rise at room temperature for about two hours, or until double in bulk. Bake in a hot oven, 425° for 12 to 15 minutes.

GARLIC TWISTS

Yield: 120
Cooking Time: 7 - 8 minutes
Freeze: Overnight

"Lengthy process, but good results."

3 packages Ballard or
    Pillsbury biscuits
    (country style)
1 cup salad oil
1 tbsp. Parmesan cheese
2 tbsp. oregano
1$\frac{1}{2}$ tbsp. garlic powder
2 tbsp. parsley flakes
salt
pepper

Cut one package of biscuits at a time into quarters. Roll with fingers into long thin pieces and tie in a knot. Bake on ungreased cookie sheet in preheated 450° oven until lightly tanned (7-8 minutes). Mix all other ingredients in large bowl and let set. When biscuits cool, toss in above mixture. (Note: Ingredients settle to bottom; therefore, spoon over biscuits.) Remove biscuits with slotted spoon. Drain on paper towel and then freeze. Reheat before serving.

Desserts

CHERRIES IN THE SNOW

Serves: 8 - 10
Chill: 2 - 4 hours

"A great dessert!"

1 large can (1 lb., 14 oz.)
    fruit cocktail, drained
1 small can (8 oz.) crushed
    pineapple, drained
1 pt. sour cream
small bag (10½ oz.) miniature
    marshmallows
small bag (4 oz.) crushed
    walnuts
maraschino cherries

Mix all ingredients in serving dish. Top with maraschino cherries and chill in refrigerator before serving.

RASPBERRY CHERRY DELIGHT

Serves: 4 - 6

"Nice summer dessert."

1 pt. raspberry sherbet,
    slightly softened
1 can (1 lb.) dark, sweet,
    pitted cherries, drained
2 tbsp. brandy (optional)

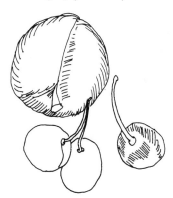

Soften sherbet slightly; drain syrup from cherries, reserving ½ cup. Add brandy to syrup, if desired. Layer sherbet and cherries in 4 - 6 parfait glasses. Spoon syrup mixture over each and serve at once. <u>Note</u>: To flame, heat 90-proof brandy, add to dessert, and ignite.

FRESH PEACH DESSERT

Serves: 6 - 8
Cooking Time: 3 - 5 minutes

"Perfect ending to a meal."

4 cups fresh peaches (fresh blueberries or seedless white grapes may be substituted), sliced
2 tbsp. lemon juice
2 tsp. sugar
1 pt. sour cream
¼ cup brown sugar

Place fruit in a 10-inch Pyrex pie plate. Sprinkle with lemon juice and sugar. Frost with sour cream, completely covering fruit. Cover sour cream with brown sugar. Put under broiler, 6 inches from heat. Cook until the brown sugar melts. Chill. Draw liquid before serving.

FRUIT CUP

Serves: 10 - 12

"Nice choice of fruits for an old standby."

1 melon
2 slices pineapple, ½-inch thick
3 oranges
1 package (10 oz.) frozen sliced strawberries
2 large bananas
4 fresh or canned peaches
1 small can apricot nectar

Add any other fruits in season (but never apples or grapefruit). Cut all fruits in uniform size pieces, except pineapple. This should be shredded or cut in slivers.

AMBROSIA

Serves: 7 - 10
Cooking Time: 15 minutes

2 pt. sour cream
2 cans (11 oz.) mandarin oranges, sliced
½ package (10½ oz.) miniature marshmallows
1 can (3½ oz.) shredded coconut

Mix all ingredients together. Refrigerate before serving in order to heighten flavor.

FRESH FRUITS IN GINGER SAUCE

Serves: 6 - 8
Cooking Time: 30 minutes
Chill: At least 2 hours

"Great light dessert after a heavy meal. Looks pretty too!"

1 small pineapple
½ lb. seedless green grapes
1 pt. strawberries
2 tbsp. sugar
1 cup fresh orange juice
⅓ cup sugar
1 tbsp. lemon juice
2 tbsp. dark rum
1 tbsp. minced crystallized
   ginger

Peel, quarter, and core the pine-apple. Cut each quarter in half lengthwise. Cut into very thin fan-shaped slices. ·Slice the grapes in half lengthwise and add to the pineapple. Gently rinse the strawberries, remove the hulls, and slice in half. Put the berries in a small separate bowl, sprinkle with two table-spoons of sugar and chill. In a small sauce pan, mix the orange juice with ⅓ cup of sugar and lemon juice. Bring to a boil, lower the heat and simmer for 20 minutes. Remove from heat, stir in the rum and ginger. Add the sauce to the pineapple and grapes. Chill. Add the strawberries and their juice just before serving.

FRUIT COMPOTE

Serves: 16 - 20
Cooking Time: 30 minutes

"Serve hot or cold."

2 boxes (12 oz. each) pitted
   prunes
walnuts, shelled
1 can (29 oz.) fruit for salad
1 can (11 oz.) mandarin oranges
1 can (20 oz.) pineapple chunks
1 can (21 oz.) cherry pie
   filling
1 package (11 oz.) dried
   apricots
¾ cup apricot brandy

Stuff walnuts in prunes. Drain fruit for salad and mandarin oranges. Combine all ingredi-ents; add brandy. Put in uncov-ered casserole and bake thirty minutes at 350°.

SWEET AND SOUR STEWED FRUIT

Yield: 4 pints
Cooking Time: 3 hours

"Always on hand — use as you need it."

2 grapefruit
1 lemon
1½ qt. water
1 large can (29 oz.) Alberta
  peaches
1 cup yellow raisins
1 cup dark raisins
1 cup brown sugar
few pinches salt

Scrub grapefruit and lemon thoroughly. Cut up into ½-inch squares after removing all seeds. Boil water and immerse fruit. Open can of peaches. Add peaches and yellow and dark raisins. Boil very slowly for two hours, then add brown sugar and salt. Boil another hour, slowly. Cool and put in jars. Refrigerate.

HOT FRUIT COMPOTE

Serves: 8
Cooking Time: 30 minutes

"Serve as a side dish with meats also."

12 macaroons, crumbled, stale,
  and dry
4 cups canned fruit (peaches,
  pears, apricots, pineapple,
  bing cherries — apricots
  should definitely be
  included — even if you omit
  one of the other fruits),
  drained
½ cup almonds, slivered and
  toasted
¼ cup brown sugar
½ cup sherry
¼ cup butter or margarine,
  melted

Grease a 2½ - quart casserole. Cover the bottom with macaroon crumbs. Alternate fruit and macaroons in layers, ending with macaroons on top. Sprinkle with almonds, sugar, and sherry. Bake at 350° for 30 minutes. Add melted butter and serve hot. May be used as a food accompaniment or as a dessert.

FRUIT DESSERT FOR HEALTH AND PLEASURE

Serves: 8
Cooking Time: 45 minutes

gingersnaps
3 bananas
2 cups apple sauce
1 cup frozen orange juice
   concentrate, slightly
   diluted
margarine
vanilla ice cream (optional)
diet whipped cream (optional)

Grease a 9-inch deep-dish pie plate. Place gingersnaps flat at cover bottom and halved around the rim, circled part standing up. Slice three bananas evenly to cover crackers. Pour over this apple sauce, moisten with orange juice. Dot top of mixture with margarine. Bake slowly for 3/4 hour at 325°, or until brown and adhering to the sides. Serve hot with dollop of vanilla ice cream or whipped cream. Slice in wedges, enjoy yourself, and have no qualms about the ingredients.

WHIPPED CREAM SALAD OR DESSERT

Serves: 6 - 8
Chill: 1 hour

1/2 pt. heavy cream, whipped
1 large banana, sliced
10-12 dates, halved
1/2 - 3/4 cup miniature marshmallows (or large, quartered)
1/4 - 1/2 cup walnuts
1 medium apple, diced

Whip cream, adding sugar to taste. Stir in other ingredients and mix. Chill and serve.

CHERRY PUDDING

Serves: 4 - 6
Cooking Time: 15 minutes

"Great dessert."

½ cup butter, room temperature
⅔ cup sugar
4 eggs
¾ cup almonds, ground
1 tsp. lemon peel, grated
1 cup zwieback, crushed finely
   with rolling pin
2 cups cream
2 cups black bing cherries,
   drained and pitted

Cream butter and sugar together until light and lemon colored. Separate eggs, reserving whites, and add yolks to the butter-sugar mixture. Add almonds, grated lemon, zwieback crumbs, and one cup of cream, mixing well. Beat egg whites until they peak and fold into batter. Pour half of batter into well-buttered oven-proof casserole (approximately 8 inches in diameter) and bake at 350° for 15 minutes. Remove from oven and cover pudding with cherries. Pour over the remaining batter and continue baking for 20 minutes or until firm. Serve with remaining cream.

APPLE PUDDING

Serves: 6 - 8
Cooking Time: 1 hour

"We love this one. Very special on holidays."

6 eggs, separated
2½ to 3 lb. MacIntosh apples,
   sliced
juice of 1 lemon
1⅓ cups sugar
pinch salt
⅔ cup matzo meal
¼ cup oil
honey
sugar
cinnamon
nuts, chopped

Beat egg whites until stiff. Coat apple slices with lemon juice. Beat egg yolks, salt, sugar until lemon colored. Add matzo meal, oil, and apples. Add beaten egg whites. Pour into greased Pyrex baking dish, drizzle with honey and top with mixture of sugar, cinnamon, and nuts. Bake at 350° for 1 hour.

Fancy and Easy Dessert

Serves: 4

1 box (4½ oz.) Jello Soft
  Swirl, vanilla
Tia Maria, crème de cacoa, or
  your favorite cognac or
  brandy

Prepare soft swirl according to package directions. Chill in champagne glasses. Before serving, add Tia Maria, crème de cacoa or your favorite cognac or brandy.

Apple Bread Pudding

Serves: 4 - 6
Cooking Time: 45 minutes

"The kids will love this."

5 eggs
1½ cans (14½ oz.)
  evaporated milk
3 cups milk
½ cup sugar
1 tsp. vanilla
5 slices white bread, cut in
  cubes
3 large MacIntosh apples,
  peeled and cut into small
  pieces
3 tbsp. butter

Beat eggs, add evaporated milk, milk, sugar, vanilla, bread cubes, and apples. Mix well. Turn into a shallow baking dish, well buttered. Mix again. Dot with butter and bake at 450° for 45 minutes or when silver knife inserted in middle comes out clean.

Rice Pudding

Serves: 6 - 8
Cooking Time: 1 hour

¾ cup rice
4 eggs
½ cup sugar
1 qt. milk
1 tsp. vanilla

Cook rice, set aside. Mix eggs and sugar, add milk, vanilla, and rice. Stir all together. Pour into casserole. Set casserole in a shallow pan of water and bake in 350° oven for one hour.

RICE PUDDING LIKE CAKE

Serves: 10 - 12
Cooking Time: 30 minutes

"Here's a place for that leftover rice."

butter
6 eggs, beaten
½ pt. sour cream
2 cups cooked rice
2 cups milk
1 cup sugar
cinnamon

Grease a 9 x 13 x 2-inch casserole with butter. Combine ingredients and bake at 350° for 30 minutes.

BREAD PUDDING

Serves: 10
Cooking Time: 1 hour

"Basic and Easy."

8 eggs
1 cup sugar
1 qt. milk
1 tsp. vanilla
5-6 slices white bread, cubed
raisins (optional)
cinnamon

Preheat oven to 350°. Using egg beater, beat eggs until foamy and creamy yellow. Add sugar and beat until sugar is dissolved. Add milk, vanilla, and mix. Fold in cubed bread to above mixture. Add raisins. Pour into 2½-quart, deep baking dish. Sprinkle top with cinnamon. Set dish in another pan containing water, Bake 45 minutes to one hour. To test when pudding is done, insert knife in center. Knife must be clean when withdrawn. May be served with hard sauce or fresh strawberries and whipped cream or garnish to taste.

LEMON MOUSSE

Serves: 4 - 5

"Delightfully light after a heavy meal."

1 cup heavy cream
1 envelope unflavored gelatin
¼ cup water
4 eggs, separated
⅔ cup sugar
¼ cup lemon juice
2 tbsp. lemon rind

Beat cream until stiff and refrigerate. Soften gelatin in water over hot water. Beat egg yolks, add sugar gradually, and beat until frothy. Beat whites until stiff and set aside. Add lemon juice and rind and gelatin to yolks. Fold in egg whites and beaten cream. Garnish with lemon slices, mint, strawberries, or whipped cream.

MOCHA MOUSSE

Serves: 6
Refrigerate: 1 hour or more

"Coffee adds a new touch."

1 package (6 oz.) semisweet
   chocolate
5 tbsp. boiling water or
   liquid coffee
4 eggs, separated
2 tbsp dark rum

Put semisweet chocolate into blender with the water or coffee. Cover and blend at high speed for 10 seconds, or until smooth. To this add four egg yolks and then the rum. Cover and blend five seconds, or until smooth. Beat egg whites until stiff and fold chocolate mixture into it. Put into serving dishes and chill in refrigerator at least one hour.

CHOCOLATE MOUSSE

Serves: 5
Cooking Time: 15 minutes

"Just an old favorite."

1 package (6 oz.) Nestle's
   semisweet chocolate bits
4 eggs, separated
2 tbsp. cognac
dash salt

Melt chocolate in top of double boiler. After chocolate is melted add egg yolks and then cognac. Blend well. Beat egg whites until stiff, not dry, put in dash of salt. Fold into chocolate mixture. Refrigerate, covered, until ready to serve. Serve with whipped cream.

CHOCOLATE SOUFFLÉ

Serves: 4 - 5
Cooking Time: 25 - 35 minutes

"This French favorite has won a place in Americans' hearts."

1 tsp. butter
1 tbsp. sugar, for soufflé
   dish
4 tbsp. sugar
4 tbsp. flour
1/8 tsp. salt
1 cup milk
4 egg yolks
4 oz. sweet or semisweet
   chocolate, melted
6 egg whites

Butter and sugar a one-quart soufflé dish, tie a wax paper collar around it. Preheat oven to 375°. Put sugar, flour, and salt in heavy sauce pan. Add milk gradually to make a smooth mixture. Put mixture on low flame to cook. Bring to a boil stirring constantly. When sauce thickens, remove from flame. Beat egg yolks with a whisk until light in color. Add sauce to yolks gradually and stir briskly. Add melted chocolate. Up to this point, soufflé can be done ·well in advance. Forty minutes before serving time, beat egg whites until stiff but not dry. Fold half of whites into chocolate mixture. Finish by folding in remainder of whites. (Do not overfold.) Pour mixture into soufflé dish and bake on middle rack of oven for 35 minutes for dry soufflé, 30 minutes for a slightly moist one, and 25 minutes for a moist soufflé. Serve with whipped cream.

UNCOOKED CHOCOLATE CREAM

Serves: 6 - 8

"This is good."

6 oz. sweet or bittersweet
   chocolate
6 tbsp. water
2 tsp. vanilla
2 cups heavy cream
1 cup chopped nuts
ladyfingers
rum

Place chocolate and water into sauce pan and stir over low heat until smooth. Cool chocolate. Add vanilla. Whip cream until stiff. Fold in chocolate mixture and nuts. Line a bowl with the ladyfingers and generously sprinkle with rum. Fill bowl with cream.

ULTRASMOOTH CHOCOLATE FUDGE

Yield: 32 pieces
Cooking Time: 25 minutes

1 package (12 oz.) semisweet
   chocolate bits
2 tbsp. butter
1 can condensed milk
$\frac{1}{3}$ cup marshmallow fluff
$\frac{1}{2}$ cup miniature marshmallows
$\frac{1}{2}$ cup nuts, chopped

Melt chocolate bits and butter in top of double boiler. Add condensed milk and cook. Stir constantly for four minutes. Remove from heat. Add marshmallow fluff and stir well. Add miniature marshmallows and nuts. Pour into buttered, 8-inch square pan. Chill well before serving. Fudge must be kept in refrigerator or it will soften.

APRICOT BAVARIAN CREAM

Serves: 8
Chill: 3 hours

"Perfect ending for a heavy meal."

1 package apricot jello
   (A & P brand)
1 can (16 oz.) apricot halves,
   drained and reserve syrup
1 cup reserved apricot syrup
$\frac{1}{4}$ tsp. almond extract
1 cup heavy cream
2 tbsp. brandy
1 cup hot water

Dissolve gelatin in hot water and add apricot syrup. Crush apricot halves to make one cup. Chill gelatin until cold and syrupy. Add apricots and almond extract. Whip cream until it peaks. Fold into gelatin mixture. Chill until almost firm. Stir in brandy. Spoon into parfait or champagne glasses. Chill until firm.

TRIFLE

Serves: 8

"Very impressive and good."

2 packages ladyfingers
1 jar (12 oz.) apricot preserves
sherry, to taste
1 package each (10 oz.) frozen
    raspberries, blueberries,
    strawberries, all drained
1 can (11 oz.) mandarin oranges,
    drained
1 can (20 oz.) crushed pine-
    apple, drained
1 container prepared vanilla
    pudding
whipped cream
fresh strawberries (optional)

Line a pretty and large bowl with ladyfinger sandwiches (made by buttering ladyfinger halves with apricot preserves). Drizzle some sherry over. Add a layer of mixed fruit. Next add layer of pudding then a layer of ladyfinger sandwiches, more sherry, fruit, pudding, etc., ending with ladyfinger sandwiches and sherry. Strategically place large fresh strawberries and decorate with whipped cream.

BRULÉE

Serves: 6 - 8
Preparation Time: 20 minutes
Chill: 2 hours

"Quick way to an elegant dessert."

1 package (8 oz.) cream
    cheese, softened
1 cup heavy cream, whipped
½ cup nuts, chopped
1½ cups crushed pineapple,
    drained (#2 can or 1 lb.,
    4 oz.)
1 tsp. fresh ground nutmeg
1½ cups brown sugar, firmly
    packed

Beat softened cream cheese with whipped cream. Stir in nuts, drained pineapple, and nutmeg. Put in pan or Pyrex dish. Sift sugar over entire surface. Broil about 5 inches below heat until sugar melts and begins to bubble. Cool about three minutes, then put into refrigerator for one to two hours. Tap crust to break sugar and serve.

Baked Alaska

Serves: 12
Cooking Time: 1 hour

"For spectacular finale, ignite with flaming brandy and elegantly slice and serve at the table!"

½ cup nuts, chopped
2 squares unsweetened chocolate
¼ lb. butter, melted
1⅔ cups sugar
2 eggs
1 tsp. vanilla
¾ cup flour
½ tsp. baking powder
1 qt. chocolate ice cream, slightly softened
1 qt. coffee ice cream, slightly softened
5 egg whites, room temperature

Note: For a speedy Alaska, use prepared brownie mix. Ice cream and cake may be prepared, put together and kept in freezer for several weeks. However, meringue must be prepared the day of serving. It may be prepared 6-8 hours before serving, spread over cake and ice cream and then returned to freezer.

Prepare 9-inch baking pan and 2-quart bowl, 7 to 8-inches wide. Chop nuts. Take chocolate ice cream from freezer to soften.

Melt together chocolate and butter. Combine in mixer one cup sugar, eggs, and vanilla. Add melted chocolate and butter. Gradually add to moist ingredients the flour and baking powder. Add chopped nuts to batter. Bake in 9-inch pan at 325° for 30-35 minutes. Cool on cake rack. Then transfer to oven-proof cake plate or board.

Spread a one-inch layer of softened chocolate ice cream over bottom and sides of bowl. Place mold in freezer and remove coffee ice cream to soften. Fill center of mold with coffee ice cream. Cover with foil. Press with hands to smooth top. Freeze firm. When firm, remove foil and invert over cake.

Have egg whites at room temperature. Beat egg whites stiff, gradually adding ⅔ cup sugar, until peaks form. Quickly cover cake and ice cream with meringue, swirling it in peaks. Be sure to spread plenty of meringue around the edge where ice cream and cake meet.

Remove from freezer about ½ hour before serving. Place on lowest rack in hot oven (500°) and bake about 3 minutes or until meringue is browned. Let stand a few minutes for easier cutting. Cut in wedge-shaped slices.

CRÈME CARAMEL

(CARAMEL CUSTARD)

Serves: 8 - 10
Cooking Time: 1 to 1½ hours

"Careful cooking produces excellent results."

1½ cups sugar
1 qt. milk
6 eggs
¼ tsp. salt
2 tsp. vanilla
¼ cup slivered almonds
 (optional)

Caramelize one cup sugar in heavy pan over low flame, stirring constantly, until golden brown. Don't let sugar get too dark, as it will become bitter. Pour into warm, two-quart mold, coating all sides. Scald milk and cool a little. Beat eggs. Add ½ cup sugar, salt, and vanilla to eggs, then slowly add milk. Pour into mold. Bake in pan of hot water in 325° oven 1 to 1½ hours, until knife comes out clean. Cool, then refrigerate a few hours before serving. Invert on platter and unmold. Spoon syrup that runs on the platter back over custard. Sprinkle over with slivered almonds.

WATERMELON SHERBET

Serves: 4
Freeze: 4 hours

"Great for summertime entertaining."

1 envelope unflavored gelatin
¼ cup cold water
4 cups watermelon, diced
¾ cup sugar
2 tbsp. lemon juice
2 or 3 drops red food coloring
1 drop yellow food coloring
2 egg whites

Soften gelatin in cold water and dissolve over hot water. Put one cup of melon in blender with sugar, lemon juice; add dissolved gelatin and coloring; blend until smooth. Add rest of melon. Blend. Beat egg whites very stiff. Fold into melon mixture. Put in freezer and stir two or three times while freezing.

STRAWBERRY ICE CREAM

Serves: 6 - 8
Freeze: 4 - 5 hours

1 cup sugar
¼ cup orange juice
1 tbsp. lemon juice
¾ cup water
2 qt. strawberries
1 cup heavy cream

Stir the sugar, orange juice, lemon juice, and water together, stirring steadily to a boil, then cook until syrupy. Allow to cool. Blend the berries in an electric blender or put through a sieve. Mix the berries with the cool syrup. Whip the cream and fold in. Pour into two dry ice trays or into a mold. Cover. Place in freezer for 4-5 hours or until firm.

BUTTER NUT ICE CREAM SAUCE

Yield: 1 cup

¾ cup dark corn syrup
¼ cup sugar
¼ tsp. salt
¼ cup peanut butter
2 tbsp. hot water

Mix syrup, sugar, and salt together. Boil gently until candy thermometer registers 232°, or mixture forms a very soft ball when tested in cold water. Remove from heat. Stir in the peanut butter and water. Continue to stir until mixture is smooth.

CHOCOLATE SAUCE

"The sauce is out of this world. Use it anywhere."

4 oz. German sweet chocolate
4 oz. bitter chocolate
½ pt. heavy cream
1 cup sugar

Cook all ingredients in a double boiler until thick, using only half of cream to start. Add balance of cream to achieve pouring consistency.

Words To The Wise About Baking:

1. Cake pans are placed on racks as near the center of the oven as possible. Pans should not touch each other or the sides of the oven.

2. Cake is done when it is lightly browned, fully risen, and begins to shrink slightly from the edge of the pan.

3. Test doneness by pressing finger lightly on top of the cake. If it springs back not leaving an impression, the cake is done.

4. One teaspoon of flavoring extract added to cake mixes improves their flavor.

5. Cakes baked in ungreased pans should be cooled in the pan upside down before unmolding. Cakes baked in greased pans should be allowed to cool for a few minutes before removal.

6. An artist's metal spatula, small and flexible, is especially useful for frosting cakes.

7. If using Pyrex pans, lower oven temperature 25°.

But It Happened Anyway:

DISASTER	BUTTER CAKES	SPONGE CAKES
too dry	too little butter too little liquid too little sugar overbeaten egg whites overbaked overmixed	overbeaten egg whites too much flour too much sugar overbaked oven temperature too low
too coarse	improperly combined ingredients insufficient mixing too much sugar too much leavening wrong oven temperature	underbeaten eggs too little mixing oven too hot
heavy	too much mixing lack of leavening too much butter too much sugar underbaked	loss of air in mixing
sticky crust	too much sugar damp flour underbaked	too much sugar damp flour underbaked
cracked crust	oven too hot batter too stiff wrong size pan	batter too stiff overbeaten eggs oven too hot

Apple Cake

Serves: 8 - 10
Cooking Time: 1¼ to 1½ hours

"Layered apple cake. May be served with a side dish of sour cream."

2 cups sugar
1 cup salad oil
4 eggs
3 cups flour
1 tsp. salt
3 tsp. baking powder
¼ cup orange juice
2½ tsp. vanilla
4-6 apples, peeled and sliced
5 tbsp. sugar
2 tsp. cinnamon

Beat together until smooth and thick the two cups sugar, oil, eggs, flour, salt, baking powder, juice, and vanilla. Grease tube pan. Put layer of batter, then layer of apples, layer of sugar/cinnamon mixture. · Make about two layers and end with sugar mixture. Bake at 350° for 1¼ to 1½ hours. Cool in pan until lukewarm.

Apple Cake

Serves: 6
Cooking Time: 35 minutes

"Apples on the bottom."

3 lb. apples (MacIntosh)
½ cup sugar
1 tsp. cinnamon
1 egg
1 cup sugar
1 cup sifted flour
½ cup butter, melted
2 tbsp. lemon juice

Cut, core, and peel apples into quarters. Lay in pan, 8 x 8 inches. Spread ½ cup sugar, which has been mixed with the cinnamon, on apples. In separate bowl beat egg well. Gradually add one cup sugar. Add flour, melted butter and lemon juice. Mix well. pour over apples. Bake at 400° for 35 minutes.

APPLE CRUMB CAKE

Serves: 10 - 12
Cooking Time: 1¼ hours

"Crumby and good."

3 lb. green apples
1 cup sugar
¼ lb. butter
1 egg
1¾ cups flour
1 tsp. baking powder
1 tsp. vanilla
cinnamon

Peel and slice apples. Cream together ½ cup sugar, ⅛ pound butter and one egg. Add to creamed ingredients one cup flour baking powder, and vanilla. Line bottom and sides of 10-inch spring form pan (buttered) with dough. Fill with sliced apples. Combine ½ cup sugar, ¾ cup flour, and ⅛ pound butter and cinnamon and spread this crumb mixture evenly over apples. Bake for 1¼ hours at 350°.

DUTCH APPLE CAKE

Serves: 12
Cooking Time: 35 - 40 minutes

2 cups flour
3 tsp. baking powder
½ tsp. salt
4 tbsp. sugar
4 tbsp. shortening
1 egg
⅔ cup milk
2-3 cups apples
2 tbsp. butter

Topping:

½ cup sugar
1 tbsp. cinnamon

Sift flour; add baking powder, salt, and sugar. Sift into a bowl. Add shortening and cut in with pastry blender or two knives until mixture looks like coarse meal. Combine egg and milk. Stir into flour mixture with fork. Divide dough in half and spread in two 8- or 9-inch pie plates. Pare, core, and slice apples. Arrange slices in rows and press into top of dough. Spread with two tablespoons butter. Mix topping and sprinkle on top. Bake at 375° for 35-40 minutes.

Upside Down Dutch Apple Cake

Serves: 6
Cooking Time: 45 minutes

"Good, old-fashioned apple cake."

6 large or 7-8 small apples,
   cut into eighths
sugar and cinnamon mixed
2 eggs
¾ cup sugar
1 cup flour
½ cup melted shortening
1 tsp vanilla

Place apples in greased pie plate and cover with cinnamon and sugar. Mix eggs, sugar, flour, shortening, and vanilla in bowl. Then pour over apples. Sprinkle with cinnamon and sugar again. Bake at 375° for 45 minutes.

Sour Cream Banana Cake

Serves: 6 - 8
Cooking Time: 45 - 60 minutes

"The quickest and easiest banana cake we've ever seen!"

½ cup butter
1½ cups sugar
2 eggs
3 ripe bananas, mashed
½ cup sour cream
1 tsp. baking soda
2 cups flour
1 tsp vanilla

Cream butter and sugar. Add eggs. Add mashed bananas. Add sour cream, baking soda, flour, and vanilla. Bake at 350° for 45-60 minutes. You may use one 8-inch square pan or two layer pans.

"Dump-It"

Serves: 10 - 12
Cooking Time: 1 hour, 10 minutes

"Easy and great. Try it with chocolate ice cream."

2 cans cherry pie filling
1 can (12 oz.) crushed
   pineapple
1 box yellow cake mix
½ cup crushed pecans
¼ lb. butter, dotted on top

Open the cans and packages of above ingredients in the order given and simply "dump-it," layer by layer into a 9 x 13 inch pan. Bake at 350° for one hour, ten minutes. Top with whipped cream if desired.

BLUEBERRY BATTER CAKE

Serves: 8
Cooking Time: 45 - 50 minutes

"Unusual preparation."

2 cups blueberries (if
  canned, drained)
juice from ½ lemon
¾ cup sugar
3 tbsp. shortening
½ cup milk
1 cup flour
1 tsp. baking powder
¼ tsp. salt

Topping:

½ cup sugar
1 tbsp. cornstarch
¼ tsp. salt

Place blueberries in well greased 8 x 8 x 2-inch pan. Sprinkle lemon juice over berries. Cream sugar and shortening, add milk and flour (with baking powder and salt) alternately. Spread evenly over berries. Sprinkle topping over cake. Add one cup boiling water over cake. Bake in 375° oven for 45-50 minutes. Serve warm.

THE BEST SOUTHERN CHERRY CAKE

Serves: 10 - 12
Chill: Overnight

"Old family recipe."

1 can (#2) tart, pitted red
  cherries, strained
1 package red jello
⅓ to ½ cup sugar
1 pt. heavy cream, whipped
1 large or 2 small ready-made
  angel food cakes (sliced
  in 3 layers)

Drain cherry juice into measuring cup. Add sufficient water to make 1¾ cups. Prepare jello with juice and water. Chill in refrigerator for ½ hour. Mash cherries and add sugar. Mix with cream (already whipped) and jello until blended. Using an angel food-type of pan (2 pieces), lightly oil bottom and sides of pan. Line bottom with slices of cake. Place slices of cake (lady-finger size) along sides of pan, about one inch apart. Spoon in ½ of cherry mixture. Repeat this procedure, leaving a layer of cake on top. Place in refrigerator overnight. Unmold and serve.

BLACK FOREST CHERRY CAKE

Serves: 8
Cooking Time: 1 hour

"Worth the effort."

½ cup butter or margarine
1 cup sugar
6 eggs, separated, at room
  temperature
4 squares (1 oz. each) semisweet chocolate, melted
  and cooled
6 tbsp. kirsch (domestic)
1½ cups toasted filberts,
  grated
¼ cup all-purpose flour,
  unsifted
3 cups heavy cream
⅓ cup sifted confectioner's
  sugar
chocolate curls

Cream butter and sugar; beat in egg yolks, one at a time. Blend in melted and cooled chocolate and two tablespoons kirsch. Mix together filberts and flour. Stir into butter mixture. Beat egg whites until stiff, but not dry. Fold into batter. Turn into greased and floured 8-inch spring form pan. Bake at 375° for one hour or until cake tests done. Cake may be slightly cracked. Cool ten minutes. Remove and cool thoroughly on wire rack. Using a long sharp knife, cut into three layers. Place top layer, inverted, on cake plate. Spread with Cherry Filling. Whip cream in large bowl and electric mixer, gradually adding confectioner's sugar and remaining kirsch. Spread generously over cherry filling; assembly remaining layers. Decorate top with reserved cherries from filling and chocolate curls.

Cherry Filling:

1 jar (1 lb.) red maraschino
  cherries, drained, re-
  serving syrup and 13
  cherries for decoration
kirsch
1½ tsp. cornstarch
1 tbsp. lemon juice

Slice cherries in half. Combine cherry syrup and enough kirsch to measure ¾ cup. In sauce pan, gradually blend syrup mixture into cornstarch. Add the lemon juice. Stir over medium heat until mixture boils ½ minute. Add sliced cherries and cool. Yield: 1⅓ cups.

LEMON CAKE

Serves: 10 - 12
Cooking Time: 1 hour

"Rich and beautiful."

1 package yellow cake mix
  (Duncan Hines)
1 package (3 oz.) lemon
  jello
$\frac{2}{3}$ cup cool water
$\frac{2}{3}$ cup salad oil (Wesson)
4 eggs
juice of $\frac{1}{2}$ lemon

Combine everything and beat at high speed for no less than five minutes. Bake in greased angel food pan at 350° for one hour. Test with toothpick. Cool on rack.

Icing (Optional):

1 cup powdered sugar
grated rind of 1 lemon
juice of 1 lemon

Mix and spread around cake. Serve with lemon sherbet.

LEMON CHIFFON CAKE

Serves: 10
Chill: 3 - 5 hours

"Can be made the day before."

6 eggs, separated
1 cup sugar
3 lemons
1 envelope gelatin
$\frac{1}{4}$ cup cold water, scant
2 packages ladyfingers
sweet cream

Place egg yolks in top of double boiler. Beat well with sugar and juice of three lemons and rind of two lemons. Add gelatin, which has been dissolved in less than $\frac{1}{4}$ cup cold water, and cook until thickened. Let mixture cool and beat egg white until stiff, adding a pinch of salt. Pour yolk mixture into whites and fold gently together. Line 9-inch spring form pan with ladyfingers. Pour in mixture and refrigerate. Decorate top with whipped cream.

VIENNESE PLUM CAKE

Serves: 6 - 8
Cooking Time: 30 - 35 minutes

"Plummy and different. Like grandma used to make."

½ cup butter
½ cup sugar
2 eggs
1 cup flour
1 tsp. baking powder
¼ tsp. salt
10 red or blue fresh plums,
   cut into halves, pitted
½ cup sugar
2 tsp. cinnamon

Cream the butter in a bowl; add sugar, cream until fluffy. Add one egg at a time, beating well after each addition. Sift the flour, baking powder, and salt; add to first mixture beating until well blended. Spread in a buttered deep pie plate, or into a square pan (8 x 8 inches). Place the halved plums, skin side down, pressing into the top of the batter. Mix the second half cup of sugar with the cinnamon; spoon into each plum. Bake in a 350° oven for 30 to 35 minutes. Serve hot.

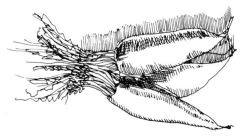

DESSERT CARROT CAKE

(MIX IN ORDER)

Serves: About 18 - 20
Cooking Time: 50 - 55 minutes

"Vitamin A-plus."

1¼ cups Wesson oil
2 cups sugar
4 eggs
4 small jars carrots
   (baby food, strained)
3 cups sifted flour
2 tsp. baking powder
2 tsp. baking soda
1½ tsp. cinnamon
1½ cups nuts, chopped

Mix well, place in greased 9 x 13-inch baking pan. Bake at 325° for 50-55 minutes.

248

CARROT PUDDING CAKE

Serves: 12
Cooking Time: 1 hour

"This does not taste like carrots."

1½ cups Crisco
1 cup brown sugar
4 eggs, separated
2½ cups flour, sifted
1 tsp. baking powder
2 tsp. baking soda
1 tsp. salt
2 tsp. vanilla
2 tsp. water
1 tsp. lemon juice
2 cups raw carrots, finely
  grated

Cream Crisco with brown sugar. Add egg yolks, flour, baking powder, baking soda, salt, vanilla, water, and lemon juice. Beat thoroughly. Add four egg whites, beaten. Lastly, add carrots. Mix until smooth (it will be a bit lumpy). Bake in a well-greased tube pan (9 or 10 inches) at 350° for 45 to 60 minutes.

PUMPKIN CAKE

Serves: 8 - 10
Cooking Time: 1 hour

"Great icing on a pumpkin lover's cake. Try this icing on your favorite cake too!"

4 eggs
2 cups sugar
1 cup Crisco oil
2 cups flour
2 tsp. baking soda
½ tsp. vanilla
½ tsp. salt
2 tsp. cinnamon
1 cup pumpkin (solid pack)
½ cup raisins
1 cup walnuts, crushed

Mix eggs, sugar, and oil, beat well. Add flour and rest of ingredients, beat well. Add raisins and walnuts; mix well. Bake at 325° for one hour in a 10-inch greased tube pan.

Icing:

2¼ cups confectioner's sugar
¼ tsp. vanilla
1 package (3 oz.) cream cheese
4 tbsp. butter

Mix and spread on cooled cake.

POUNDCAKE

Serves: 20 - 24
Cooking Time: 90 minutes

"Excellent!"

¼ lb. butter
¼ lb. margarine
1 cup Crisco
2 cups sugar
2 cups flour
6 eggs
1 tbsp. vanilla

Cream all shortenings together with sugar until smooth. Add eggs and flour alternately. Beat well. Add vanilla and beat again. Pour into greased and floured 16-inch long loaf pan (or two 8-inch loaf pans). Bake at 325° for 1½ hours.

APRICOT BRANDY POUNDCAKE

Serves: 8 - 10
Cooking Time: 1½ hours

"Apricot brandy adds sensational flavor."

1 cup margarine
3 cups sugar
6 eggs
1 cup sour cream
½ cup apricot brandy
1 tsp. vanilla flavoring
½ tsp. rum flavoring
1 tsp. orange extract
¼ tsp. almond extract
½ tsp. lemon extract
3 cups flour
¼ tsp. baking soda
½ tsp. salt

Cream margarine and add sugar. Add eggs (one at a time), beating thoroughly. Combine the next seven ingredients. Sift together flour, baking soda, and salt. Alternately, add flour and sour cream mixture to the sugar mixture. Mix well until blended. Pour into greased and floured large, tube cake pan. Bake at 325° for about 1½ hours (no peeking). Test with toothpick.

CREAM CHEESE RAISIN POUNDCAKE

Serves: 10
Cooking Time: 1¼ hours

"Good plain or with confectioner's sugar sprinkled on top."

1 cup butter or margarine
1 package (8 oz.) cream cheese
1½ cups sugar
2 tsp. vanilla
4 eggs
2¼ cups flour
2 tsp. baking powder
¼ tsp. salt
1½ cups halved raisins (use scissors)

Cream butter and cream cheese until light and soft. Beat in sugar. Add vanilla and eggs, one at a time. Sift flour, baking powder and salt; blend into creamed mixture. When mixture is silky, fold in halved raisins. Transfer to a well-greased Bundt pan. Bake in a slow 300° oven for 1¼ hours. Cool in pan ten minutes.

CHOCOLATE ANGEL CAKE

Serves: 14 - 16
Chill: Overnight

"Uses leftover cakes."

2 packages (6 oz. each) semi-sweet chocolate bits
2 tbsp. sugar
3 eggs, separated
2 cups heavy cream, whipped
1 small angel food cake (8 oz.) leftover or bought

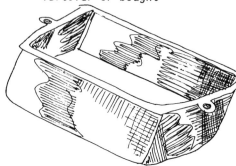

Melt chips with sugar over hot water and remove from heat. Add beaten egg yolks and cool five minutes (until it stiffens). Beat egg whites stiff; fold beaten egg whites and whipped cream into chocolate mixture. Break angel food cake into bite-size pieces; sprinkle a layer in bottom of a buttered 8 x 12 x 2-inch baking dish (use about ½ of cake). Cover with layer of chocolate mixture. Dot this with rest of cake pieces. Top with remainder of the mixture. (Chopped nuts can be added on top, if desired.) Chill overnight. Cut in small pieces to serve.

YUM YUM CAKE

(CHOCOLATE)

Serves: 10 - 12
Cooking Time: 35 minutes

1½ cups cold water
1 cup sugar
½ cup butter
1 cup raisins
½ tsp. cinnamon
½ tsp. cloves
2 squares chocolate
1 tsp. baking soda
salt
2 cups sifted flour
1 tsp. vanilla
chopped nuts

Boil together water, sugar, butter, raisins, cinnamon, cloves, and chocolate. Cool. Dissolve baking soda in two tablespoons cold water and add to cooled mixture, plus a little salt, flour, and vanilla. Blend well. Pour into square pan (9 inch). Bake at 350° approximately 35 minutes (or until toothpick does not stick). Nuts may be added after flour if desired.

Icing:

1 package (8 oz.) cream cheese
2 tbsp. confectioner's sugar
2 or 3 drops desired flavoring
   (vanilla or almond)

Blend all ingredients.

"MAMA'S MOIST CHOCOLATE CAKE"

Serves: 10 - 12
Cooking Time: 40 minutes

"Vinegar makes the difference."

½ cup milk
2 tbsp. vinegar
1½ tsp. baking soda
½ cup butter, soft
2 cups sugar
4 squares chocolate, melted
1 cup boiling water
2 eggs, beaten
2 tsp. vanilla
2 cups flour, sifted

Combine milk, vinegar, and baking soda. Cream butter and sugar. Add chocolate and water, mix. Add milk mixture; add eggs and vanilla; add flour. Mix with beaters until smooth. Batter will be thin. Bake, in greased 11-inch oblong pan, at 375° for 40 minutes. Decorate with sifted confectioner's sugar if desired.

CHOCOLATE BUNDT CAKE

Serves: 6 - 8
Cooking Time: 50 - 55 minutes

"This cake has won raves all over Long Island."

1 package Duncan Hines dark
  chocolate cake mix
1 package instant chocolate
  pudding
¾ cup water
½ cup salad oil
4 eggs
8 oz. sour cream
1 package (6 oz.) chocolate
  chips

Place first six ingredients in bowl. Beat at low speed to moisten, beat at medium speed until creamy. Fold in chocolate chips. Grease tube or Bundt pan. Bake at 350° for 50-55 minutes. Test by inserting toothpick until it comes out clean.
Note: Be sure toothpick is hitting into cake and not into a melted chocolate chip.
Optional: Dust with confectioner's sugar.

"FLORA'S CHOCOLATE CAKE"

Serves: 8
Cooking Time: 30 minutes

"The most chocolatey cake ever."

¼ lb. butter
1¾ cups sugar
2 eggs
½ pt. sour cream
2 cups flour
pinch of salt
½ tsp. baking powder
1 tbsp. baking soda
½ cup boiling coffee
½ cup cocoa
1 tsp. vanilla

Cream butter and sugar together. Add eggs and sour cream. Cream well. Add flour, salt, and baking powder to egg and butter mixture. Dissolve baking soda in boiling coffee and stir in cocoa. Add vanilla. Then add cocoa mixture. Bake in two round, 9-inch cake pans at 350° for 30 minutes.

Frosting:

1 cup sugar
3 tbsp. cornstarch
1½ cups milk
3 squares baking chocolate,
  unsweetened
2 tbsp. butter
1 tsp. vanilla

Mix sugar and cornstarch together. Add milk. Melt chocolate in double boiler. Combine these two mixtures and cook until thick. Add butter and vanilla.

CHOCOLATE CAKE

Serves: 10
Cooking Time: 45 minutes

*"You think you are ruining it, but do not be alarmed! The
raw batter also tastes terrible, but is
delicious when cooked."*

½ cup butter
1 lb. brown sugar
2 eggs, beaten
2 squares unsweetened
   chocolate, melted
½ cup buttermilk
2 tsp. vanilla
2¼ cups cake flour, sifted
½ tsp. salt
1 cup boiling water
2 tsp. baking soda

Preheat oven to 375°. Cream butter; gradually add sugar, creaming until light and fluffy. Add eggs and beat hard. Stir in melted chocolate, the buttermilk and vanilla. Gradually add sifted cake flour and salt, beating thoroughly after each addition. Lastly, stir soda into boiling water and stir into batter. Batter will be extremely thin. Bake in a greased 9 x 12 x 2-inch pan at 375° for 15 minutes, then at 350° for about 30 minutes.

CHOCOLATE CHIP CAKE

Serves: 8 - 10
Cooking Time: 50 minutes to 1 hour

¼ lb. butter, soft
1 cup sugar
2 eggs
½ pt. sour cream
1 tsp. vanilla extract
2 cups flour
1 tsp. baking soda
1 tsp. baking powder
1 small package (6 oz.)
   chocolate chips

Mix all ingredients as listed, fold into greased and floured spring form pan.

Topping:

3 tbsp. butter
4 tbsp. sugar
1 tsp. cinnamon

Melt butter; add sugar and cinnamon, mixing well. Spread over batter. Bake for 50 minutes to one hour in a preheated oven, at 350°.

ROULAGE LEONTINE

(CHOCOLATE ROLL)

Serves: 10 - 12
Cooking Time: 17 minutes

"For the more experienced baker."

½ lb. dark sweet chocolate
1½ cups heavy cream
3 tbsp. confectioner's sugar
1 tsp. vanilla (or vanilla
    bean)
8 eggs
⅓ cup cold water
1 cup superfine sugar
cocoa

Oil an 18 x 12-inch jelly roll pan. Cover with wax paper extending ½ inch at ends. Do not oil paper. Break chocolate into pieces in heavy sauce pan. Whip cream until it thickens with the confectioner's sugar and vanilla. Beat until stiff, place in refrigerator. Add water to chocolate and melt over low flame, stirring with a wooden spoon. Separate eggs. Put yolks in mixer bowl and start mixer. Add sugar to yolks and beat until pale and fluffy. Add chocolate (which is now cool). Beat egg whites until they form soft peaks. Fold the chocolate mixture into egg whites with rubber spatula. Spread evenly over prepared pan. Bake at 350° for 17 minutes (do not overcook). Remove from oven and cover top with two layers of wet paper towels and one layer of dry paper. Cool at room temperature 20 minutes. When cool, peel off paper towels carefully. Loosen by running knife along side. Now lift extension of wax paper a little way, one side at a time. Dust top with dry cocoa. Place two overlapping pieces of wax paper, length of pan with one nearest you on top. Flip pan over quickly. Lift off and gently peel off wax paper. Spread cream evenly. Roll up, lifting paper nearest you. Roll up in paper and shape it. Remove paper and sprinkle generously with cocoa. Serve from wooden board.

Chocolate Mousse Icebox Cake

Serves: 12
Refrigerate: 3 hours

"No problem to make and looks lovely."

1 Sara Lee poundcake
7 eggs, separated, room
  temperature
2 packages (12 oz.) Nestle's
  chocolate chips, semisweet
  or sweet
2 tbsp. rum extract
½ pt. heavy cream, whipped

Line an 8 x 11-inch pan with aluminum foil. Slice poundcake lengthwise into 6 slices. Place 3 slices next to each other in pan for first layer. Separate eggs. Put yolks in large bowl, whites in smaller one. Beat yolks slightly. Melt chocolate chips over hot water. Add extract to melted chocolate. Add chocolate mixture to egg yolks and beat very well. Beat egg whites until they form peaks. Now fold into chocolate mixture. Then fold in whipped cream. Pour ½ mixture over cake in pan. Add last 3 slices for second layer, then pour in rest of chocolate mixture. Refrigerate for at least three hours. Remove from pan, take off foil and decorate (optional) with nuts or coconut, etc.

Pistachio Swirl Cake

Serves: 10
Cooking Time: 1 hour

"Pistachio pudding and chocolate syrup are used here."

1 package yellow cake mix
1 package instant pistachio
  pudding
1 cup club soda
½ cup oil
4 eggs
½ cup nuts, chopped
¾ cup Fox's U-Bet chocolate
  syrup

Mix all ingredients except nuts and chocolate syrup. Fold in nuts. Set aside two tablespoons of batter. Mix with chocolate syrup. Pour into greased, 10-inch tube pan (not Bundt). Pour syrup mixture onto cake mixture and marbleize. Bake at 350° for 55-60 minutes.

MARBLE CAKE

Serves: 6 - 8
Cooking Time: 25 - 30 minutes (or 45 - 60 minutes)

½ cup butter
1 cup sugar
2 eggs
2 cups cake flour, sifted
2 tsp. baking powder
1 cup milk
1 tsp. vanilla
2 squares bitter chocolate,
   melted

Cream butter, sugar, and eggs. Sift flour, baking powder together. Add alternately with milk to creamed mixture. Pour ½ of batter into two greased, 8-inch square pans. Using large spoon, to remaining batter add melted chocolate. Mix well. Spoon chocolate mixture into the pans. Create marble effect by swirling light and dark mixtures together with butter knife. Bake at 350° for 25-30 minutes. Frost as desired. (May also be baked in tube pan at 350° for 45-60 minutes.)

WALNUT LOAF CAKE

Serves: 10
Cooking Time: 40 - 45 minutes

"Chewy."

½ cup shortening
1 cup brown sugar
2 eggs
1 tsp. vanilla
1¾ cups sifted flour
1 tsp. baking powder
½ tsp. salt
¾ cup milk
1 cup chopped walnuts

Cream shortening and sugar. Add eggs, one at a time, add vanilla. Add flour combined with baking powder and salt, alternately with milk. Add chopped walnuts. Pour into well-greased, floured loaf pan. Bake at 350° for 40-45 minutes.

SPONGE CAKE

Serves: 8 - 10
Cooking Time: 55 minutes

"Serve with strawberries and whipped cream."

6 large eggs, separated
1½ cups sugar
½ cup orange juice
1½ cups all-purpose flour
1 tsp. baking powder
rind of 1 lemon

Beat whites, starting on low spead and building up to high, until very stiff. Set aside. Beat yolks well, gradually adding sugar, alternately with orange juice. Beat until thick and lemon colored (about 10 minutes). Add flour, baking powder and rind of lemon. Mix thoroughly. Fold in beaten egg whites. Bake in an ungreased, 10-inch tube pan. Place in cold oven and turn on to 350°. Leave in oven a total of 55 minutes. Invert pan until cool.

KIRSCH CAKE

Serves: 6 - 8
Cooking Time: 1 hour

"An old-fashioned cake that turns out to have a surprise finish — custard on the bottom and cake on the top!"

1½ tbsp. butter
¾ cup sugar
3 egg yolks
3 tbsp. flour
¼ cup kirsch
1 cup milk
3 egg whites
pinch of salt

Preheat oven to 350°. Grease an 8-inch porcelain quiche pan or baking pan. Beat butter and sugar until fluffy. Add egg yolks, flour, kirsch, and milk. Beat egg whites with salt until stiff. Fold egg whites into first mixture. Pour into baking dish and bake for one hour.

KISS ME CAKE

Serves: 8
Cooking Time: 40 - 50 minutes

"Very interesting cake."

1 large orange, pulp and peal
1 cup raisins
1/3 cup walnuts
2 cups sifted flour
1 tsp. soda
1 tsp. salt
1 cup sugar
1/2 cup shortening
1 cup milk
2 eggs, unbeaten

Topping:

1/3 cup orange juice
1/3 cup cinnamon
1/4 cup walnuts, chopped

Grind together orange, pulp and peal (reserve juice for topping), raisins, and walnuts. Sift together flour, soda, salt, sugar. Add shortening, 3/4 cup milk. Beat two minutes at medium speed. Add eggs, unbeaten, 1/4 cup milk. Beat two minutes. Fold orange-raisin mixture into batter. Pour into well-greased and lightly floured 12 x 8 x 2-inch pan. Bake in moderate oven (350°) 40 to 50 minutes. Drip orange juice over warm cake. Combine cinnamon and chopped walnuts. Sprinkle over cake. Can be decorated with orange slices.

PRALINE GOLD CAKE

Serves: 6 - 8
Cooking Time: 35 minutes

"A true Southern secret."

2 cups sifted Swan's Down
    cake flour
2 tsp. Calumet baking powder
1/4 tsp. salt
1/2 cup butter
1 cup sugar
3 egg yolks, beaten until very
    thick and lemon colored
3/4 cup milk
1 tsp. vanilla

Sift flour once, measure. Add baking powder and salt; sift 3 times. Cream shortening, add sugar gradually. Cream until light and fluffy. Add egg yolks, beat very well. Add flour alternately with milk, in small amounts; beat very thoroughly. Add vanilla. Bake in greased 9 x 9 x 2-inch pan, dusted with flour. Bake at 350° for 35 minutes, or until done. Note: Do not line pan; leave cake in pan.

Topping:

1/4 cup brown sugar, firmly
    packed
2 tsp. cake flour
2 tbsp. butter, melted
1 tsp. water

Combine ingredients. Spread on top of cake and broil a few minutes.

TUNNEL CAKE

Serves: 8 - 10
Cooking Time: 55 - 60 minutes

"Frosting is inside the cake."

1½ cups soft butter (3 sticks)
6 eggs
1½ cups sugar
1½ cups all-purpose flour
1 package Pillsbury Double Dutch
  frosting
2 cups chopped walnuts

Preheat oven to 350°. Grease Bundt pan. Beat butter at high speed until fluffy. Beat in eggs, one at a time. Gradually beat in sugar; beat until fluffy; By hand, stir in flour, dry frosting mix, and walnuts, until blended. Bake 55 - 60 minutes, until top is dry and shiny. Cool in pan for two hours.

DELUXE AND DELICIOUS CAKE

Serves: 8 - 10
Cooking Time: 45 - 50 minutes

"This cake warrants its name."

1 package yellow cake mix
1 package vanilla instant
  pudding
¾ cup salad oil
¼ cup whiskey (rye)
½ cup whole milk
5 medium eggs
3 heaping tbsp. sour cream
1 package (6 oz.) butterscotch
  bits
½ cup walnuts or pecans,
  chopped

Preheat oven to 350°. Blend all but last two ingredients in bowl. Mix 3-4 minutes at medium speed. Add butterscotch bits and nuts. Bake in 10-inch greased tube pan for 45-50 minutes. Cool right side up about 25 minutes then remove from pan. Butterscotch bits may stick to pan. Scrape with knife and use as crumbs on cake. For Variety: Use chocolate cake mix, chocolate pudding, and chocolate bits. Any mix can be substituted; other ingredients may be coconut, etc.

ICE CREAM CAKE

Serves: 12

"Sensational. Keep one in your freezer at all times."

2 boxes (8½ oz. each)
  chocolate wafers
1 cup butter or margarine,
  melted
2 pt. vanilla ice cream
2 pt. pistachio ice cream
2 pt. chocolate ice cream
coconut flakes

Anytime up to two weeks before serving, make crumbs from wafers in blender or with rolling pin. Combine crumbs and melted butter, reserving ⅔ cup of crumbs. Firmly press remaining crumbs over bottom and up sides of a 9-inch spring form pan. Freeze until firm (15 minutes). Remove from freezer and spread vanilla ice cream in an even layer. Sprinkle with ⅓ cup crumbs. Return to freezer until ice cream is firm. Repeat layering ice cream, pistachio then chocolate, in the same manner, omitting crumbs at the end. Cover top with foil and freeze. Early on serving day put serving plate in freezer to chill. Ten minutes before serving, invert pan onto plate, release catch, and remove sides and bottom. Garnish with coconut flakes.

DOBOSCHE TORTE

Serves: 6 - 8

"Quick and easy. Great for summer entertaining. No baking."

1 Sara Lee poundcake
1 bar (4 oz.) Baker's German
  chocolate
½ pt. sour cream

Partially thaw cake. Cut horizontal slices about ¼ to ½-inch thick. Lay each slice upside down as you cut it, so cake winds up upside down. Leave last slice on plate. Melt chocolate in top of double boiler. Remove from flame and add sour cream. Mix thoroughly. Frost layers, returning so cake is now right side up. Frost top and sides and refrigerate.

BLUEBERRY SOUR CREAM TORTE

Serves: 8
Cooking Time: 40 - 45 minutes

"Nice moist cake."

4 eggs
1 box Pillsbury yellow cake
  mix
½ cup water
½ cup oil
1 cup sour cream
1 cup blueberries (fresh or
  canned)
1 cup coconut
confectioner's sugar

Preheat oven to 350°. Beat whole eggs in mixer until double in bulk, stir with spatula until well mixed. Add cake mix, water, oil, and sour cream. Beat until well blended. Mixture will be thick. Grease well a large tube or Bundt pan. Spread half of mixture into pan. Spread berries over batter, then coconut. Add rest of batter evenly over all. Bake for 40-45 minutes. Let cool Turn out on serving dish. Sprinkle with confectioner's sugar.

COFFEE-GLAZED WALNUT TORTE

Serves: 10
Cooking Time: 20 minutes

"Fantastic dessert!"

6 eggs
1¼ cups sugar
1½ cups ground walnuts
¼ cup bread crumbs
1 tsp. baking powder
1 tsp. vanilla
½ tsp. cinnamon
½ tsp. nutmeg
½ tsp. salt (sprinkle)
2 cups heavy cream, whipped

Glaze:

1 cup confectioner's sugar
½ tsp. instant coffee
1 tbsp. margarine
2 tbsp. water

Separate eggs. Let egg whites stand at room temperature for one hour. Preheat oven to 350°. Line bottoms of three 8-inch layer cake pans with wax paper. Beat egg whites and add ½ cup sugar. Beat egg yolks and add remaining sugar. Add walnuts, bread crumbs, baking powder, vanilla, cinnamon, nutmeg, and salt. Add egg whites and pour into pans. Bake for 20 minutes. Cool one hour and remove from pans. Make Glaze: Combine confectioner's sugar, coffee, and margarine with water. Mix with wooden spoon. Put cake layers together with ⅔ of the whipped cream. Spread glaze over top and cover with rest of whipped cream on the side. Garnish top with walnuts. Refrigerate torte.

SWEET CREAM CAKE

Serves: 10 - 12
Cooking Time: Approximately 50 minutes

"Make sure to use self-rising flour."

1½ cups sugar
4 eggs
1¾ cups self-rising flour
1 cup heavy cream
1 tsp. vanilla

Beat sugar and eggs until very thick and pale in color. Fold in flour and cream alternately. Stir in vanilla. Grease and flour 9-inch pan. Bake at 400° exactly 15 minutes, lower to 350° for 30 minutes. Cool about ten minutes and loosen from bottom of pan. Half an hour later, with spatula, release bottom of cake.

Topping:

3 tbsp. butter or margarine
3 tbsp. brown sugar
2 tbsp. heavy cream
½ cup coconut

Melt butter or margarine, brown sugar; mix well. Add heavy cream, mix. Add coconut and spread on top. Broil two to four minutes.

CHEESE CAKE

Serves: 8 - 10
Cooking Time: 1 hour

"Vanilla wafers make your crust."

2 lb. cream cheese
1¼ cups sugar
6 eggs
1 tbsp. flour
1 tbsp. melted butter
1 tsp. vanilla
1 cup sour cream

Cream the cream cheese and sugar. Add remaining five ingredients and mix well. Pour into a spring form baking pan. Bake at 300° for at least one hour. Turn off oven and leave the cake to cool (in the oven). Should be light in color.

Crust:

½ box Nabisco vanilla wafers, crushed
1½ tbsp. melted butter
1 tsp. sugar

Combine ingredients in bottom of pan and press down firmly. Pour batter on top.

263

ARLENE'S CHEESECAKE

Serves: 12
Cooking Time: 1 hour

Crust:

1¾ cups graham cracker crumbs
¼ cup walnuts, chopped
½ tsp. cinnamon
½ cup melted butter

Mix together. Reserve three tablespoons for topping. Press remainder into bottom and sides of 9-inch spring form pan.

Filling:

3 eggs
2 packages (8 oz. each) cream cheese
1 cup sugar
2 tsp. vanilla extract
3 cups sour cream
½ tsp. almond extract

Combine eggs, cheese, sugar, and flavorings. Beat until smooth. Blend in sour cream. Pour into crust. Top with reserved crumbs. Bake at 375° for one hour. Chill 4-5 hours before serving.

CHERRY CHEESECAKE

Serves: 12
Cooking Time: 30 minutes (1 hour in oven, turned off)

"Roslyn raves about this cake."

1 lb. cream cheese
1 cup sugar
3 eggs
1 tsp. vanilla
1 pt. sour cream
1 can Comstock cherries

Beat cheese with sugar; add eggs, vanilla, sour cream. Pour mixture into pie crust. Top with can of Comstock cherries. Bake at 375° for 30 minutes. Leave in oven with door closed, oven turned off, for one hour.

Crust:

1¼ cups graham crackers
2 tbsp. sugar
2 tbsp. margarine, melted

Line 8-inch spring form pan with crust.

CHERRY CROWN CHEESECAKE

Serves: 12 - 18
Cooking Time: 2 hours

"Zwieback for the crust. Best when made 12-24 hours before serving."

Crust:

1½ cups zwieback crumbs
  (about 18 pieces)
3 tbsp. brown sugar
1 tsp. cinnamon
6 tbsp. butter or margarine,
  melted

Mix zwieback crumbs with brown sugar and cinnamon in small bowl; blend in melted butter or margarine. Press evenly over bottom and sides of buttered 9-inch spring form pan. Set pan in 12-inch long piece of double-thick foil. Fold up around sides to catch any butter mixture that may leak out as cake bakes. Chill.

Filling:

3 packages (8 oz. each) cream
  cheese
1½ cups sugar
4 eggs
2 cups dairy sour cream
1 cup heavy cream
2 tbsp. lemon juice
1 tsp. grated lemon rind
½ tsp. vanilla

Soften cream cheese in large bowl; gradually beat in sugar until fluffy. Add eggs, one at a time, beating well after each. Beat in remaining ingredients; pour into prepared crust. Bake in a 350° oven one hour; turn off heat. Let cake remain in oven with door closed one hour longer. Remove from oven; cool in pan on wire rack. (Cake will settle slightly in center as it cools.) Remove foil wrapping. Loosen cake around edge with knife, release spring, and carefully lift off side of pan. Place cake on plate.

Topping:

1 can (21 oz.) cherry pie
  filling

Spoon topping over cake. Chill.

Chocolate Cheesecake

Serves: 8 - 10
Cooking Time: 2 hours

"Popular favorite."

2 packages (8 oz.) cream
   cheese
1 cup sugar
6 eggs, separated
1 tsp. vanilla
1 tbsp. orange juice
1 cup heavy cream, whipped
1 square unsweetened
   chocolate
1 graham cracker crust for
   9-inch spring pan

Blend cheese and sugar and add yolks, one at a time, beating well. Stir in vanilla and orange juice. Beat whites stiff and spoon into cheese mixture. Fold in whipped cream. Melt chocolate in separate pot. Using a lightly greased spring form pan, pat the graham cracker crust into place. Spoon in 1/3 of batter, dribble some chocolate in and swirl around with knife. Repeat until mixture is all used up. Bake at 300° for one hour. Leave in oven one hour longer with door closed and oven turned off. Remove, cool, refrigerate.

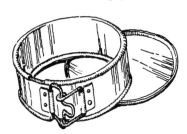

Lemon Icebox Cake

Serves: 6 - 8
Cooking Time: 10 minutes

"Bake and chill. Very easy."

1 can (14 oz.) sweet
   condensed milk
2 eggs
1/2 cup lemon juice
lemon rind

Blend all ingredients and pour into crust. Bake for ten minutes at 300°. Serve cold.

Crust:

1 cup graham cracker crumbs
1/2 tsp. cinnamon
3 tbsp. brown sugar
3 tbsp. margarine

Blend well and press into bottom of a 9-inch pie plate.

266

BABKA

Serves: 10 - 12
Cooking Time: ¾ hour

"Not easy to make, but worth the effort. Will stay fresh, wrapped, for a week."

1 package dry yeast
¾ cup sugar
¼ tsp. salt
3¾ cups flour
¼ cup warm water
¾ cup warm milk
½ cup butter
3 eggs
½ cup raisins

Dissolve yeast, one tablespoon sugar, salt and one cup flour in warm water and milk. Let rise. When light, cream butter and sugar, add eggs and yeast mixture. Beat. Add raisins and rest of flour. Make a thick batter. Allow to rise until double. Pour into two well-greased loaf pans and fill ⅓ full. Brush top with butter and Streusel Topping. Bake at 375° for ¾ hour.

Streusel Topping:

¼ cup brown sugar
2 tbsp. flour
2 tbsp. butter
½ tsp. cinnamon
¼ cup nuts

Rub ingredients together with fingers and put on cake.

SOUR CREAM COFFEE CAKE

Serves: 12
Cooking Time: 1 hour

"Chocolate bits are a great addition to coffee cake."

1 tsp. baking soda
1 cup sour cream
¼ cup butter or margarine
1 cup sugar
3 eggs
2 tsp. vanilla
2 cups flour
1 tsp. baking powder

Filling:

½ cup walnuts, chopped
1½ tsp. cinnamon
½ cup sugar
¾ cup chocolate tidbits
  (keep aside)

First, add one teaspoon baking soda to sour cream and let sit. Cream butter and sugar. Add eggs and vanilla (one at a time). Add baking powder to flour. Add to mixture, alternating flour and sour cream. Grease spring pan. Combine the first three ingredients of the filling. Put in half of the batter, about half the filling, add about half the chocolate tidbits (save some for top). Add rest of batter. Finish with topping and chocolate tidbits. Bake at 350° for one hour.

FLEUDEN

(RUSSIAN COFFEE CAKE)

Yield: 24 pieces
Cooking Time: 55 minutes

3 cups flour
1½ tsp. baking powder
¾ cup sugar
¾ cup Crisco
3 eggs

Filling:

1 lemon, juice and grated
   rind
6-8 apples, peeled and grated
¼ cup bread crumbs
1 jar jelly
1 cup raisins
1 cup chopped nuts (on the
   large side)
sugar
cinnamon

Blend flour, baking powder, sugar with Crisco. Add eggs and knead well. Cover with dish until filling is done. Divide dough into four parts.

Sprinkle the juice and grated lemon peel onto the apples. Grease pan and shake on flour. Roll dough and line pan. After shaking bread crumbs on dough, spread jelly, apples, raisins, nuts, alternately. Follow with dough / layer of filling / dough/ layer of filling and top with dough. Sprinkle with sugar and cinnamon. Bake at 350° for 45 minutes, remove, cut squares, and bake ten minutes more.

CHOCOLATE COFFEE CAKE

Serves: 20
Cooking Time: 60 minutes

"Easy and good results."

½ lb. butter or margarine
   (margarine is best)
1 cup sugar
2 eggs
2 cups sifted flour
1 tsp. cinnamon
¼ cup chopped walnuts
½ cup brown sugar
1 tsp. baking powder
1 tsp. baking soda
1 tsp. vanilla
1 cup sour cream
½ package (6 oz.) chocolate
   bits, melted
2 tbsp. cocoa, melted
4-5 tbsp. milk

In mixer, cream butter and sugar. Add eggs, beat well. Add dry ingredients, sour cream, and vanilla, alternately. Add half brown sugar mixture and put into greased 9 x 13-inch pan. Melt chocolate bits with milk and cocoa. Marbleize dough with half melted chocolate. Top with rest of brown sugar mixture and dribble rest of chocolate on top. Bake at 350° for 60 minutes.

Costigan's Old Mill Road P.T.A. Crumb Cake

Serves: 8
Cooking Time: 50 minutes

"No one will know you cheated with a mix."

1 box Duncan Hines golden
  butter recipe cake mix
¼ lb. Blue Bonnet margarine,
  instead of butter

Make cake according to directions. Pour into greased and floured 9 x 12-inch pan. Bake 25 minutes.

Crumb Mixture:

2 cups flour
½ lb. Blue Bonnet margarine,
  room temperature
½ cup sugar
¼ tsp. salt
1 tbsp. cinnamon

Mix with fingers until fluffy and form crumbs. Sprinkle crumbs on hot cake and return to oven for an additional 25 minutes. Sprinkle confectioner's sugar over hot cake. Cool and serve.

Maple Nut Butter Frosting

Preparation Time: 10 minutes

"Try this frosting on Flora's Chocolate Cake, page 253."

⅓ cup soft butter
3 cups confectioner's sugar
½ cup maple syrup
¼ cup nuts, finely chopped

Blend butter and sugar. Stir in maple syrup and nuts. Fills and frosts two 8- or 9-inch layers or one 13 x 9-inch cake pan.

Cake Portion Guide:

Pan Size	Yield
13 x 9 x 2 inches	24 2-inch squares
13 x 9 x 2 inches	12 3-inch squares
8-inch square loaf pan	6 servings
9-inch square loaf pan	6 - 8 servings
8-inch round layer pan	8 servings
9-inch round layer pan	8 - 10 servings
10-inch torte	10 - 12 servings
10-inch tube pan	8 - 10 servings

Editors' Note:
   This can be used for Beef Wellington by omitting almond extract, nuts, and sugar glaze.

Danish Puff Pastry

Serves: 6 - 8
Cooking Time: 1¼ hours

1 cup butter
2 cups flour
1 cup plus 2 tbsp. water
1 tsp. almond extract
3 eggs
nuts, chopped

Heat oven to 350°. Cut ½ cup butter into one cup of flour. Sprinkle 2 tablespoons water over mixture; mix. Round into ball, divide in half. On ungreased baking sheet, put each half into strips 12 x 3 inches. Strips should be about 3 inches apart. Heat ½ cup butter and one cup water to rolling boil in medium sauce pan. Remove from heat and quickly stir in almond extract and one cup flour. Stir vigorously over low heat until mixture forms a ball, about one minute. Remove from heat. Beat in eggs (all at once) until smooth and glossy. Divide in half, spread each half evenly over strips. Bake about 60 minutes or until topping is crisp and brown. Cool. Frost with Confectioner's Sugar Glaze and sprinkle with nuts.

Confectioner's Sugar Glaze:

1½ cups confectioner's sugar
2 tbsp. butter, softened
1½ tsp. vanilla
1 to 2 tbsp. warm water

Mix all ingredients together until smooth.

CHEESE TARTS

Yield: 18 - 20 tarts
Cooking Time: 10 - 15 minutes

"Creamier filling for those who like it that way."

Nabisco vanilla wafers
1 lb. cream cheese
2 eggs
¾ cup sugar
1 tsp. vanilla
1 can Comstock cherry pie
   filling

Place one Nabisco vanilla wafer into each foil muffin cup. Put muffin cups in muffin pans. Beat together the cream cheese, eggs, sugar, and vanilla and bake in 350° oven for 10-15 minutes. Remove from oven and, while still hot, open one can Comstock cherry pie filling and place one tablespoon on each tart. Refrigerate overnight.

FRUIT TARTS

Serves: 8
Chill: Several hours

"Just mix. No cooking."

1 cup (4 oz.) Cool Whip
1 package (8 oz.) cream cheese
1 tsp. vanilla
8 packaged graham cracker tart
   shells
1 can pie filling (blueberry,
   cherry, etc.)

Mix Cool Whip, cream cheese, and vanilla. Beat until fluffy and creamy. Pour into shells. Top with pie filling and refrigerate several hours.

CREAM CHEESE PETIT FOURS

Yield: 30 small, 12 regular size
Cooking Time: 12 minutes

"Great for last minute preparation."

1 egg
½ lb. farmer cheese
½ lb. cream cheese
½ cup sugar
graham cracker crumb mix
petit four cups
1 can Lucky Leaf pie filling
   (fruit of your choice)

Mix first four ingredients in blender, using egg first. Place petit four cups in muffin tins and sprinkle with graham cracker crumbs. Spoon cheese mix on top. Bake 12 minutes at 350°. Cool and top with pie filling. May be frozen.

Pecan Tarts

Yield: 24
Cooking Time: 15 minutes

"Easy dough preparation. Delicious filling."

Crust:

1 package (3 oz.) cream cheese
¼ lb. butter
1 cup flour

Cream butter and cream cheese together. Blend in flour and form into ball. Refrigerate until ready to use.

Filling:.

1 cup pecans, chopped
¾ cup brown sugar
1 tbsp. melted butter
1 egg
1 tsp. vanilla
pinch of salt

Add and mix all filling ingredients together. Take dough from refrigerator and cut into 24 pieces. Work into small muffin tins to form a cup; add one teaspoon filling. Bake at 375° for 15 minutes. Cool; sprinkle with powdered sugar; serve.
Note: "Small muffin tin" is the extremely small type used for pastries.

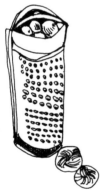

Jay's Cheese Pie

Serves: 8
Cooking Time: 30 minutes

"Baked sour cream topping."

1⅓ cups fine graham cracker
  crumbs
¼ cup melted butter
3 packages (3 oz. each) cream
  cheese, room temperature
½ cup plus 5 tbsp. sugar
2 eggs, beaten, room temperature
1 tsp. vanilla extract
2 cups sour cream
⅛ tsp. ground cinnamon

Mix crumbs and butter well with hands. Press onto bottom and sides of 9-inch pie pan. Bake in preheated moderate oven (350°) for five minutes. Cream cheese well. Gradually beat in ½ cup sugar. Add eggs and ½ teaspoon vanilla, beat well. Pour into prepared pan. Bake in slow oven (325°) for 20 minutes or until firm. Mix sour cream, ½ teaspoon vanilla, five tablespoons sugar, and cinnamon. Pour over top. Return to oven and bake for five minutes more. Chill and serve.

CREAMY CHEESE PIE

Serves: 6 - 8
Chill: 3 - 4 hours

"Fruit topping."

1 package (8 oz.) cream cheese
1⅓ cups condensed milk (15 oz. can)
⅓ cup lemon juice
1 tsp. vanilla
1 graham cracker crumb crust
1 can prepared pie filling (your choice)

Soften cream cheese to room temperature, whip till fluffy. Gradually add condensed milk, while continuing to beat until well blended. Add lemon juice and vanilla extract; blend well. Pour into crust. Chill 3-4 hours before serving. Top with pie filling.

CHERRY CHEESE PIE

Serves: 8
Refrigerate: Several hours

"Simple! Delicious! No bake! Sure hit!"

1 package (8 oz.) cream cheese
1 cup powdered sugar
1 pt. heavy cream, whipped
1 tsp. vanilla
1 graham cracker crust
1 can cherry pie filling

In a bowl, cream the cheese and sugar together. In a second bowl, whip the cream and vanilla. Add mixture from first bowl to second bowl slowly. Put combined mixture into pie crust. Gently pour can of cherry pie filling over mixture. Refrigerate several hours.

PINEAPPLE CREAM PIE

Serves: 6 - 8
Chill: 2 hours

"From an excellent baker."

1 package (8 oz.) cream cheese, softened to room temperature
¼ cup sugar
1 cup heavy cream, whipped
1½ cups crushed pineapple (Dole #2 can or any 1 lb., 4 oz. can)
9-inch graham cracker pie shell

Whip softened cream cheese and sugar well. Fold in whipped cream and add pineapple (well drained). Spoon into pie shell. Chill thoroughly, about 2 hours, or until filling is set. Garnish with pineapple chunks or rings.

Editors' Note:
This is a basic pastry recipe and can be used with the filling of your choice.

PASTRY

Serves: 8 - 10
Cooking Time: 1 hour

¼ lb. butter
¼ cup sugar
1 egg yolk
grated rind 1 lemon
1¼ cups flour
peaches, plums, or apricots
¼ cup brown sugar
butter

Blend butter and sugar together. Add egg yolk, then grated lemon rind; then add flour. Turn out into 9- or 10-inch spring form pan. Pat with hand to line bottom and bring dough up on sides about one inch. Fill with plums, peaches, or apricots. Sprinkle brown sugar over fruit and dot with butter. Bake at 350° for one hour.

CRANBERRY MINCEMEAT PIE

Serves: 8
Cooking Time: 35 minutes

"This is great for Thanksgiving dinner and can be served with whipped cream or slightly softened ice cream!"

½ package (10 oz.) pie crust mix
1 can (1 lb.) whole cranberry sauce
1¼ cups prepared mincemeat
1 cup pecans, finely chopped
2 tbsp. sugar
2 tbsp. butter, melted
3 tbsp. brandy

Preheat oven to 425°. Prepare pie crust according to package directions. Roll out pastry to an 11-inch circle. Use to line a 9-inch pie plate. Trim, crimp edge decoratively. In medium bowl, combine cranberry sauce with mincemeat, mixing well. Turn into prepared pie shall. In small bowl, lightly toss pecans with sugar and butter. Sprinkle evenly over cranberry mixture. Bake pie 35 minutes or until crust is golden brown and filling is bubbly. Cool on wire rack one hour. Just before serving, heat brandy in small sauce pan, over very low heat. Ignite with a match. Pour flaming brandy over pie. Serve at once.

FRESH PEACH PIE

Serves: 8
Cooking Time: 40 minutes

"Takes time, but it's worth it! Use favorite pie crust mix or your own recipe for crust and lattice top."

1 cup sugar, sifted
¾ cup water
⅛ tsp. salt
2 lb. peaches
3 tbsp. cornstarch, dissolved
   in ¼ cup water
3 tbsp. bread crumbs
9-inch pie crust plus dough
   for top

Mix sugar and ¾ cup water in a sauce pan. Add salt and cornstarch mix. Cook slowly until thickened and clear. Slice peaches. Pour glaze over sliced peaches. Sprinkle crumbs into bottom of pie crust in 9-inch pan. Pour in peaches, with glaze. Brush edges of crust with one tablespoon milk or egg yolk. Make lattice top. Bake at 400° for 40 minutes.

FRAN'S RASPBERRY PIE

Serves: 6 - 8

"There will be no leftovers."

1 package (3 oz.) raspberry
   gelatin
¼ cup granulated sugar
1¼ cups boiling water
1 package (10 oz.) frozen
   raspberries
1 tbsp. lemon juice
1 package (3 oz.) cream cheese,
   softened
⅓ cup sifted confectioner's
   sugar
1 tsp. vanilla
dash salt
1 cup heavy cream, whipped
9-inch baked pastry shell,
   cooled

Dissolve gelatin and granulated sugar in boiling water; add frozen berries and lemon juice. Stir until berries thaw; chill until partially set. Blend cream cheese, confectioner's sugar, vanilla and salt. Fold in small amount of whipped cream, then fold in remainder. Spread half the white cheese mixture over bottom of pastry shell. Cover with half the gelatin (red) mixture. Repeat layers. Chill until set.

Banana Split Pie

Serves: 25
Cooking Time: 15 minutes

"Great for a crowd."

Crust:

2 packages (13 oz. each) graham
   cracker crumbs
2 sticks margarine, softened

Grease bottom of sheet pan. Blend cracker crumbs with margarine. Spread into prepared pan. Bake 15 minutes at 375°. Cool.

Filling:

2 sticks margarine
2 eggs
2 cups confectioner's sugar
2 tsp. vanilla

Cream all ingredients together at high speed on mixer for 10 minutes. Spread on the graham cracker crust.

Topping:

6 or 7 bananas
1 large can (20 oz.) crushed
   pineapple
1½ pt. heavy cream
½ cup confectioner's sugar
½ cup walnuts or pecans,
   finely chopped
maraschino cherries

Slice the bananas into thirds, lengthwise. Lay on top of filling. Drain pineapple and sprinkle on bananas. Whip together heavy cream and sugar. Spread on top. Sprinkle with nuts and dot with halved maraschino cherries.

Apricot Chiffon Pie

Serves: 8
Chill: 1 hour

"Easy and good."

1 tbsp. gelatin
¼ cup cold water
4 eggs, separated
1 cup sugar
½ tsp. salt
1½ cups apricot pulp*
1 tbsp. lemon juice
9-inch pie shell. baked
whipped cream (optional)

*I use one large (#2) can of halved apricots which I put through a sieve. A small amount of juice can be added in case there is not quite 1½ cups pulp.

Soften gelatin in cold water, set aside. Combine egg yolks, sugar, salt, apricot pulp, and lemon juice in sauce pan. Cook over low heat until thickened. Add gelatin and mix. Cool. Beat egg whites until stiff and then fold them into apricot mixture. Pour into baked pie shell and chill. Garnish with whipped cream, if desired.

LEMON CHIFFON PIE

Serves: 8
Chill: 2 hours

"A favorite dessert."

1 envelope gelatin, unflavored
1 cup sugar
⅛ tsp. salt
4 eggs, separated
½ cup lemon juice
¼ cup water
2 tsp. grated lemon rind
9-inch pie crust, baked
whipped cream

Mix gelatin, ½ cup sugar, and salt in top of double boiler. Beat egg yolks, lemon juice, and water and add to gelatin. Cook in double boiler, stirring constantly, until all is dissolved (five minutes). Remove from heat. Stir in lemon rind. Chill until mixture mounds slightly when dropped from spoon. Set in refrigerator until cool. Check every five minutes (less than 20 minutes). Beat egg whites until stiff. Beat in ½ cup sugar. Fold in gelatin mixed with egg whites. Turn into pie shell. Chill until firm. Garnish with whipped cream.

ORANGE CHIFFON PIE

Serves: 8
Cooking Time: 10 minutes

"Chiffon pie always makes a nice refreshing dessert."

3 tbsp. flour
3 egg yolks
2 tbsp. lemon juice
¼ cup sugar
1 cup orange juice
½ tbsp. grated orange rind
3 egg whites
1 baked pie shell

Cook over hot water, the flour, yolks, lemon juice, sugar, orange juice and orange rind. Cook till thick. Cool. Whip whites and fold into orange mixture. Pour into pie shell and bake at 400° for ten minutes.

VIENNESE CHOCOLATE PIE

Serves: 10
Cooking Time: 1 hour

"Very, very, elaborate."

Shell:

3 egg whites
¼ tsp. cream of tartar
¾ cup sugar
dash salt
1 tsp. vanilla
chopped pecans

Beat whites with cream of tartar. Gradually add sugar, salt, and vanilla until egg whites peak. Put in pie plate; build up on sides. Bake at 275° for one hour. When cool, line bottom of shell with chopped pecans.

Filling:.

8 oz. sweet chocolate bits
1 tsp. instant coffee, dissolved in ¼ cup boiling water
2 cups whipped cream (1 pt. heavy cream)
powdered sugar
1 tsp. vanilla
chocolate curls

Melt chocolate and coffee in double boiler or small pan set in another pan of water. When melted add one cup whipped cream using a whisk. Pour into cool pie shell and, when thick and cool, decorate with one more cup of whipped cream, sweetened with powdered sugar and vanilla. Add chocolate curls, if desired.

COCONUT CREAM PIE

Serves: 8
Refrigerate: 6 hours

"Helen didn't want to part with this one."

1 cup coconut, fresh or canned
1 cup milk
¾ lb. marshmallows
3 cups heavy cream, whipped stiff
2 cups coconut, freshly grated
1 9-inch pie shell, baked

Soak one cup coconut in milk for one hour. Strain mixture through double thickness of cheesecloth, pressing out all the milk. Cook the coconut milk with marshmallows over low heat until marshmallows melt. Cool in bowl. Refrigerate until mixture starts to jell (35 minutes to one hour). Beat the jellied mixture until frothy with an electric mixer. Combine this with the whipped cream. Blend in one cup freshly grated coconut. Pile the mixture into the pie shell. Cover entire top of pie with remaining one cup coconut. Refrigerate for at least six hours.

Brandy Alexander Pie

Serves: 8
Chill: Overnight

"A delicious, very rich dessert!"

1 envelope Knox unflavored
  gelatin
1/2 cup cold water
2/3 cup sugar
1/8 tsp. salt
3 eggs, separated
1/4 cup cognac
1/4 cup crème de cacoa
2 cups heavy cream, whipped
1 9-inch graham cracker crust
chocolate curls

Sprinkle gelatin over cold water in a sauce pan. Add 1/3 cup sugar, salt, and egg yolks. Stir to blend. Over low heat, stirring constantly, dissolve gelatin and let mixture thicken. Do not boil. Remove from heat and stir in cognac and crème de cacoa. Chill in refrigerator while beating egg whites until stiff. Gradually beat in remaining sugar. Fold all into the chilled mixture. Fold in one cup whipped cream. Turn into crust. Chill overnight or at least several hours. Garnish with chocolate curls and whipped cream.

Chocolate Mousse Pie

Serves: 10
Refrigerate: 2 - 3 hours

"Bananas added to chocolate make a nice rich dessert."

1 package (12 oz.) bittersweet
  chocolate bits
6 eggs, separated
2 tbsp. sugar
2 pt. heavy cream
1 box Nabisco graham cracker
  crumbs
3 bananas, sliced

Melt chocolate bits in top of double boiler. Cool. Beat yolks one at a time, into chocolate, beating well after each. Beat whites until frothy. Gradually beat sugar into egg whites. Beat 1/4 of the egg whites into chocolate. Fold in the rest. Whip heavy cream and fold into chocolate. Make crust according to package directions. Put in a spring form pan. Pour in 1/2 of the mixture, add a layer of bananas, add remaining mixture and top with remaining bananas. Refrigerate for 2-3 hours.

BUTTERSCOTCH SQUARES

Yield: 1 dozen
Cooking Time: 30 minutes

"Brownies go Scotch."

1 package (6 oz.) Nestle's
   Butterscotch morsels
1/8 lb. butter
1 cup dark brown sugar
2 eggs
1/2 tsp. vanilla
3/4 cup flour
1 tsp. baking powder
dash salt
3/4 cup walnuts, chopped

Melt butterscotch morsels and butter together in top of double boiler. Remove from heat and stir in brown sugar. Stir in eggs and vanilla. Sift flour, baking powder, and salt together and stir into mixture. Add nuts. Grease a 10 x 6½ - inch pan. Spread mixture in pan and bake at 350° for 30 minutes (just until golden). Cut while warm and keep covered to keep chewy and moist.

APPLE NUT SQUARES

Yield: 24 (2 x 2-inch squares)
Cooking Time: 50 minutes

"Delicious and easy. Everyone asks for this recipe."

2 cups flour
2 cups sugar
2 tsp. baking soda
1/2 tsp. salt
1 tsp. cinnamon
1/2 tsp. nutmeg
4 cups raw apples, finely diced
1/2 cup butter or margarine,
   softened
1/2 cup nuts, chopped
2 eggs
confectioner's sugar

Combine flour, sugar, baking soda, salt, cinnamon, nutmeg. Add the apples, butter, nuts, and eggs and beat until just combined (it will be thick). Grease a 9 x 13 x 2-inch pan; turn into pan and spread evenly. Cook at 325° oven for 50 minutes. Cut into squares and just before serving, top with confectioner's sugar.

LEMON BARS DELUXE

Yield: 30
Cooking Time: 45 minutes

2 cups sifted flour
½ cup confectioner's sugar
1 cup butter
4 eggs, beaten
2 cups granulated sugar
⅓ cup lemon juice
¼ cup flour
½ tsp. baking powder

Sift together the flour and congectioner's sugar. Cut in butter until mixture clings together. Press into 13 x 9 x 2 - inch pan. Bake at 350° for 20-25 minutes or until lightly browned. Beat together eggs, granulated sugar, and lemon juice. Sift together the flour and baking powder, stir into egg mixture. Pour over baked crust. Bake at 350° for 25 minutes longer. Sprinkle with additional confectioner's sugar. Cool. Cut into squares.

CHEESECAKE DIAMONDS

Yield: 16
Cooking Time: Approximately 40 minutes

5 tbsp. butter
⅓ cup brown sugar
1 cup all-purpose flour,
   sifted
¼ cup walnuts, chopped
½ cup granulated sugar
1 package (8 oz.) cream cheese,
   softened
1 egg
2 tbsp. milk
1 tbsp. lemon juice
½ tsp. vanilla

Cream butter and brown sugar. Add flour and nuts, and mix well. Set aside one cup of this mixture for topping. Press remaining mixture in bottom of 8 x 8 x 2-inch baking pan. Bake at 350° for 12-15 minutes.

Blend granulated sugar and cream cheese until smooth. Add egg, milk, lemon juice, vanilla, and beat well. Spread over cooked crust. Sprinkle on reserved topping. Return to oven and bake another 25 minutes. Chill. Cut into diamonds.

LIGHT BROWNIES

Yield: 4 - 5 dozen
Cooking Time: 30 minutes

⅔ cup margarine
1 lb. light brown sugar
3 eggs
2⅔ cups flour
2½ tsp. baking powder
½ tsp. salt
1 cup walnuts, chopped
1 cup chocolate bits

Melt margarine in sauce pan large enough to hold all ingredients. Add brown sugar and stir well. Let stand ten minutes to cool. Add eggs, one at a time, beating well after each. Add flour, baking powder, and salt. Mix well. Then add chopped walnuts and the chocolate bits. Spread in greased and floured jelly-roll pan and bake 30 minutes at 350°. Let cool and cut into pieces.

BROWNIES

Yield: 12
Cooking Time: 35 minutes

1 cup sifted flour ⎫
¼ tsp. salt   ⎬ OR 1 cup Presto flour, sifted
¼ tsp. baking powder ⎭
1 cup sweet butter or margarine, softened
2 cups sugar
4 eggs
4 squares baking chocolate, melted
1 tsp. vanilla
½ cup walnuts

Sift together flour, salt, and baking powder. Beat together butter or margarine and sugar. Add eggs, melted chocolate. Add flour mixture, vanilla, and walnuts. Bake at 325° for 35 minutes in greased 9 x 14-inch Pyrex dish.

BUTTER PECAN BARS

Yield: 36
Cooking Time: 40 minutes

"Brownie-like texture. Good finger cake.

½ lb. sweet butter
2½ cups all-purpose flour
1 lb. light brown sugar
2 large eggs, beaten
1 tsp. vanilla extract
1½ tsp. baking powder
pinch salt
1 cup pecans, coarsely chopped

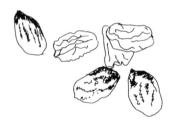

Combine ½ cup butter, 1¼ cups flour, and ⅓ cup sugar and press mixture (with floured fingers) on bottom of 9 x 13-inch pan. Bake at 350° for 15 minutes. While the crust is baking, prepare the filling in a sauce pan: Combine remaining sugar and butter. Cook on low heat just until both are completely dissolved. Slowly stir this hot mixture into beaten eggs, then add extract, remaining flour, baking powder, salt, and finally pecans. Pour over crust and bake for 25 minutes. Allow to cool completely. Remove and cut with serrated knife.

HONEY WALNUT DROPS

Yield: 7 - 8 dozen
Cooking Time: 10 - 12 minutes

"Sweet and luscious."

1 cup sugar
1 cup honey
⅔ cup shortening
3 eggs
3¾ cups all-purpose flour
1 tsp. soda
1 tsp. salt
1 cup commercial sour cream
1 cup walnuts, chopped
¾ cup coconut flakes
1 tsp. vanilla

Cream sugar, honey, shortening, and eggs. Measure unsifted flour and pour onto wax paper. To this add soda and salt. Stir to blend, do not sift. Add blended dry ingredients alternately with sour cream to creamed mixture. Stir in walnuts, coconuts, and vanilla. Drop by teaspoonful onto greased baking sheet. Top each cookie with a walnut half. Bake at 375° for 10-12 minutes.

SALT BUTTER COOKIES

Cooking Time: 10 - 15 minutes

½ lb. salt butter, softened
½ cup confectioner's sugar
1 tsp. vanilla
2 cups flour

Cream butter and sugar and add other ingredients. Roll dough into marble-size balls and bake in preheated 350° oven for 10-15 minutes. While cookies are warm, roll in powdered sugar, if desired.

CARMELA'S BUTTER BALLS

Cooking Time: 10 minutes

"Stays forever."

½ lb. butter
½ cup confectioner's sugar
1 tsp. vanilla
2 cups flour
1 tsp. baking powder
1 cup walnuts, chopped

Mix together butter, confectioner's sugar, and vanilla. Add flour, baking powder, and walnuts. Mix well. Roll into balls and bake at 350° until lightly brown.

SWEDISH BALL COOKIES

Yield: 4 dozen
Cooking Time: 5 - 10 minutes

"The children will love them."

1 cup butter
1 cup sugar
2 egg yolks
2 cups flour
pinch salt
2 egg whites, stiffly beaten

Cream butter and sugar. Add egg yolks, then flour and salt. Form into small balls and roll them in stiffly beaten egg whites. Bake on cookie sheet, 5-10 minutes at 350°.

SUGAR COOKIES

Yield: 4 dozen
Cooking Time: 10 minutes

½ cup sweet butter
1 cup sugar
2 eggs
2 tsp. vanilla
2 tsp. baking powder
3½ cups flour

Cream butter and sugar. Add eggs to vanilla. Put baking powder in flour. Mix all ingredients together thoroughly. Roll dough, cut with assorted cookie cutters. Bake at 350° for 10 minutes.

VANILLA WAFERS

Yield: 50 cookies
Cooking Time: 8 - 10 minutes

¼ lb. lightly salted butter
½ cup sugar
1 egg
1 cup flour
½ tsp. salt
1 tsp. vanilla
pecans

Cream butter. Gradually add sugar, egg, flour, salt, vanilla. Drop by teaspoon, two inches apart on greased cookie sheets. In center of each cookie, press ½ pecan. Bake 8 to 10 minutes at 375° until brown around edge. Remove immediately from pans and cool on wire rack.

GEORGIAN BUTTER COOKIES

Yield: 4 dozen
Cooking Time: 10 minutes

½ cup sweet butter
½ cup Crisco
2 cups flour
¾ cup sugar
vanilla
3 egg yolks

Rub butter and Crisco into flour. Add sugar, vanilla; egg yolks last. Roll into foot-long rolls with a 1-inch diameter. Wrap in wax paper. Freeze or slice into 1-inch thick slices and bake at 400° for ten minutes.

CHOCOLATE CHIP COOKIES

Yield: 48 cookies
Cooking Time: 10 - 12 minutes

½ cup butter
½ cup granulated sugar
¼ cup brown sugar, firmly
  packed
1 egg
1 tsp. vanilla
1 cup cake flour, sifted
½ tsp. salt
½ tsp. soda
1 package (6 oz.) semisweet
  chocolate bits

Cream butter until soft. Add sugars gradually, continuing to cream, until light and fluffy. Add egg, vanilla, and beat well. Sift flour, salt, soda together and beat until smooth. Fold in chocolate bits and drop from teaspoon 2 inches apart on ungreased cookie sheet. Bake 10-12 minutes in moderate oven (350°).

POWDERED COOKIES

Yield: 2 dozen
Cooking Time: 10 - 12 minutes

1 lb. sweet butter
3½ cups unbleached flour,
  sifted
1 egg yolk
2 tbsp. confectioner's sugar
1 jigger brandy or whiskey

Combine all ingredients, mix well. Shape into crescents and bake at 350° until brown. When cold, saturate in confectioner's sugar.

CHINESE ALMOND COOKIES

Cooking Time: 8 - 10 minutes

1 cup flour, sifted
½ cup butter
½ tsp. salt
¼ cup plus 2 tbsp. sugar
½ tsp. almond flavoring
1 egg yolk
1 tbsp. water
¼ cup blanched almonds

Place flour in a bowl, cut in shortening (finely). Use hands to work in salt, sugar, and flavoring. Shape into a long roll one inch in diameter and wrap in wax paper. Chill about one hour. Heat oven to 400°. Cut into ¼-inch slices. Place one inch apart on lightly greased baking sheet. Brush each slice with mixture of yolk and water. Press almond on top of each. Bake 8-10 minutes.

MAGIC MARSHMALLOW CRESCENT PUFFS

Yield: 16 rolls
Cooking Time: 10 - 15 minutes

"Hidden marshmallow melts like magic and leaves a hollow puff."

¼ cup sugar
1 tsp. cinnamon
16 Kraft jet-puffed marshmallows
¼ cup margarine, melted
2 cans (8 oz. each) crescent
  dinner rolls
powdered sugar glaze
¼ cup nuts, chopped (optional)

Combine sugar and cinnamon. Dip marshmallows in melted margarine; roll in sugar-cinnamon mixture. Wrap a crescent triangle around each, completely covering marshmallow and squeezing edges of dough tightly to seal. Dip in margarine, place in muffin pans. Put on foil and bake at 375° for 10 to 15 minutes until golden brown. Immediately remove, drizzle with glaze. Sprinkle with nuts, if desired.

KEVIN'S CHOCOLATE COOKIES

Cooking Time: 8 - 10 minutes

½ lb. butter
½ cup sugar
2 cups flour
2 tsp. baking powder
2 egg yolks
3 squares semisweet chocolate,
  melted
1 tsp. vanilla

Beat butter with sugar. Add flour, baking powder. Mix alternately with eggs and melted chocolate. Add vanilla. Mix well, then form into a roll. Slice roll into ¼-inch slices, bake on cookie sheet 8-10 minutes at 350°.

CRESCENTS

Yield: 8 dozen
Cooking Time: 15 - 20 minutes

½ lb. pure sweet butter
5 tbsp. sugar
1 tbsp. cold water
2 tsp. vanilla
pinch of salt
2 cups flour
2 cups pecans, chopped

Cream butter and sugar together. Add water and vanilla. Next add salt and flour. Add nuts last. Mix well. With hands, shape small pieces of dough into tiny rolls. Twist on cookie sheet to from crescents. Bake at 325° for 15-20 minutes.

FILBERT BONBON COOKIES

Yield: 120
Cooking Time: 12 - 14 minutes

"Enjoy!"

1 cup butter
¾ cup sugar
1 egg
2½ cups flour
½ tsp. baking powder
⅛ tsp. salt
1 tsp. vanilla
whole filberts

Cream shortening and sugar, add egg. Sift dry ingredients and blend in. Add vanilla. Wrap and refrigerate until firm. Using less than one teaspoon dough, roll around nut and shape into balls. Bake at 350° until golden, about 12 -14 minutes. Cool and dip into Glaze.

Glaze:

2 tbsp. butter, melted
1 tbsp. unsweetened cocoa
1 cup confectioner's sugar
⅛ cup cold coffee

In small bowl, place melted butter, add cocoa, sugar, and coffee alternately. Mix well. Dip top of cookies into glaze, then roll in chopped nuts, coconut, or coarse sugar. Let top harden before storing or serving. May be frozen.

STAR COOKIES

Yield: 4 dozen
Cooking Time: Varies — 1 - 1½ hours

"From a star cook."

1 cup flour
½ tsp. salt
1-3 tsp. sugar
1 egg
1 cup milk
confectioner's sugar
cookie iron*
oil, for frying

*Irons are available at Bloomingdales ($2.00).

Mix above ingredients. Heat oil. Dip hot iron into mixture, then in oil. Scoop cookies out when golden, drain on paper towels. Sprinkle with confectioner's sugar.
Hint: While oil is heating, keep iron in pan. After batter has been placed in oil, it will fall away from iron itself. If it sticks, rap iron on side of pan. Electric fry pan is a great help in keeping oil at a constant temperature. The cooking process will shorten as you gain skill at using the iron, as you will again and again.

MERINGUE COOKIES

Yield: 2 dozen
Cooking Time: 1 hour

"Light and airy."

2 egg whites
½ cup sugar
½ cup walnuts, chopped
½ cup milk chocolate bits

Beat egg whites until stiff, add sugar gradually. Fold in nuts and chocolate. Drop onto greased cookie sheet. Bake one hour at 250°.

HOLIDAY SNOWBALL COOKIES

Yield: 3½ dozen
Cooking Time: 12 - 15 minutes

"Festive fare."

1 cup butter
⅓ cup sugar
2 tsp. milk
2 tsp. vanilla
2 cups sifted flour
½ cup walnuts, chopped
confectioner's sugar

Cream butter and sugar until light and fluffy. Mix in milk and vanilla. Add flour and nuts, mix well. Chill dough thoroughly. Form into balls about one inch in diameter. Place on ungreased cookie sheet and bake at 375° for 12 - 15 minutes. Remove from cookie sheet; cool. Roll in confectioner's sugar.

Editors' Note:
The following three rugelach recipes vary in the fillings.

SCHNECHEN

Yield: 3 dozen
Cooking Time: 30 minutes

2½ cups flour
1 cup shortening
¾ cup sour cream
1 egg yolk
salt

Mixture:

1 cup sugar
1 tbsp. cinnamon
½ cup walnuts, chopped

Blend flour and shortening. Add sour cream and egg yolk. Mix well. (You can knead with fingers.) Refrigerate at least two hours. Divide into fourths and roll out into a circle on some of the mixture. Sprinkle some mixture on top. Cut like pie wedges and roll. Bake at 350° for about 30 minutes or until done.

Austrian Pastries

Yield: 100
Cooking Time: 15 minutes

3 cups flour
1 package dry yeast
½ lb. butter or margarine,
  room temperature
3 egg yolks
1 cup sour cream

In large bowl add flour, sprinkle the yeast over it. Add, at room temperature, butter or margarine. Blend with pastry blender until well mixed and crumbly. In separate bowl combine egg yolks and sour cream. Mix well. Add to above mixture and mix well. Wrap in wax paper and refrigerate overnight.

Filling:

1½ cups granulated sugar
1½ tsp. cinnamon
1 package (6 oz.) sliced
  almonds, crumbled

Divide dough into five sections. Roll, one section at a time on filling (instead of flour), to ⅛-inch thick. Cut into narrow pie-shaped wedges and roll toward center. Bake on ungreased cookie sheet at 350° about 14 minutes until golden. Freezes and ships well.

Rugelach

Yield: 3 dozen
Cooking Time: 25 - 30 minutes

½ lb. butter
½ lb. cream cheese
2 egg yolks
8 tbsp. sugar
2 tsp. vanilla
¼ tsp. salt
2 cups flour

Paste:

apricot preserves
nuts
cinnamon
sugar

Cream first six ingredients, add flour. Form into ball of dough. Divide ball into four parts. Roll each part into circle. Spread paste. Cut into wedges. Roll up wedges and shape into horns. Do not grease sheet. Bake at 350° for 25-30 minutes.

PINIOLLATI

Cooking Time: 5 - 6 minutes

4 cups flour
½ tsp. salt
4 eggs
¾ cup sugar
4 heaping tbsp. Crisco
¼ cup water
1 large jar (16 oz.) honey

Sift flour with salt. Mix in 4 eggs. Melt sugar and Crisco with water. Mix in and knead. Roll out into long snakelike pieces. Cut into ¼ inch size and deep fry till golden brown. Coat with melted honey.

QUICK ITALIAN DUMPLINGS

Serves: 4
Cooking Time: 5 minutes

1 cup Presto flour
1 cup milk, warm
1 egg

Mix all ingredients together. Prepare small pot with 3 inches hot oil. Keep flame high. Put in one tablespoon of above batter at a time. Turn as they brown. Drain and put into a dish with powdered and granulated sugar. Serve immediately.

ANNETTE'S ZIPPLE

Cooking Time: 5 minutes

"Deep fried, and soft inside."

1 lb. pot cheese
3 eggs, slightly beaten
3 tbsp. sugar
4 tsp. baking powder
1 cup flour
¼ tsp. salt
powdered sugar
hot oil

Mix together pot cheese, eggs, sugar, and baking powder. Let stand for one hour. Then add flour and salt. Mix well. Drop by spoon into hot oil until brown. Sprinkle with powdered sugar.

DIMPLE DOLLIES

Chill: 2 hours
Cooking Time: 12 - 14 minutes

1 lb. butter
1 lb. cream cheese
1 lb. flour, sifted
½ tsp. preserves (your choice)
confectioner's sugar

Mix together butter, cream cheese and flour. Make sure mixture is mixed well. Shape into a roll and refrigerate for two hours. Cut off small pieces and roll out paper thin on floured board. Cut squares, as large or as small as you wish. Dot each square with preserves. Fold opposite corners to center and pinch closed. Bake at 400° until light brown. Sprinkle well with confectioner's sugar.

RUM BALLS

Yield: 40 balls

"I always double this recipe. If you make the balls smaller you increase the yield. Fun for Christmas giving or dinner party treat."

½ lb. vanilla wafers
1 cup confectioner's sugar
2 tbsp. cocoa
1 cup pecans, finely chopped
½ cup light corn syrup (Karo)
¼ cup rum

Grind or roll wafers very fine. Mix dry ingredients; add nuts, syrup, and rum. Stir well until stiff. Roll into balls the size of a walnut. Coat hands with powdered sugar to shape balls. Let stand on wax paper for an hour to dry a bit. Roll again in confectioner's sugar. These will keep in a tin container for weeks. In fact, they have more of a rum taste after at least one week, stored airtight.

GREEK NUT ROLLS

Yield: 2 - 3 dozen
Cooking Time: 35 minutes

"Can be made ahead and dipped in syrup just before serving."

1 cup pecans, finely chopped
1 cup walnuts, finely chopped
1 cup almonds, finely chopped
¼ cup sugar
½ tsp. cloves
½ tsp. cinnamon
1 package filo pastry
½ lb. sweet butter
honey or rose water syrup,
    see page 294

Preheat oven to 350°. Combine nuts, sugar, cloves, and cinnamon. Brush two sheets of filo pastry with melted butter and arrange one sheet on top of the other. Sprinkle with 2-3 tablespoons of nut mixture. Repeat this procedure until there are three layers of nuts and three layers of pastry. Roll up like a jelly roll. This recipe will give you three such rolls. Cut each roll into 1-inch slices. Place the slices on a buttered baking sheet. Bake the slices for about 20 minutes, then turn them over and bake for another 15 minutes, or until both sides are golden brown. Cool. While the pastry is baking, prepare the syrup. You can use either one. Dip the cooled pieces of nut roll in the syrup, top with a dab of unsweetened whipped cream, and serve with strong black, coffee.

COCONUT MACAROONS

Yield: 1½ dozen
Cooking Time: 20 minutes

1 can (3½ oz.) coconut
⅓ cup sugar
2 tbsp. flour
⅛ tsp. salt
2 egg whites
½ tsp. almond extract

Combine coconut, sugar, flour, and salt in bowl. Stir in egg whites and almond extract and mix well. Drop by teaspoon onto lightly greased baking sheets. Bake at 325° for 20 minutes or until brown at edges. Remove from baking sheets immediately.

Lithuanian Pastries

Chill: 2 hours

"Pig's ears."

1 cup confectioner's sugar
1 tbsp. cinnamon
4 eggs, beaten
⅔ cup sugar
⅓ cup milk
⅓ cup shortening, melted
3½ cups flour
½ tsp. salt
½ tsp. baking powder
¼ tsp. nutmeg
1 qt. oil, very hot

Sift confectioner's sugar and cinnamon together and leave in a bowl. Cream eggs and sugar until light. Add milk and cooled shortening. Add flour, sifted with salt, baking powder, and nutmeg. Beat until smooth. Chill two hours. Roll dough ¼ inch thick on floured surface. Cut in oblong strips 4 x 1 inch wide. Cut a split down center, then put ends through split and pull slightly. Fry in oil 3-5 minutes. To test temperature of oil, drop a small piece of dough in; it should become crisp immediately. Fry a few at a time. Drain on brown paper. Sift sugar and cinnamon mixture over ears while still warm. When finished, allow oil to set for a while. Remove sediment and reuse oil for cooking purposes.

Grandma's Apple Strudel

Cooking Time: 45 - 55 minutes

"Difficult to roll thin dough, but not as hard as it sounds. Always a treat to serve. Leftover dough can be made into cookies."

4 cups flour, sifted
1⅓ cups sugar
1⅓ tsp. baking powder
4 eggs
1⅓ tsp. vanilla
1⅓ cups Crisco
1 jar preserves
4 cans Comstock apples
walnuts, chopped
butter
oil

Sift flour, sugar, and baking powder together. Add eggs, vanilla, and Crisco. Knead with fingers to form dough. Roll ⅓ of dough and place in bottom and sides of a greased 9 x 13 x 2-inch pan. Spread with preserves; add two cans apples and nuts; dot with butter. Add second layer of dough, repeat preserves, apples, etc. Cover with top crust. Rub oil on top, make a slit for escaping steam. Bake at 450° for ten minutes then reduce heat to 350° and bake 35-45 minutes.

ICE CREAM DANISH

Serves: 4 dozen
Cooking Time: 30 minutes

"Unusual batter yields unusual pastry treat."

½ lb. butter
1 cup vanilla ice cream
2 cups all-purpose flour
preserves of your choice
chopped walnuts
golden raisins
toasted coconut
chocolate chips

To make dough, melt butter. Add ice cream. Add flour and blend well. Mix and divide dough into four balls (wrap in foil or Saran Wrap) and refrigerate at least two hours. May be made day before using. Roll each ball into rectangle Spread with the preserves. Then sprinkle with either chopped walnuts, golden raisins, toasted coconut, or chocolate chips, or any combination of above. Roll covered dough into long jelly-roll strips and place on ungreased cookie sheet, two on each tray. Cut slices half way through, 10-12 slices per roll. Bake in preheated 375° oven 25-30 minutes until golden. Freezes well after cutting into individual pieces.

MONDEL BRODT

Yield: 42 pieces
Cooking Time: Approximately 1 hour, 15 minutes

"Traditional Russian recipe."

1 cup sugar
½ cup Crisco or Spry
3 eggs
1 tsp. vanilla
½ tsp. salt
2 tsp. baking powder
3 cups flour (does not have to
  be sifted)
½ cup toasted, slivered almonds
  (Blue Diamond)
sugar and cinnamon, mixed

Cream sugar and shortening. Mix next six ingredients in order listed. Divide into three parts. Flour hands. Shape into three flat loaves. Bake for 20-25 minutes in 350° oven or until light brown (on a cookie sheet). Test with a toothpick. When brown, take out and cut into pieces on an angle. Lay each piece on its side and sprinkle with cinnamon and sugar mixed together. Toast at 225° for 30 minutes or 275° for 20 minutes. Repeat procedure. You should get at least 42 pieces of Mondel Brodt. Let cool before serving.

MUERBE TEIG WITH LEKVAR

Yield: 2 - 3 dozen
Cooking Time: 35 - 45 minutes

"This old European recipe resembles a prune and butter danish. Very, very good."

½ lb. butter
¼ cup sugar
2 egg yolks
½ lemon, pulp and rind
¼ cup cold water
3 cups flour

Combine butter, sugar, and egg yolks in mixer. Chop up lemon in blender with cold water, then add to beaten mixture. Gradually add flour. Butter a cookie sheet. Then spread dough on cookie sheet ¼ inch thick. Set in refrigerator for at least 20 minutes or up to 8 hours. Bake 25-30 minutes. When cool spread with filling.

Filling:

½ lemon, pulp and rind
¼ cup cold water
1 jar lekvar (prune butter)
2 egg whites, beaten stiff
¼ cup confectioner's sugar
1 cup walnuts, chopped

Chop up lemon with cold water in blender. Combine with lekvar. Spread over dough. Combine egg whites, confectioner's sugar, and walnuts and spread over lekvar filling. Bake at 400° until light brown, approximately 10-15 minutes. When cool, cut into 2-inch squares.

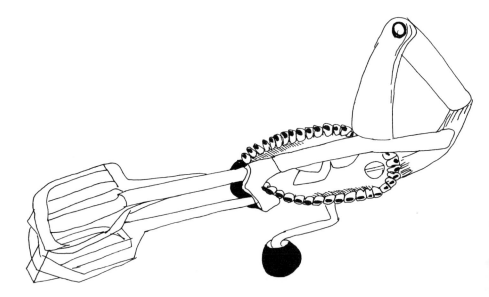

EQUIVALENTS AND MEASURES

3 tsp.	1 tbsp.	1 tsp.	1/6 oz.
4 tbsp.	1/4 cup	1 tbsp.	1/2 oz.
5 1/3 tbsp.	1/3 cup	2 tbsp.	1 oz.
12 tbsp.	3/4 cup	1 cup	8 oz.
16 tbsp.	1 cup	1 pt.	16 oz.
2 cups	1 pt.		
2 pt.	1 qt.		
4 qt.	1 gal.		

8-oz. can	.... 8 oz.	.... 1 cup
# 1 can	.... 1 lb.	.... 2 cups
# 2 can	.... 1 1/4 lb.	.... 2 1/2 cups
# 2 1/2 can	.... 1 3/4 lb.	.... 3 1/2 cups
# 3 can	.... 2 lb.	.... 4 cups
#10 can	.... 6 1/2 lb.	.... 13 cups

* * * * * * *

ALMONDS, unshelled, whole .. 1 lb. .... 1 3/4 cups nutmeats
ALMONDS, blanched, whole ... 1 lb. .... 3 1/2 cups nutmeats
APPLES .... 1 lb. .... 3 1/2 cups pared
    and sliced
APRICOTS .... 1 lb. .... 3 cups dried;
    6 cups cooked
BANANAS .... 1 lb. (3 medium) .. 2-2 1/2 cups sliced
BEANS, kidney, dried .... 1 lb. (2 1/3 cups) .. 9 cups cooked
BEANS, lima, dried .... 1 lb. (2 1/3 cups) .. 6 cups cooked
BEANS, lima, in pod .... 1 lb. .... 2/3 cup shelled
BEETS .... 1 lb. (4 medium) .. 2 cups diced and
    cooked
BREAD .... 1 slice .... 1/4-1/3 cup dry
    crumbs
BREAD .... 1 slice .... 3/4-1 cup soft
    crumbs
BUTTER (or margarine) ...... 1/4-lb. stick, 4 oz. 8 tbsp.
BUTTER (or margarine) ...... 1 lb. .... 2 cups (32 tbsp.)
CABBAGE .... 1 lb. .... 5 cups shredded
CANDIED FRUITS and PEELS ... 1/2 lb. .... 1 1/2 cups cut up
CARROTS .... 1 lb. (8 - 10) ..... 2 3/4 cups sliced
    or diced
CELERY .... 1 lb. (2 medium
    bunches) ... 4 cups diced
CHEESE, cream .... 3 oz. .... 6 tbsp.
CHEESE, hard .... 1 lb. .... 4 cups grated
CHICKEN .... 3 1/2 lbs. .... 2 cups cooked and
    diced
CHOCOLATE, unsweetened ..... 1 square .... 1 oz. (1 tbsp.
    melted, 5 tbsp. grated)
CORNMEAL .... 1 cup, uncooked ... 4 cups cooked
CRACKERS, graham .... 15 .... 1 cup fine crumbs
CRACKERS, soda .... 22 .... 1 cup fine crumbs
CRANBERRIES .... 1 lb. .... 4 cups
CREAM, heavy .... 1/2 pt. (1 cup) .... 2 cups whipped

```
DATES ..................... 1 lb. ............. 2 cups pitted
EGG WHITES ................ 8 - 11 ............. 1 cup
EGG YOLKS ................. 12 - 16 ............. 1 cup
FIGS ...................... 1 lb. ............. 2¾-3 cups
                                                      chopped
FLOUR, all-purpose ........ 1 lb. ............. 4 cups sifted
FLOUR, cake ............... 1 lb. ............. 4½ cups sifted
GARLIC .................... 1 medium clove ..... ¼ tsp. chopped
GELATIN ................... ¼-oz. package ..... 1 tbsp.
LEMON or LIME ............. 1 medium .......... 3-4 tbsp. juice
LEMON, rind .............. 1 medium .......... 1½-2 tsp.
                                                      grated
MACARONI .................. 1 cup (¼ lb.) ..... 2 cups cooked
MEAT ...................... 1 lb. ............. 2 cups diced
MILK, evaporated .......... 14½-oz. can ....... 1⅔ cups
MILK, sweetened, condensed .. 14-oz. can ......... 1¼ cups
MUSHROOMS, fresh .......... ½ lb. ............. 2½ cups sliced
NOODLES ................... 8 oz. ............. 4 cups cooked
ONIONS .................... 1 medium .......... ½ cup chopped
ORANGE .................... 1 medium .......... ⅓ cup juice
ORANGE, rind ............. 1 medium .......... 2 tbsp. grated
PEANUTS, unshelled ........ 1 lb. ............. 2-2½ cups
                                                      nutmeats
PEAS, in pod ............. 1 lb. ............. 1 cup shelled
                                                      and cooked
PEAS, split .............. 1 lb. ............. 2 cups
PECANS, unshelled ........ 1 lb. ............. 2¼ cups
                                                      nutmeats
POTATOES .................. 1 lb. (3 potatoes) . 2½ cups sliced
                                                      or diced;
                                                      2 cups mashed
PRUNES, dried ............ 1 lb. ............. 2½ cups, 4
                                                      cups cooked
RAISINS ................... 1 lb. ............. 3 cups
RICE, raw ................. 1 cup (½ lb.) ..... 3 cups cooked
RICE, precooked ........... 1 cup ............. 2 cups cooked
SHALLOTS .................. 1 medium .......... 1 tbsp. minced
SPAGHETTI ................. 1 lb. uncooked ..... 7 cups cooked
SUGAR, brown .............. 1 lb. ............. 2¼ cups packed
SUGAR, confectioner's ..... 1 lb. ............. 3½-4 cups
                                                      sifted
SUGAR, granulated ......... 1 lb. ............. 2½ cups
TOMATOES .................. 1 lb. (3 medium) ... 1 cup juiced,
                                                      chopped pulp
WALNUTS, in shell ......... 1 lb. ............. 1⅔ cups
                                                      nutmeats
WALNUTS, shelled ......... 1 lb. ............. 4 cups nutmeats
```

Dried herbs and fresh herbs are interchangeable. The ratio is
1 part dried herb = 3 parts fresh herb.

ABBREVIATIONS

Teaspoon	.... tsp.	Gallon	gal.
Tablespoon	.... tbsp.	Ounce	oz.
Pint	.... pt.	Pound	lb.
Quart	.... qt.	Monosodium glutamate .... M.S.G.

And More Words To The Wise

1. To tell a stale egg from a fresh one, place the egg in a pan of water. The fresh egg will sink to the bottom, while the stale one will rise to the top.

2. Never cook eggs in boiling water — just simmer them to desired consistency. A pinch of salt added to the water will prevent the yolk from escaping through a crack you may have inadvertently made in the egg shell.

3. Unused egg whites may be kept frozen in a covered container for four to five months.

4. Always be sure to remove even the tiniest bit of egg yolk from separated egg whites that are to be beaten. Even the smallest amount of yolk can prevent the whites from rising well.

5. Dip tomatoes in boiling water for ten seconds and then in cold water for easy peeling.

6. An unlit match stick held between your teeth, striking end out, when slicing onions will prevent those onions tears. Try it! It really works!

7. Put wilted carrots and celery in a bowl of ice water and refrigerate to perk them up.

8. Leftover parsley, chives, and dill can be washed, pat dried, stored in plastic containers or bags, and frozen for future use. Just remove the quantity needed and replace the rest.

9. Cabbage leaves are easily separated when the head is first cored and then placed in a freezer one to two nights.

10. Overcooking brussel sprouts will cause them to have a strong and unpleasant flavor. Ideally, if fresh, boil in a small amount of salted water for three minutes, and then cook covered three to eight minutes.

11. A little lemon juice added to cauliflower cooking water will keep the flowerlets white. The addition of a piece of bread will reduce the cooking odor. Overcooking cauliflower will discolor it.

12. Dried beans have a pantry life of up to two years. However, the older they are, the longer they must be soaked before using.

13. Dipping citrus fruit in hot water before squeezing will double and triple the amount of juice the fruit yields.

14. A large piece of citrus peel placed in a box of brown sugar will keep it moist and lump free.

15. White orange fibers are easily removed after the unpeeled orange is first placed in a hot oven for a few seconds and then in cold water.

16. Dip peeled avocado, banana, or apple in lemon juice or other citrus juice to prevent its discoloration.

17. Chill melons in paper bags in the refrigerator to prevent the spread of their odors.

18. Peel and individually wrap those bananas that are a little too ripe for your family in aluminum foil and freeze. The result is a treat that closely resembles ice cream. Just serve them to the children in rolled down foil. You may also dip them in chocolate sauce and then in nuts and freeze them that way.

19. Potatoes should be started cooking in boiling salted water, rather than cold, and drained immediately. Cover lightly with a clean dish towel to keep them warm, but never put a lid on the pot or they will get soggy.

20. Add two or three tablespoons of olive oil or vegetable oil to the water when cooking pasta to prevent sticking.

21. Any hard vegetable may be French fried. Try a tempura batter.

22. To remove excessive salt from food, add one teaspoon each of sugar and vinegar to the pot; or in soup, add a few slices of raw potato.

23. Add Knorr bouillon cubes to chicken soup for extra body when the soup seems a little thin. For that matter, add them to rice cooking water, gravies, and sauces for a delicious added flavor.

24. Save yourself lots of time browning quantity meatballs. Place them in a Pyrex dish for twenty minutes in a 400° oven. You'll never juggle that fry pan again.

25. Add one tablespoon of oil to butter when pan browning to prevent the butter from burning.

26. Add ice water to chopped meat to make it light and fluffy. If the recipe calls for milk, be sure it's cold and the meat will stay light. Handle the chopped meat as little as possible to prevent clumping.

27. When broiling steak, brush both sides very lightly with either olive oil or butter to seal in the juices.

28. Potted or stew-type dishes when made in advance and then reheated always improve in flavor. It's always nice to double the quantity and freeze the remainder for some harried day ahead.

29. Do not use running water to clean fish or shellfish, but rather dip them in cold, salted water and pat them damp dry with paper towel.

30. When prebaking a pastry crust, place another pan in the crust or fill the crust with raw rice to prevent it from rising and shrinking.

31. To cut marshmallows easily, dip the scissor to be used in confectioner's sugar or hot water to prevent sticking and tearing.

32. Two level tablespoons is the standard coffee measure per cup.

33. Add clean, washed eggshells and a pinch of salt to coffee grinds for clear, flavorful coffee. However, the best efforts for good coffee are doomed for failure unless all residual coffee oils are removed from the pot. To do so, place a small amount of dishwasher detergent in the grinds basket and proceed to perk as you would normally. You'll be amazed at the amount of residue oil that will be rinsed away.

34. Try this for a delicious mellow coffee: Use one tablespoon of coffee per cup and add $\frac{1}{4}$ teaspoon cocoa and 2 or 3 dashes of salt to the water per eight cups.

INDEX

311